Retooling the Rural Church for the Twenty-First Century

Retooling the Rural Church for the Twenty-First Century

A Rural Church Institute Resource

Glenn Daman AND Jeffrey Clark

Foreword by Ed Stetzer

WIPF & STOCK · Eugene, Oregon

RETOOLING THE RURAL CHURCH FOR THE TWENTY-FIRST CENTURY
A Rural Church Institute Resource

Wipf & Stock
An Imprint of Wipf and Stock Publishers
199 W. 8th Ave., Suite 3
Eugene, OR 97401

www.wipfandstock.com

PAPERBACK ISBN: 979-8-3852-7640-0
HARDCOVER ISBN: 979-8-3852-7641-7
EBOOK ISBN: 979-8-3852-7642-4

VERSION NUMBER 04/09/26

Rural Church Institute is a ministry of the Wheaton College Billy Graham Center: https://wheatonbillygraham.com/rural-church-institute/.

I would like to dedicate this book to my wife, Rebecca, who has been a faithful companion, unfailing friend, unwavering encourager, and a vibrant coworker in the ministry. Even when confronted with stage 4 cancer, she demonstrated the love and peace of Christ and a passion to see people come to Christ through her journey. —Glenn Daman

I would like to dedicate this book to my wife, Melva. She is the joy of my life and the one who makes it possible for me to serve as I do. I also want to dedicate this book to my daughters, Rachel and Hannah, as well as my granddaughter, Maggie. Just being around them keeps me going when times are difficult. Thank you for being there for me! —Jeffrey Clark

Contents

Foreword

In the Acts, Luke has a habit of describing through a general summary the events in the early church at that moment. These summaries either followed or preceded concrete examples. After Peter's specific instance of preaching at Pentecost, while other disciples spoke of God's work (Acts 2:11), Luke summarized things in 2:42–47. Then we read of the healing of a lame man in Acts 3, and Peter preached again; we read in Acts 4 how more came to Christ, persecution came in response, and the church gathered to pray. Luke follows that with another summary in 4:32 and following. We see this device used several other times before we come to Acts 11:19–26. In this case, Luke gives the summary first: believers are scattered from Jerusalem because of persecution. As they go, they share Christ first with Jews and then Gentiles. Luke follows this with the specific instance of Barnabas coming to see what the Spirit was doing in Antioch.

He found a church planted there. He encouraged them and provided specific leadership.

In Acts 13, we read of the first missionaries sent by a church; they are sent from Antioch.

Whether you read Luke's general descriptions or more specific content, you see a consistency of devotion to the gospel and its spread. You see churches planted. You see lives changed. This happens in cities and towns, among Jews and Greeks.

It seems that most of the talk today about churches and church planting focuses on the cities. And indeed, our cities need Jesus. But 60 million people also live in rural areas in the United States. The gospel is needed there as well.

In our day of either-or, good vs. evil, binary approaches to politics and other areas, we can create tension where none is needed. We champion the megachurch or the microchurch, but sometimes in doing so, we denigrate one to promote our own preference. Another example in the church world is the urban-rural church binary. It seems the emphasis has shifted so far to urban centers for church planting that the rural church has been pushed to the side.

When Scripture says Jesus loved the church and gave himself for her (Eph 5:25), the Bible does not add "rural" or "urban" or "mega" or "micro" as a modifier. It simply says "church." And that should be the focus of believers, on Christ's church, on our one Lord, one baptism, one Spirit, and one Father above.

That said, it is appropriate and helpful to explore ways to help churches in specific settings to be more effective, so a focus on rural, or urban, or other categories is understandable in that sense. But we must do so in a way that encourages all churches, because we are all one in Christ.

We must admit that the lion's share of resources today and most of the focus is aimed at the urban church. That is why we launched the Rural Churches Institute in my time at Wheaton College. One of the authors of this book, Jeff Clark, was its first director. His coauthor, Glenn Daman, has written a number of important works on the rural church.

We need to help pastors in rural communities to become more effective in reaching the lost in their world. Pastors and churches need encouragement and equipping. This book does both.

Rural churches historically have often been more than the place of worship on Sundays. They have served in some towns as the community center, the place for everything from education to medical help.

The gospel never changes. How we apply the gospel in an urban, suburban, or rural context does change. Let this book help you share the timeless gospel in timely ways.

Introduction

In 2024, the church I (Glenn) attended in my youth celebrated its seventy-fifth anniversary. The church looks much the same as it did when I attended fifty years ago. The large wooden pulpit, crafted by a church member from a previous generation, still stands in front. Descend into the basement and the cement floor is still painted with the same green paint present when I was young. Even the chairman's last name remains the same. Fifty years ago, my father served as chairman for many years. Today, the role is passed on to my brother and will soon be passed on to his son.

Tensed, the small town surrounding the church, has the same population (approximately ninety) it did when my brothers and I would trick-or-treat through the streets. The streets remain unpaved, and the potholes persist in the same locations. The only noticeable difference is that the name of the small market is no longer Clem's Store, as the Clem family sold the store years ago. Now it is ironically named The Big Store, however, there is nothing big about it.

Driving down the country roads, most of the houses that dotted the landscape fifty years ago are still present. While a few new homes have been built and a few have been abandoned over time, most retain their original appearance from the 1960s and 1970s. If one community exists where the march of time has slowed to a crawl, it would be Tensed.

Three miles south of the town and another two miles down a gravel road sits the farm where I was raised. At the entrance is a granite rock engraved with the statement "Daman Farms established in 1934," testifying to the year the Dust Bowl led my grandfather and father to sell their farm in South Dakota and move to Idaho to establish a new farm in this location. Today, the farm is still operated by my brothers and will soon be passed on to the next generation, as my two nephews prepare to take over the operation. The small one-bedroom house where my grandfather lived until his death, which we boys took over as our "bunkhouse," still remains, with his fishing boat still parked in the lean-to on the side of the house. The barn my father built in the '30s still stands, although it is slowly decaying over time.

Like many rural communities, driving through Tensed would lead one to assume little has changed in the last fifty years. The outsider would conclude it typifies what we often assume about rural areas: they are untouched by time and by the dynamic changes occurring in the rest of American culture.

However, upon closer examination, we find that the community is vastly different from what it was fifty years ago. Fifty years ago, most of the community's population made their living through their connection with the land. The people who lived in the community were either farmers, loggers, or operated businesses supporting these industries. In the valley, there were thirteen operating farms. While a couple of farmers cultivated one to two thousand acres, most (like my father) farmed three to four hundred acres. Farmers used tractors from four different manufacturers: John Deere, Case, International Harvester, and Steiger. Tensed had two family-owned and operated sawmills that processed the local timber and shipped the lumber to various markets.

Today, the only remaining farm is the one operated by my brothers, who now farm approximately eight thousand acres. They absorbed the other farms in the area as the next generation moved to the city rather than remaining on the farm. The two sawmills have been shut down long ago, as regional sawmills have taken over the market. The community is mainly comprised of retirees who moved into the area due to its natural resources. When I was growing up, the local school (twenty miles away) would send two large school buses to bus the sixty-plus kids who lived in the valley to school. Today, they use one small twenty-passenger school bus.

Fifty years ago, my dad would consider a good day of baling to be approximately twenty tons of hay. He used a 54 hp Ford tractor to pull a Massey baler with an 18 hp two-cylinder Wisconsin motor, which would produce fifty-pound bales. The hay would be primarily used for his own cattle; any excess would be sold to neighbors for their livestock. Today, my brothers raise three thousand acres of Timothy hay and no longer have any cattle on the farm. Their hay is all exported to Korea or Japan. They use four large 350-horsepower tractors. On a typical day, they will bale and stack 1,000 tons of hay, with each bale weighing 1,200 pounds. In reality, Tensed today shares little in common with Tensed of 1970. It still has the same name, but it is not the same community.

We often hold fast to the myth that rural communities are unchanging and untouched by the cultural and moral change occurring around them. But the reality is far different. The changes observed in Tensed and rural communities across North America are not limited to demographic shifts or farming methods. These only serve to illustrate and point to a greater change that has occurred, namely, the transformation in the very nature of rural communities. Contrary to the popular myth that rural communities are static, driven by unchanging traditions, they have undergone massive changes throughout their history.

The Age of Accelerated Change

When I entered the ministry, my first computer was a Compaq Portable with an 8088 processor and two floppy disks. Its average performance was between .33 and 1 million instructions per second. The laptop that I am using today can process 18 trillion operations per second. This would be like pitting a Model T, with a top speed of 20 mph, against a Hennessey Venom F5, which can reach speeds of up to 311 mph, in a drag race. Yet, my current laptop pales in comparison to the quantum computers under development, which can perform in 200 seconds what would take a traditional computer 10,000 years to process.

The changes occurring in the computer industry serve to illustrate how rapid change has become a pervasive feature of our culture. Over the last twenty years, our nation has undergone a profound shift in its moral compass. What was unthinkable twenty years ago has become accepted and celebrated today.

In the past, the changes confronting a generation could be described as predictable and acceptable. Incremental change was desired because it is foreseeable and directly related to existing knowledge. Like a slow bend in the road on a flat plain, people want to see far enough down the road that they can still envision the future. Today, however, we live in a world Regele describes as "chaotic change." He writes,

> The underlying dynamic of chaotic change is discontinuity. Unlike the more predictable rhythmical nature of continuous change, discontinuous change does anything but flow with predictable continuity. It is not incremental. It is usually radical and transformative.[1]

In such a world, Erich Hoffer warns, "In times of change, learners inherit the earth, while the learned find themselves beautifully equipped to deal with a world which no longer exists."[2]

In the past, we were taught how to develop our ministry based on both past and present experiences. Today, we face a chaotic and erratic world, a world in which the methods and programs that worked in the past or even in the present will no longer be effective in the future. We are facing a world not only of tumultuous cultural and technological change, but also a world of chaotic spiritual and moral change. Nick Oberlensky points out,

> From a context point of view, then, the pace of change has outstripped by far the leadership assumptions we have. This means we are living in a large period of discontinuity: we have changed the context within which we lead faster than we can change our assumptions about what leadership is.[3]

In a chaotic world, we are now facing a new civil war. This is not a war between rural and urban, or between states or races. It is a war of ideology and morality. James Davison Hunter describes this new battlefield:

> The divisions of political consequence today are not theological and ecclesiastical in character but the result of differing worldviews. That is to say, they no longer revolve around specific doctrinal issues or styles of religious practices and organizations but around our most fundamental and cherished assumptions about how to order our lives—our own lives and our lives together in this society.[4]

In 1999, Leonard Sweet warned of the coming tsunami of change when he wrote,

1. Regele, *Death of the Church*, 47.
2. Regele, *Death of the Church*, 52.
3. Oberlensky, *Complex Adaptive Leadership*, 19.
4. Hunter, *Culture Wars*, 42.

> The seismic events that have happened in the aftermath of the postmodern earthquake have generated tidal waves that have created a whole new world out there. In your lifetime and mine, a tidal wave has hit. We are now in transit and transit out of terra firma (if ever there were such a thing) and into terra incognita (i.e., unfamiliar territory). A sea change of transitions and transformations is birthing a whole new world and a whole new set of ways of making our way in the world. We have moved from the solid ground of terra firma to the tossing seas of terra aqua.[5]

In describing this tsunami of change, futurist Bob Johansen writes, "After centuries of stability and slow, incremental change, in less than a generation, our world has become . . . volatile, uncertain, complex and ambiguous."[6] Our culture is now in turmoil as competing views of morality vie for supremacy. The Pew Research Center reports that in assessing the seventeen most economically advanced countries in the world, the United States stands out as the most conflicted nation.[7] It seems as if the only thing people can agree upon today is that we cannot agree upon anything. These changes are not just changes in urban culture and morality; they are changes affecting even the most remote communities in rural areas. In recent years, Christendom has not only lost its grip on our culture, but it has been altogether abandoned.

The Loss of the American Soul

In the Adamic fall, humanity tried to become equal to God. Throughout history, people ignored God. Today, we live in a world where humanity despises God. When Adam and Eve first sinned, an awareness of God's position in heaven and a desire to connect with him still remained in the hearts of sinful humanity. Even morally corrupt Cain still had within him a desire to connect with God, albeit on his terms. However, by the time we arrive at Gen 6, humanity had become completely disconnected from God. They had completely thrown off the moral constraints still present even after Adam and Eve were driven from the garden. As we look about our country, we are quickly becoming "like the days of Noah" (Matt 24:37). However, today we have not only abandoned any consideration of God and rejected the moral teaching of God; we now live in

5. Sweet, *SoulTsunami*, 17.
6. Bolsinger, *Canoeing the Mountains*, 27.
7. Connaughton, "Americans See Stronger Societal Conflict," para 1.

a culture that demonizes God. To the secularist, the God of the Bible is evil, written by culturally biased writers who were governed by their unenlightened bigotry.

In this world, the church is increasingly becoming marginalized. Where churches were once considered the bedrock upon which the community was built, the church is now seen as an intrusion and an outsider whose presence is more of a menace than a necessity. As Tod Bolsinger points out,

> When cities are now considering using eminent domain laws to replace churches with tax-revenue generating big-box stores, when Sundays are more about soccer and Starbucks than about sabbath, when Christian student groups are getting derecognized on university campuses, when the fastest growing religious affiliation among young adults is "none," when there is no moral consensus built on Christian tradition, when even a funeral in a conservative beach town is more likely to be a Hawaiian style "paddle out" than a gathering in a sanctuary, then Christendom as a mark of society has clearly passed.[8]

In his book *Life in a Negative World*, Aaron Renn rightly points out that we have moved from a culture governed by a Judeo-Christian ethic, in which the church was seen as the guardian of public ethics, to a postmodern world in which the church is seen as a threat to the social ethic. In the past, Christianity was embraced and centralized; now it is viewed with suspicion and is becoming an outcast.[9] No longer is the church seen as the moral backbone of society; it is now considered a threat. We have entered a new era. Yet, as Renn rightly points out, "Evangelicals are largely operating as though they're still living in the lost positive and neutral worlds. . . . Evangelicals had not—and to a great extent still have not—recognized what we now live in the negative world."[10] This is most evident in urban communities, but it is also becoming increasingly apparent in rural communities.

The abandonment of a Judeo-Christian ethic and morality is not just about specific moral issues (such as abortion, homosexuality, race, etc.); it is a conflict centered upon different moral visions.[11] While sociologists and historians have debated whether or not we were established as

8. Bolsinger, *Canoeing the Mountains*, 12.

9. Renn, *Life in the Negative World*, 6–7.

10. Renn, *Life in the Negative World*, 33.

11. Hunter, *Culture Wars*, 48.

a Christian nation, there is no longer any debate that we are now entering the realm of being a post-Christian society, where morality is determined by popular opinion rather than any recognized universal standard established by a creator. Within the cultural climate of the day, we are not only the product of changing physical evolution, but we are also the product of a shift in moral evolution.

Rural communities tend to view these issues and the changing morality as urban problems confronting the metropolitan church, disconnected from the rural community and church. While the urban church wrestles with these issues, many rural communities believe they can continue to maintain the status quo. Yet this is a fantasy. Just as the Industrial Revolution changed urban centers and impacted rural areas, so, too, is the tsunami of moral upheaval rapidly descending upon rural communities. While the rural community may remain politically conservative, it is increasingly becoming spiritually ambivalent. For years, the church has operated under the assumption, "If we build it, they will come."[12] In the past, people highly valued the church and would identify with and attend a local congregation. However, even in rural communities, this is no longer the case. Rural people are equally abandoning the church. According to the Cooperative Election Study, 54 percent of rural Americans identify as Christians, which is only a few percentage points above the 51 percent of urban residents. Furthermore, 36 percent of both rural and metro people identify as atheist, agnostic, or "nones."[13]

While rural people may be more morally and politically conservative, that does not translate into a redemptive relationship with Christ. The spiritual wind sweeping across the nation is equally blowing across rural communities. What Bolsinger states in general is equally relevant in rural ministry: "In every field, in every business, every organization, leaders are rapidly coming to the awareness that the world in front of us is radically different from everything behind us."[14] He goes on to point out,

> All that we have assumed about leading Christian organizations, all that we have been trained for, is out of date. We have left the map, we are in uncharted territory, and it is different than we expected. We are experienced river rafters who must learn to be

12. Robinson, *Field of Dreams*.

13. Melotte, "Rural People Don't Practice Religion," para. 4.

14. Bolsinger, *Canoeing the Mountains*, 27.

> mountaineers. And some of us face "the most terrible mountain we have ever beheld."[15]

We were prepared to be pastors who preached in the church, organized the programs and ministries, and provided pastoral care to those in need. While these are still important, in the changing world, they will not be enough. What Richard Critchfield writes is especially applicable to the church: "The faster change comes, the less the old solutions and rules apply and the more new solutions and rules have to be invented, which can be a worry and confusing experience."[16] Just as farmers have had to adapt and change their farming methods over the past one hundred years, so, too, will the church need to find new solutions and methods to minister effectively in a rapidly changing rural culture.

In this new world, the church needs to regroup and reequip for a whole different ministry. When I attended seminary in the early '80s, I was equipped to serve churches in a Christian culture that valued the church, where I had a voice in the broader community. It was a time when pastors were seen as an essential part of the community and valued and respected. It was still standard fare for pastors to be able to golf free on Mondays, and Wednesdays were reserved by the community and schools for church functions. The local pastor was invited to speak at the high school baccalaureate program and lead the community in prayer at community functions. In the '70s, it was the world that was being "left behind."[17]

Today, even in rural communities, the church is being left behind, and the pastor is viewed as an outsider. In this rapidly changing world, two things are certain. First, our message and mission remain relevant and unchanged. The one thing we cannot do is change the message we proclaim and the mission of advancing the kingdom of Christ. Second, current methods of conducting ministry and engaging with the community will no longer be relevant. While the message and mission remain the same, rural pastors will need to refocus and restructure their approach to fulfill the mission.

15. Bolsinger, *Canoeing the Mountains*, 28.

16. Critchfield, *Trees, Why Do You Wait?*, 35.

17. The phrase "left behind" became popular in the 1970s to describe people who were left after the rapture portrayed in the "Left Behind" movie series produced by Mark IV pictures: *A Thief in the Night* (1972), *A Distant Thunder* (1978), *Image of the Beast* (1981), and *The Prodigal Planet* (1983).

Book Outline

The purpose of this book is to provide the foundation for reexamining rural ministry and recognizing that the rural church can no longer be effective by merely being the little white church in the dale. The hope is to spark a new discussion about rural ministry, exploring new avenues of ministry.

Section 1 examines the rapid changes in rural America. To guide the church forward, it is essential to understand how rural communities have evolved and how broader societal shifts have affected the fabric and makeup of rural communities.

Section 2 will discuss recent changes in rural churches, noting a growing disconnect between churches and their communities. Recognizing the rural church as crucial to ministry, we should shift from an internally focused, business-like approach to a gospel-focused, missional model.

Section 3 will focus on the future to examine how the rural church needs to reorient its ministry within the new context. We will explore the essential characteristics required to undergird the church's ministry if it is to be effective in the future. The most crucial decision in orchestrating change and adapting to a new world is to determine what we cannot change.

Section 4 focuses on developing a philosophy of ministry suited to a post-Christian world, highlighting the need for new methods and approaches. This includes adopting new methods and adapting our mission and ministry to a post-Christian world.

The last section sets forth the road map for how the rural church needs to change its ministry to be effective today. In a changing world, we need to be adaptive and innovative in our ministry as we move the ministry of the church into the community. We can no longer assume the community will come to the church; instead, we need to develop a ministry that engages the community with the gospel.

A popular saying today states, "Insanity is doing the same things over and over again and expecting a different result." This is true within the rural church. If we continue to do things the same way, then we will increasingly find ourselves marginalized from the community. While the gospel message must remain unchanged, contextualizing the gospel for the local community will require the church to adapt, becoming a missional rather than a maintenance-oriented church. This journey will challenge us not to change the gospel or the church's nature but to rethink and adapt how we effectively minister within the local setting.

Part 1

The Changing Rural Culture

1

Navigating a World in Flux

THE 2016 PRESIDENTIAL ELECTION had numerous ramifications for the entire United States, particularly for the 19 percent of the population residing in rural areas. For the first time in many years, people who lived in the flyover areas of the country, the small towns and remote rural regions making up the countryside between the East Coast and the West Coast, were brought to the forefront as, suddenly, they were seen as kingmakers—or in this particular situation, president-makers.

The results hurled the US media out of their coastal cities and into the heartland to discover who these people were and why they voted as they did. For some, this served as an indictment of rural people. Upon reflection, one liberal writer described the problem with rural America as such:

> Rural Americans don't understand the causes of their own situations and fears, and they have shown no interest in finding out. Another problem with rural Christian white Americans is they are racists. . . . Their white god made them in his image, and everyone else is a less-than-perfect version, flawed and cursed. . . . For us "coastal elites" who understand evolution, genetics, and science, nothing we say to those in flyover country is going to be listened to because not only are we fighting against an anti-education belief system, we are arguing against god.[1]

1. Forsetti's Justice, "Rural Christian White America," para. 2, 7, 10.

On May 26, 2017, the *Wall Street Journal* published an article titled, "Rural America is the New 'Inner City.'" The article asserted rural America has more poverty-related issues, more drug problems, more health problems, more divorces, and more teen pregnancies than the rest of the US.

> In terms of poverty, college attainment, teenage births, divorce, death rates from heart disease and cancer, reliance on federal disability insurance and male labor-force participation, rural counties now rank the worst among the four major U.S. population groupings (the others are big cities, suburbs, and medium or small metro areas).[2]

Along with the rising interest among secular groups, the Christian community began to develop an interest in rural ministry as well. Since 2016, a plethora of books have been published on rural and small-town ministry, such as *The Forgotten Church* by Glenn Daman (2018), *Small Town Jesus* by Donnie Griggs (2016), and *A Big Gospel in Small Places* by Stephen Witmer (2019), to name a few. While a few rural organizations have existed for many years focusing on rural ministry (such as the Rural Home Missionary Association and Village Missions), several new rural networks and training events have emerged in recent years. The development of the Rural Church Institute at Wheaton College and organizations such as Dirt Roads Network are examples of resources recently developed for rural churches.

To gain an accurate picture of rural America today, it is essential to examine three major social influences and their impact on rural America since World War II. The three forces of mechanization, mobilization, and media have shaped rural America over the last two generations and continue to exert significant influence on rural communities today.

Mechanization

World War II is considered a turning point for rural America. For more than three hundred years before World War II, the family farm was the backbone of the US economy. In 1800, 83 percent of the US population was involved in farming.[3]

Family farms required lots of man-hours to survive. Thus, it was helpful to have large families to work the fields. For example, in the 1800s,

2. Adamy and Overberg, "Rural America," para. 5.
3. Huston, "Early National America," abstract.

one farmer could feed three to five people.[4] That meant one farmer could provide enough food for his immediate family and just barely make enough to survive. The more children he had, the more he could produce and the more money he could make.

Starting in the 1930s, tractors became more affordable for the average farmer as manufacturers began to develop machinery designed for the family farm. As World War II began, the young men who had been providing manual labor on the farm left to fight in the war. The increasing needs for supplies to feed and clothe these soldiers, along with the growing nation, caused commodity prices to rise, providing farmers with the resources needed to purchase tractors, combines, and other mechanized farm equipment. Where a farm in the 1940s could only feed twenty people, today, with modern machinery, a farm can produce enough food for 165 people.[5] The machinery that allowed the family farm to become more efficient caused fewer family members to be needed to run the farm.

Another example of mechanization and its effect on rural life was the rise of the automobile, both cars and trucks. Along with the growth in the manufacturing of farm machinery, the end of World War II saw a sharp increase in the number of automobiles produced. Cars evolved from simple designs, such as the Ford Model A before the war, to sleek, modern-designed vehicles like the 1949 Ford sedan, which could travel great distances in comfort. Farmers previously isolated in rural areas could now drive into town to shop, dine, and attend the movies. Their sons and daughters could now live in a nearby city and travel easily to visit the rural family farm.

Let me provide a personal example. My dad grew up in the 1940s, about eight miles from the nearest town. He went to town once a month with his family, where, if he was lucky, he bought a soft drink and went to the movies. Today, he lives on the same farm but makes the trip into town at least once a day to visit a local gas station, grab a cup of coffee, or shop at Walmart or the local co-op to pick up items needed for the farm.

The unintended consequences of the automobile on rural life are not to be overstated. Small mom-and-pop grocery stores that once dotted the countryside, within walking distance for most people, closed as people could now go into town to large chain stores to buy groceries. Modest community-based schools shuttered as they were consolidated

4. Progressive Rancher, "Growing the Number of People," para. 1.

5. Progressive Rancher, "Growing the Number of People," para. 1.

with other rural schools, and their students were bused to the one large school in town.

In just a few decades, mechanization was able to turn rural life upside down. The rise of the automobile stretched the boundaries of where one could travel in a day, and isolated communities lost their identity as their stores, schools, and churches closed. As tractors and combines grew larger, farms also expanded, allowing farmers to work more land with fewer people. In 1930, the average farm size was 151 acres.[6] By 2020, the average farm size had mushroomed to 444 acres.[7] Thus, farming morphed from family farms into agri-businesses requiring specialized training and machinery.

Urban Migration

At the end of World War II, more than 3 million soldiers returned from the war and began searching for employment. These men grew up in the 1930s on small, labor-intensive family farms across the US. Upon returning to the US after the war, they discovered they had been replaced by tractors, combines, and other mechanized equipment. So, by the thousands, they began to migrate to the cities to find work.

A tidal wave of migration began at the end of World War II and continues to this day. Young men and women graduate from high school, go off to universities, with no intention of returning to the farm. With no work available on the farm, they go where they have opportunities to make money.

The migration of young people to cities produces a domino effect, impacting almost every part of rural life for those left behind. The first domino is the "brain drain." Some college graduates from rural areas return to their rural roots. However, many more potential leaders "go off to college and never come back." Please note that this is not intended to disparage those who choose to remain in rural areas to pursue their vocation. Intelligent, articulate, and capable leaders remained in many places. However, urban migration reduces the pool of possible leaders from rural communities.

The second domino is the closing of stores, hospitals, and professional services in rural America. It is almost impossible to visit a small

6. Nations Encyclopedia, "United States—Agriculture," para. 2.

7. Farm Progress, "Number of Farms in U.S.," para. 1.

town in rural America today without seeing shuttered buildings that once housed schools, banks, lawyers' offices, and doctors' offices. Because many of these businesses relocated to larger towns with the advent of the automobile, a lack of job opportunities exists for people who specialized in these fields, resulting in many smaller towns and villages becoming little more than ghost towns.

As businesses close in rural areas and jobs become scarce, the third domino of poverty falls. The doctor's office that left also took with it jobs for a nurse, secretary, billing manager, and janitor. Low-paying jobs are all that remain, keeping many workers in small towns below the poverty level.

The last domino to fall because of urban migration is the rise in social issues, including drug and alcohol abuse, spousal and child abuse, teen pregnancy, and suicide. Rural America leads the country in the percentage of people dealing with each of these issues. The saddest part is that most rural areas are ill-equipped to deal with these increased social issues. Most do not have counselors or treatment facilities. Often, these services are too far away to make them feasible for many living in rural areas. Also, rural communities offer no privacy, and the stigma of going to counseling or treatment centers can be overwhelming to deal with in a community where everyone knows everyone's business.

Media

The third significant influence in rural America has been the rise of media since World War II. Prior to the 1940s, people in many rural areas lived in isolation. For example, people living in the heart of Appalachia moved into the hills and hollows starting in the mid-1700s up to around 1850. They lived isolated and unaffected by the outside world for more than 100 years. The few visitors to the area were introduced to a culture and language harkening back to the 1700s and early 1800s. For multiple generations, this area maintained a different culture and dialect from the rest of the U.S.

Starting with the advent of the radio, remote rural areas, such as Appalachia, the farming regions of the Midwest, rural fishing communities on the coasts, and Cajun country in Louisiana, were all introduced to the larger world. By the 1940s, many in these rural areas had radios in their homes to stay informed about the war, hear the latest prices for grain and livestock, and listen to shows like *Fibber McGee and Molly* as well as other popular radio programs.

Another significant media influence was the rise of movie theaters. People in rural America could now drive into town and watch the same movie as people in New York City. They also watched newsreels featuring the battles of World War II and the Korean War. By watching films and various newsreels, rural people could keep up with the latest fashions in New York and Los Angeles.

By the end of the 1950s, television had begun to make inroads into rural areas. People could watch Walter Cronkite and see the Vietnam War from their own homes. TV shows and advertisements let people know the latest fads and helped rural teenagers connect with what their urban counterparts were doing. By the 1980s, the satellite dish allowed rural people to choose from hundreds of channels, and the world came flooding into their homes via the magic of television.

Finally, the advent of the internet meant that rural people could not only watch but also interact with people from literally around the world. The internet has provided access to significant amounts of information that were previously unavailable. By Googling, it was now possible to find thousands of websites with information concerning a given subject.[8]

The impact of the media cannot be overestimated in rural areas. Communities previously isolated from the rest of the world are now open to the influences, both good and bad, of the world at large. The flood of information resulted in a loss of identity for many rural cultures. The language, mores, and defining characteristics of many rural, isolated communities are eroding as the influence of the media has homogenized the world. Farmers living in remote villages in Nebraska, coal miners in Eastern Kentucky, and fishermen off the coast of Alaska can literally talk with one another in real-time. They can watch almost anything they want on demand. Much of their machinery now uses the internet to be more effective in production. As the world moves toward one global community, isolated, rural communities are losing their local identities.

The influence of media also means major influencers in rural communities have changed. In previous generations, the local pastor, doctor,

8. An argument can be made that the internet is more than just media; it could be seen as a possible fourth influence. The internet affects rural America in the way rural people shop, interact with others, learn, and communicate. It is more than just a media source. (This concept comes from conversations with Dallas Powell, a church planting catalyst in Nebraska.)

and teachers were the major influencers in the community. Now, media personalities found on YouTube and TikTok are heralded as sources of wisdom and information.

With the influence of media comes many good things for rural communities, such as more knowledge for farming, fishing, coal mining, and other rural work; knowledge of what is going on in the world; and better materials for local teachers, doctors, and business owners, etc. However, many negative things for rural areas have also resulted from the rise of media, such as loss of community, increased addictions to harmful internet activities, such as pornography and gambling, and distractions that waste time.

Effects on the Rural Church

The results of these three major social issues on rural life cannot be overestimated. Their effects can specifically be felt by rural churches. Each issue has reshaped the local church context in ways that make pre-war churches unfamiliar to rural church members today. The little country church of the first half of the twentieth century is now long gone, and a new era has emerged due to mechanization, urban migration, and the advent of media.

Mechanization

As described earlier, the impact of mechanization on farming practices has been tremendous since the end of World War II. Farmers have been able to be more productive than ever before. However, the impact of mechanization on rural churches has been devastating. As mechanization increased on the farm, so did mobility. The rise of automobiles on the farm meant that rural people could travel farther for shopping and entertainment, as well as for worship. They were no longer limited to the local general store or the nearest church. They could now go into town to get what they needed, both physically and spiritually.

Increased mobility has led to the rise of the "Walmart" church. Just as Walmart moved into market towns and subsumed small businesses in rural areas, larger, well-funded churches with professionally trained staff in nearby towns have drawn leadership from rural, community-church members who can now travel into town for worship.

In today's world, someone going to church will pass at least one church on their way to the church of their choice. Personally, my wife and I pass four churches on our way to the church we attend. Before World War II, people attended church based on their geographical location. They could only go as far as they could walk or ride in a wagon. After the war, and with the increased mobility provided by mechanization, people began to go to church based on affinity.

The observation above is not a criticism of larger "in-town" churches. It is merely a description of the realities of rural church life since 1945. Mechanization and the resulting mobilization have provided people in rural areas with more choices than ever before. The rural church today simply cannot expect people in the immediate community to come to their church just because it is in the community.

Urban Migration

The effects of urban migration on rural churches have also been devastating. When people leave rural areas in search of "greener pastures" in the city, they leave behind small churches struggling just to stay open with limited leadership and the financial resources needed to thrive in their communities.

With dwindling pools of leadership and physical resources drying up, many small rural churches get caught in a slow death spiral. The decline begins with the elimination of ministries due to limited budgets. Ministries to youth and children are often among the first to be cut. As fewer people are reached due to ministries being reduced, fewer resources remain. Families with children and money go into town, where the church has opportunities for the entire family.

The next step is to lower the pastor's salary, as many tithing families have moved to larger churches, which causes the pastor to search for a place to serve where proper support can be found. The search for a bivocational pastor begins, which means the pastor has less time to invest in the struggling church, resulting in even more people defecting to the larger in-town churches with well-trained and well-paid staff.

Finally, the church dwindles to just a few faithful older members who can remember what the church used to be like before everyone left. With the migration complete, many rural churches remain open only due to the faithfulness of a few older members, and when they pass away, the church will likely close.

Media

The media has had perhaps the most profound impact on rural churches since 1945. Rural people can now go online and see large churches with highly trained musicians and skilled pastors preaching polished sermons along with a multimedia presentation. As a result, many in rural areas seek these more "professional" church services in nearby larger towns. After all, churches in town have things for the children and teens, maintain beautiful facilities, and have pastors dedicated solely to preaching the word.

Historically, rural churches valued pastors over preachers. They could overlook mediocre sermons if they were "pastored" well. Loving and caring for the flock from birth to the grave was the primary task of the rural pastor. However, with the rise of media, the emphasis on "good preaching" has increased. It is now common for a dedicated church member to listen to multiple sermons throughout the week on Christian radio, TV, or the internet. While they realize their pastor is no J. D. Greear, listening to sermons from pastors of big churches throughout the week raises their standards for what they expect each Sunday in their own little church.

Media as entertainment has also severely affected rural churches. Before World War II, the church was the primary source of community, support, and entertainment. The church was the place in the community for people to catch up with each other, share their lives, and sing and worship together. Now, people can get many of their needs for community, support, and entertainment met online. The church is no longer the news center or the social connector for people in rural communities. People now have access to twenty-four-hour news and entertainment and can communicate with family members around the world with the tap of a few keys.

Conclusion

The compound effects of mechanization, migration, and media on rural churches have been profound. The rural church that was once the center of the community has been increasingly marginalized as people travel further to go to the church of their choice, move away for higher education and careers, and seek to be entertained by different media outlets.

Rural areas are filled with small, struggling churches and a significant number of people who claim to be Christian, but few who actually attend church on a weekly basis. For example, in Kentucky, a primarily rural state in the "Bible belt," 90 percent of the state's residents believe in God, and 73 percent believe religion is important or somewhat important in their lives. However, only 31 percent attend church on a weekly basis.[9]

Glenn Daman summarizes the situation in his book *The Forgotten Church*: "Rural America is rapidly becoming a spiritual wasteland, where churches are being closed because they are overlooked and cast aside by the larger church community as a place deemed too insignificant or unworthy of our attention."[10] Simply put, rural America is not the religious center of the nation it once was.

Rural churches in North America have undergone significant changes since the end of World War II in 1945. Yet through all the turmoil of monumental shifts in lifestyle and culture, many rural churches have survived and are still being a light to their world in many forgotten places.

Rural churches face issues such as declining membership, limited finances, and increasing social issues, such as drug use, poverty, suicide, and teen pregnancy. It seems these rural churches remain in a permanent precarious state where demise seems imminent. However, many churches have remained on the edge of extinction for decades now, hanging on through the toughest situations.

With this in mind, a great need exists to see rural America as a mission field in need of new church starts and church revitalizations. God-called pastors still need to be trained to serve in existing rural churches, working together with urban churches to fulfill God's desire to saturate the entire US and beyond with the gospel.

Currently, a reawakening to the needs of rural America can be seen across the US, especially since the 2016 election. Awareness of America and the plight of people living in the countryside has come to the forefront. And, while many issues still plague small-town America and impact rural churches, hope still abounds as God continues to work in these areas.

9. Pew Research Center, "Religious Landscape Study."

10. Daman, *Forgotten Church*, 16.

2

The Changing Rural Community

In our rapidly changing world, if we fail to adapt to the new culture and instead strive to rediscover or preserve the past, we will lose touch with the future and become marginalized within the broader culture. Without understanding the present, we cannot prepare for or understand the future. We become lost in our search for spiritual relevance. The national trends described in chapter 1 brought transformation (both good and bad) to the rural community.

As we saw in the previous chapter, changes in the broader culture had a dramatic impact on rural communities and the rural church. We often view rural communities and the rural church as fortresses of constancy. However, external changes in the broader culture were dramatically affecting rural communities and transforming rural people. But changes were also happening within the rural community. Change did not come solely from external forces but also from internal forces within the rural culture.

Rural communities, governed by tradition, represent stability in a changing world. For many (with some merit), the decline of the rural farmer has a far more significant impact than just on rural communities. Critchfield forcefully argues that "no society can get too far away from its rural origins and farming and stay healthy."[1] He goes on to write that the shift from rural to urban will fundamentally alter American society, becoming less social and less concerned about one's neighbor,

1. Critchfield, *Trees, Why Do You Wait?*, 203.

more suspicious and less trusting, less honest and more greedy, and more focused on self-indulgence than on following basic moral principles.[2]

In the past, rural was synonymous with farming, logging, and mining. Those who drew their livelihood from the earth felt a close connection with the Creator. As Wuthnow writes, "The idea that God is always present, at least in the background, was reinforced among the farmers we spoke with by their sense of being in direct daily contact with God's creation."[3] A connection existed between their work, the Creator, and the church. But this is no longer the case. Rural communities now comprise industries and tourism as well. To minister effectively in rural communities, the church needs to understand the current community, rather than what it was in the past.

Rural America: Changing from Within

When our country was first established, it was founded as an agrarian society that viewed farming as the most noble of careers. Because the land upon which the farmer dwelt did not change, nor did the products and crops they produced, it was easy to conclude that life does not change. Yet, upon closer examination, we discover the history of rural communities is a story of change and adaptation.

As the nation grew, the amount of land spread out across the continent seemed endless. Large open-range ranches were established to feed a country on an infinite horizon of grassy plains. These ranches were vast and unencumbered. The history of the cowboy and the open range became a national icon, surviving to this day (who has not watched John Wayne movies?). Men like Pierre Wibaux, who befriended Teddy Roosevelt, established an open-range ranch of 65,000 head of cattle in eastern Montana and became one of the major cattle kings in the West.[4]

In 1902, with the encouragement of Roosevelt, Owen Wister published the novel *The Virginian: A Horseman of the Plains*, and it immediately became a bestseller. It did more than just tell a story; it created a myth that the cowboy was the quintessential American. The character was a "gentleman, polite to women, kind to animals, law-abiding and honest—the antithesis of the outlaw. When he wasn't engaged in cowboy

2. Critchfield, *Trees, Why Do You Wait?*, 224.
3. Wuthnow, *In the Blood*, 78.
4. Knowlton, *Cattle Kingdom*, 235.

activities, his job was to distinguish right from wrong."[5] The myth of the noble cowboy was further established through the writings of Zane Grey and Louis L'Amour. However, the myth was vastly different from reality, for it was a kingdom that would not last, and it reached its zenith at the cost of the Native Americans who had lived on the land for generations. A growing America needed more land, and "if the Indian could not put his land to use, another would. In the process, Indian tribes declined in population and as a civilization."[6] As indelible an imprint as the cowboy era had in our national identity, it was short-lived. As Knowlton points out, "Open-range ranching was simply a broken economic model. Doomed by false assumptions, by barbed wire, and by poorly conceived land laws and widespread ranch mismanagement, the cattle industry retrenched and then slowly began to restructure and rebuild."[7]

For all its nostalgic symbols, the era of the cowboy only lasted approximately thirty-five years. It would fall prey to the same forces that have continually brought about changes in rural communities. The end of the cowboy era was less about the closing of the frontier and more about the economic evolution of the nation and the effects of a market-driven economy.[8] The wide-open ranges were replaced by small ranches, farms, and small towns.

As the cowboys faded into the past, the homesteaders began to dominate rural areas. No longer was rural defined by open range; now it would be defined by farms, fenced pastures, and small communities that would dot the landscape. Just as the cowboy displaced Native Americans, the Homestead Act would displace cowboys. As time went on, the subsistence farmer would also be displaced by the production-driven farm as it embraced mechanization. In its pursuit of increased production and reduced labor, farmers ultimately set the stage for the radical transformation of rural communities. As already pointed out, mechanization led to the decline of farming, logging, and mining, as these industries lost importance in employing rural residents.

However, these changes were not just changes in the economic foundation of the community. The changes occurring within rural America go to the core of rural culture and values. As agriculture, mining, and logging became less and less dominant, "agriculture has lost its

5. Knowlton, *Cattle Kingdom*, 337.

6. Paxson, *History of the American Frontier*, 320.

7. Knowlton, *Cattle Kingdom*, 310.

8. Knowlton, *Cattle Kingdom*, 311.

dominance, and the countryside is being transformed by people whose occupations, outlooks, and values are decidedly nonagricultural."[9] We are not in Kansas anymore, not because we left Kansas but Kansas has left us. Rural communities were soon becoming bedroom communities for people moving out of the city and into the country. The out-migration was replaced by the in-migration of people who had no connection to the land or the church. The changes seen in the rural landscape led to a shift in rural culture.

As extractive industries declined, an increasing number of people viewed rural areas as places to retire or work remotely. However, as they moved from urban areas into the rural communities, they brought different values and cultures, which conflicted with those of the rural residents. Rural communities were no longer centered on a shared value and worldview. As a result, a gulf grew within the community between the newcomers and longtime residents.

The urban to rural migration increased with the invention of the automobile. People from urban communities have always been drawn to the beauty of rural areas. When automobiles emerged, the first effect was that they drew urban people to rural communities in search of leisure. The attitude changed. Rural communities were no longer seen as sources of food; they became places for recreation and leisure. Fitchen describes the growing conflict between long-term residents and newly transplanted people moving into the country:

> When the gap between traditional assumptions and current social realities can no longer be denied, one strategy for keeping intact the collective vision of the community as a close-knit, homogenous place is to compartmentalize local residents. Unknown or unfamiliar people are lumped into generic social types under there that essentially keep them separated from "bona fide members" of the community. Year-round residents who have recently purchased village homes or moved into new housing tracts are termed "newcomers"; vacation people are called "outsiders"; and low-income renters in the apartment and trailer parks are referred to as "transients," or sometimes "foreigners." Although the valuation attached to these categories is a gradation downward, all of the people thus categorized are externalized rather than folded into the community. Residing

9. Castle, *Changing American Countryside*, 67.

> within the locality, they are nonetheless conceptually marginalized and kept as social nonmembers.[10]

This is further intensified when the newcomer's political views directly contradict the traditional political alliances within the community. The outsider is not only regarded as a new resident, but they are also perceived as a threat to the existing geopolitical world within the community.

This subtle but real gulf between newcomers and longtime residents continues to affect community engagement and the church. The church is no longer viewed as the moral backbone; it is no longer considered essential; it is viewed as a peripheral member of the community. The church is becoming an increasingly irrelevant institution in the minds of people.

The Changing Rural Values

We often view culture as static, especially in rural communities where the houses and fields seem to remain unchanged. Brown and Swanson point out that "the American public tends to see its rural population as a repository of almost sacred values and a stable anchor during times of rapid social change."[11] However, this belies the drastic shifts that have occurred recently in rural culture. Rather than rural communities being the moral backbone of the country, rural communities are decaying as rapidly as the collapsing barns dotting the landscape.

Rural communities, once the hallmark of a stable society, are becoming the poster child of community disintegration.[12] Brown and Swanson point out, "Rural people have a higher likelihood of being poor than urban residents."[13] Not only are rural children facing higher poverty rates than urban children, but they are also lagging behind national norms in educational achievement and are more likely to drop out of school before graduation.[14] In every social, moral, and economic indicator, rural children are lagging behind their urban counterparts. Young people in rural areas are more likely to use alcohol and experience a teen pregnancy. This

10. Fitchen, *Endangered Spaces, Enduring Places*, 256.

11. Brown and Swanson, *Challenges for Rural America*, 1.

12. For further discussion of the social and economic collapse of the rural community and the response of the church see Daman, *Forgotten Church*.

13. Brown and Swanson, *Challenges for Rural America*, 2.

14. Brown and Swanson, *Challenges for Rural America*, 101.

has led some to refer to rural America as the new ghetto. Thus, Lichter, Roscigno, and Condron conclude,

> Today, a large share of rural "at-risk" children may be ill-prepared for good jobs in a rapidly changing urban and bicoastal economy. Though many stay in depressed rural communities, others move on to the cities, adding to the problem of urban joblessness, poverty, family disruption, and crime, while taxing the institutional capacity of urban centers to adequately respond.[15]

In the past, rural life was often regarded as the epitome of what was best in society. Now it is characterized by what is worst!

It is not just that rural communities are collapsing economically, but they are also changing culturally. While rural communities view urban centers as distant and disconnected, they often fail to recognize that the city is expanding into the country, and cultural conservatism and uniformity are being replaced by cultural diversity and a new morality. Yet the church often continues to blissfully exist as a symbol of traditional Christianity while the community around it collapses.

As the church moves into the future, it will need to rethink its role within the local community. If the church continues to minister as it has in the past, it may find itself in the same state of disrepair and disintegration as the red barns that once symbolized agrarian life. It may continue to ring the church bell Sunday morning to call people to worship, blissfully unaware its sound is ignored by spiritually deaf people who view the church as outdated and out of touch with the present struggles in their lives. In this new world, the rural church will need to radically shift from trying to duplicate the stability and growth of the suburban church to being innovative in ministering to people on the fringe of society. Instead of being patterned after the suburban church, it will need to learn from the innovation of the inner-city church.

The Changing Spiritual Nature of Rural Communities

Nostalgia also distorts history by painting an unreal picture of the past. Just as people view rural communities as the hallmark of stability and permanence, it is easy to uphold the illusion that the rural church has

15. Brown and Swanson, *Challenges for Rural America*, 108.

remained unchanged, untouched by the moral shifts and postmodernism impacting urban congregations and ministries.

When the history of rural ministry is examined more closely, it becomes evident that the rural church has undergone continual changes since the arrival of the first Puritan pilgrims. While historians continue to debate whether or not our nation was initially established as a Christian nation, we cannot deny the reality that often, the colonies were characterized by "scenes of drunken revelry and barroom brawling, of women in risqué ball-gowns, of gamblers and rakes."[16] Finke and Stark note that in 1776, only about one in five New Englanders had a religious affiliation.[17] In the early days of the colonial period, we often focused on the religious piety of the Puritans, but this was not true of all immigrants. Bailyn points out that many of the initial immigrants were

> hardened criminals—thieves, blackmailers, pimps, rapists, embezzlers, and thugs for hire.[18] Between 1718 and 1775, the English courts forcibly transported over 50,000 criminals, most of them convicted of capital crimes, to America.[19] As America grew, a shortage of clergy existed that limited the ability to establish churches, and often, those who did come were of such character that it would have been better that "people had no minister than such as are generally sent over.[20]

The growth of the church in the new frontier was hindered by "common features of all frontier settings: transience, disorder, too many men, too many scoundrels, and too few effective and committed clergy."[21]

This is not to say Christianity did not have a considerable influence on the rural communities, for it did. However, as the church struggled to reach the expanding frontier, it faced many challenges requiring the church to be innovative in order to reach the untamed regions of expansion. Not only was there the challenge of establishing churches in the expanding countryside, but the problem of too few people spread across a vast landscape also provided a challenge for starting churches. Where the opportunities and land were rich, well-defined communities developed around the railroad stations and shipping centers that were

16. Finke and Stark, *Churching of America*, 25.
17. Finke and Stark, *Churching of America*, 25.
18. Bailyn, *Voyagers to the West*, 295.
19. Bailyn, *Voyagers to the West*, 29.
20. Bailyn, *Voyagers to the West*, 40.
21. Bailyn, *Voyagers to the West*, 43.

established. These communities evolved into thriving trading centers, featuring stores, hotels, schools, and sometimes a church. Yet in other areas, the land was marginal; one lonely family would write that they were the "only habitation in a round sky and stretch of plain."[22] In the frontier, the church faced the challenge of a scattered and transient population, where homesteaders were a "restless, uncertain human quality."[23] In this lonesome wasteland, the gospel was needed, but few ventured.

To further add to the need was the presence of the Native American tribes, who were unreached and untouched by the gospel. To meet the challenge, President Theodore Roosevelt appointed the Commission on Country Life in 1908 to address the concerns raised by the Country Life movement. After conducting interviews with rural people across the country, they concluded,

> While there are many rural churches that are effective agents in the social evolution of their communities, it is true that, as a whole, the country church needs a new direction and to assume new responsibilities. Few of the churches in the open country are provided with resident pastors.[24]

The history of the rural church is marked by the need to adopt new strategies to meet the changing culture and environment. In response to the challenges of a growing nation, denominational leaders developed innovative ministries to address these needs. Because of a shortage of pastors and funding for resident pastors, circuit riders filled the gap by traveling to different communities to minister to people's spiritual needs. These circuit riders were the full-time professionals recognized by denominational leaders. Along with these professionals, itinerant preachers came to serve local congregations. These full-time itinerants were often lay leaders who were responsible for the local church. Due to the shortage of educated clergy, Baptists and Methodists relied heavily on ministers who came from the laity and often remained part of it. They had little education and received little to no pay, yet gained in popularity as they spoke the language of the people and preached from the heart.[25]

As rural communities began to stabilize and churches were established, they became not only the religious center but also the moral,

22. Belknap, *Church on the Changing Frontier*, 32.

23. Belknap, *Church on the Changing Frontier*, 56.

24. Bailey et al., "Report of Country Life Commission," 60.

25. Finke and Stark, *Churching of America*, 76.

social, and cultural hub for the community. With a shared spiritual and cultural belief, rural communities became defined by a cohesive and shared set of spiritual and moral values. The unique isolation resulted in social isolation, which insulated them from the changes occurring in the broader culture that dominated urban centers. As a result, local circumstances and community characteristics became dominant, creating locally distinctive cultural, organizational, ceremonial, and ritual forms.[26] Each community developed its own traditions, with religious practices largely influenced by the ethnic and religious backgrounds of its people. While different institutions existed within the community—political, economic, religious, and family—they were governed by shared values and woven together in a single fabric.[27]

This single community value is no longer present today, as new people move into the community and bring new values. Rural communities are no longer isolated from the broader culture. As a result, rural churches are now ministering in communities vastly different from those of previous generations. While the church previously shared the same moral and religious values with the community, it now finds itself in a culturally diverse community with values that conflict with the church. The church can no longer assume people are accepting of its teachings and even presence in the community, as they no longer share a moral, cultural, or spiritual identity with the church.

The Changing Ministry Environment

Just as cities have become post-Christian, so have rural communities. The methods and strategies for ministry once taught in seminary were built upon the assumption that people would come to church as long as they were provided a reason to do so, through dynamic children's programs, energetic music, and sermons addressing the felt needs of people. This is no longer the case. The game has changed. The United States is no longer a Christian nation or even a Christian community. While rural communities still give assent to traditional Christian values, in reality, many are already embracing a post-Christian culture where the church is no longer seen as relevant. In this rapidly changing world, the methods churches once employed are no longer effective for the future. The Industrial and

26. Castle, *Changing American Countryside*, 374.

27. Castle, *Changing American Countryside*, 376.

Agricultural Revolutions not only changed the population of rural communities but also altered their social and moral foundations.

The tragedy is that the church has not adapted its ministry to the new reality. Many rural churches continue to operate blissfully, as they have for generations, but then lament that the community no longer identifies with or attends the church. In response to the changing rural culture, many past methodologies are no longer relevant. Pastors were trained to lead churches and develop programs in a Christian community.

A new approach to ministry is required. In the past, the church in rural communities has operated like the *Field of Dreams*: "If we build it, they will come."[28] Evangelism and outreach were based on the idea of getting people through the church doors. However, in a postmodern world, the open door remains unused. The church will need new, innovative programs and ministries that move it out into the community, rather than waiting for the community to come to the church.

Rural ministry is not, and has never been, about stability and unchanging tradition; rather, it is a story of adaptation and innovation as the church struggles to reach isolated communities and establish and maintain small congregations. Just as the church needs to adapt to the changing needs of the rural community, so, too, will it need to continue changing if it is to reach the next generation of rural people effectively.

28. Robinson, *Field of Dreams.*

3

The Changing Perception of Rural Communities

In 1905, George Santayana, a Spanish philosopher, wrote, "Those who cannot remember the past are condemned to repeat it."[1] The inference is that we must learn from our past mistakes or be doomed to repeat them.

For this chapter, the goal is not to list past mistakes from which we need to learn. Rather, the goal is to provide a quick review of how rural America has been viewed throughout our history. This history plays a crucial role in shaping our current situation, providing the necessary background to help address current issues and prevent future mistakes.

Rural Communities in the Colonial Period

In the 1700s, the situation in England (and most of Europe) was dire for anyone who made up the vast majority of the population. Before the Industrial Revolution began in England, around 1760, the British class system had a stranglehold on British society. This system traces its origins to the medieval feudal structure, which divided society into a rigid hierarchy based on land ownership and service.[2] These classes were practically impossible to transcend. The highest class was the nobility, which

1. Santayana, *Life of Reason*, 284–85.
2. Easy Sociology, "British Class System," para. 2.

owned vast estates and wielded great power. Next were knights, squires, gentlemen, and gentlewomen whose fortunes were great enough that they did not have to work with their hands for a living. Third were the yeomanry, the middle class that could live comfortably on the little savings they had built up. The bottom of the hierarchy and, by far, the class with the largest number of people were serfs and peasants, who worked the land for subsistence.[3]

Land ownership was primarily limited to the nobility, who owned vast estates and were responsible for the care of those living on their land. Nobility were not farmers but landowners who had a vast number of people working for their estates.

From this structure emerged the first great wave of immigrants to North America. Most of these immigrants were from the lowest social class, the serfs and peasants, who often came to America as indentured servants willing to work off their travel costs in the hope of one day owning land, a privilege reserved for the nobility in England and Europe. Owning your own land and being your own boss had great appeal for the working poor seeking a way to improve their lives.

Many of those coming to America did, in fact, become landowners, especially as the frontier moved west over the Allegheny mountains. The land east of the Alleghenies was quickly divided into large plantations, especially south of Virginia. Gentlemen farmers and plantation owners maintained a system similar to that of England, with strict social structures based on land ownership. However, the new breed of immigrants seeking land began to push the borders of the colonies into central Tennessee, Kentucky, and the wild frontier of Ohio, where land was either free or at least relatively inexpensive.

In 1800, 94 percent of the US population lived in rural settings.[4] Much of the population lived on homesteads on the frontier. The 1800 census shows New York state had 83,161 people. Yet Kentucky, which is entirely west of the Allegheny mountains, had 37,274 people, a substantial number of people living west of the Alleghenies, primarily on small farms.[5]

These landowners now presented a powerful political bloc that could not be ignored. Thomas Jefferson championed the yeoman farmer when he stated,

3. Historical Association, "Social Structure."
4. Census.gov, "Table 4."
5. Census.gov, "Table 4."

> Those who labour in the earth are the chosen people of God, if ever he had a chosen people, whose breasts he has made his peculiar deposit for substantial and genuine virtue. It is the focus in which he keeps alive that sacred fire, which otherwise might escape from the face of the earth.[6]

Jefferson further elaborated when he said,

> Cultivators of the earth are the most valuable citizens. They are the most vigorous, the most independent, the most virtuous, and they are tied to their country and wedded to its liberty and interests by the most lasting bands.[7]

Jefferson's view of the American farmer can also be seen in light of his lofty statement in the US Constitution, which states, "All men are created equal." This was a direct refutation of the European political hierarchy. He envisioned a country more in line with the Enlightenment ideals of the French Revolution. He saw the farmer as the ideal and equal in status (if not above) to lawyers, politicians, and other professional jobs.

After Jefferson, free land was offered through various homestead acts from 1841 to the 1930s. These land grants saw the US government give out, for free, over 160 million acres, or nearly 10 percent of the US landmass.[8] While the eastern US was quickly moving into the Industrial Age, and cities began to grow rapidly, rural expansion westward continued unabated. By 1900, the percentage of rural people in the US had dropped to 60 percent of the total population. However, this meant 46 million out of 76 million people were living in rural areas.

The high view of the American farmer promoted by Jefferson held true in the United States until well into the twentieth century. However, the seeds of change were planted around the time Jefferson made his lofty statements about the American farmer. By the turn of the nineteenth century, the US began to move away from being an agrarian country to embracing the new Industrial Age, with its large factories and advanced production technologies. The migration of people to urban centers throughout the 1800s saw some of the allure of land ownership and the yeoman farmer ideal diminish.

6. Jefferson, *Notes on the State*, 160.
7. Jefferson, "Thomas Jefferson to John Jay," para. 1.
8. Wikipedia, "Homestead Acts."

Rural Communities in the Twentieth Century

For the first time in our country's history, in 1920, more people lived in urban areas than in rural areas.[9] The allure transitioned from living in rural areas to life in the cities. Living the cosmopolitan life, now being showcased in the new media of moving pictures, and the popularity of radio became the American ideal.

By the 1940s, the perception of rural life was being shaped by movies, such as *Tobacco Road* (1941), that portrayed rural people in the South as backward and lazy. However, this movie was hailed by critics as a masterpiece. After WWII, *Ma and Pa Kettle* movies (1947–1957) began to hit the big screen, where Ma and Pa, a married couple from rural America, are placed in situations where they must learn how to live in the "modern" world. Even when movies attempted to portray a true story, such as *Sergeant York* (1941), this wartime hero from the sticks of East Tennessee comes off as a backward hillbilly ill-suited to cope with military life. Only his excellent marksmanship and his backwoods wit turned him into a military hero.[10]

Cartoons in the local paper also portrayed rural people as backward and lazy, as seen in the wildly popular comic strip *Li'l Abner*, where Li'l Abner Yokum lived in the mountain village of Dogpatch, USA. Ultimately, the strip had as many as 60 million readers and ran from 1934 to 1977.[11] With the success of *Li'l Abner* came others, such as *Snuffy Smith* and *Pogo*, all with the same framework of backward rural people.

By the time TV came along, the 1960s became the era of rural TV shows. The list of rural shows from the 1960s includes, but is not limited to, *The Beverly Hillbillies*, *The Andy Griffith Show*, *Green Acres*, *Petticoat Junction*, *Hee Haw*, *Gomer Pyle USMC*, and *The Real McCoys*. Each of these shows pokes fun at rural America, often at the expense of rural Americans. While most are meant to be satirical, each portrays rural America as being out of touch with the rest of the country. At best, rural life is depicted as an anachronism, quaint, and nostalgic. At worst, rural folk were portrayed as backward and lazy.

9. Census.gov, "Table 4."
10. Hawks, *Sergeant York*.
11. Ushchan, "43 Years of 'Li'l Abner,'" para. 2.

Stereotypes of Rural America Today

The Mayberry Myth

Currently, the view of rural America is bipolar. On the one hand, it is portrayed in the media as a bucolic paradise, thanks to TV shows like *Heartland*, *When Calls the Heart*, and almost every show on the Hallmark Channel. The quintessential TV show most people recall when thinking about the slower, idealized rural life is *The Andy Griffith Show*, where Andy keeps the peace alongside his bumbling sidekick, Barney Fife. The merry band of unique characters in this show makes Mayberry seem to be the ideal place to live. The Mayberry mystique drives much of modern media's portrayal of rural areas as the perfect setting today.

This bucolic view of rural American life can be summed up in the recent Gallup survey, which showed that nearly half of all US adults would prefer to live in a small town or rural area.[12] The key reasons for this trend include being closer to family and friends, more affordability, and the ability to work remotely.[13] Ultimately, the slower-paced, community-oriented life has great appeal to many Americans.

The living example of someone making this transition comes in the story of Christopher Ingraham, a reporter for the *Washington Post* who wrote an article after he combed through government data and looked at things such as shopping conveniences and medical care, where he declared Red Lake County, Minnesota, as "the absolute worst place to live in America."[14] Needless to say, Red Lake County was not excited about its new designation. In an interesting turn of events, county leadership invited Christopher to visit Red Lake county. Upon his brief visit to Red Lake county, he and his family fell in love with the area. Ingraham soon moved his family there to live a more tranquil life. He chronicled his adventure in a bestselling book titled *If You Lived Here, You'd Be Home by Now*.[15]

This rural mystique was popularized during the 2008 political campaign when Sarah Palin stated, "We believe that the best of America is in these small towns that we get to visit, and in these wonderful little pockets of what I call the real America. . . . This is where we find the

12. Roper, "Rural Life Desire Rises," para. 2.
13. Compeer Financial, "Where Are Young People Moving," para. 1.
14. Martin, "Throwaway Line," para. 3.
15. Martin, "Throwaway Line," para. 7.

kindness and goodness and the courage of everyday Americans."[16] Palin was pandering to a bloc of voters, but her sentiment is deeply held by many who do not live in rural America, yet maintain nostalgia and a mystique about rural life.

Modern Media Myth

Conversely, much of today's media portrays rural America as backward, bigoted, and a dangerous place to visit. Almost every horror movie made today is in a rural setting. A brief sampling includes, but is not limited to, *Children of the Corn*, *The Mist*, *Halloween*, *The Texas Chain Saw Massacre*, and *The Blair Witch Project*. (The list could include dozens more movies.) The general theme of each of these movies is don't go to rural places and never venture out into the woods alone at night.

Recent TV shows aim to portray the perceived backwardness of rural people. This would include shows such as *Here Comes Honey Boo Boo*, *Moonshine*, the wildly popular *Duck Dynasty*, as well as *Swamp People*, which is so popular that it has its own channel dedicated to watching people catch alligators.

This myth, which reports rural America as "where village idiots reside, country bumpkins gather, and rednecks tell bigoted jokes," is prevalent in North America today.[17] This myth has been promoted by no less than a president of the United States, when Barack Obama stated in a San Francisco fundraiser in April of 2008,

> You go into these small towns in Pennsylvania and, like a lot of small towns in the Midwest, the jobs have been gone now for 25 years, and nothing's replaced them. And they fell through the Clinton administration, and the Bush Administration, and each successive administration has said that somehow these communities are gonna regenerate, and they have not. And it's not surprising then they get bitter, they cling to guns or religion or antipathy toward people who aren't like them or anti-immigrant sentiment or anti-trade sentiment as a way to explain their frustration.[18]

16. Leibovich, "Palin Visits a 'Pro-America,'" para. 2.
17. Wuthnow, *In the Blood*, 129.
18. Smith, "Obama on small town Pa.," para. 1–2.

J. D. Vance published *Hillbilly Elegy* in June 2016. Vance's coarse and sometimes profane bestseller highlighted the plight of Appalachian people, both in Appalachia (particularly in eastern Kentucky) and as they dispersed across the country (particularly in Dayton, Ohio). While this book is an accurate account of J. D.'s family, it is not necessarily a portrait of all rural America, or even all rural Appalachia, and should not be used to paint all of Appalachia as being poor, ignorant, and backward.

Two Extremes

The tendency, when looking at rural America today, is to gravitate toward one of two extremes. One extreme is the Mayberry myth, where rural America is idolized. Here, life is slower, people are nicer, and Andy is the sheriff. Rural America is seen as an escape from the hectic world of today, with its scenic downtowns, rolling meadows filled with horses, men wearing plaid shirts, and everyone waving to one another.

The other extreme is to see rural America as white, uneducated, Christian, and card-carrying Republicans with guns. For those subscribing to this extreme, the only possible solutions for the modern media myth include education and repatriating rural folk to urban, more civilized places or simply ignoring them with the hopes they will eventually just go away.

The Impact of These Myths on Rural Communities

These myths have had a deleterious effect on rural communities. The Mayberry myth has enticed people to move out to the "countryside" with the hopes of living in a community with Aunt Bea, Barney, and Opie. Within a short amount of time, they realize all is not what was presented in *The Andy Griffith Show* or the Hallmark movies.

The truth in many rural communities is a façade of friendliness, where everyone waves as you pass by and is nice to you at the grocery store. However, outsiders find it difficult to go beyond the superficial with the locals, finding them standoffish when pressed. The disillusionment often develops into an "us vs. them" mentality that divides the community.

The modern media myth, where rural folks are just a bunch of bigoted rednecks, is also having a profound effect on rural America. This myth keeps businesses from investing in rural communities, keeps people from wanting to move to rural areas, and hijacks the rural narrative by a few loud voices that are actually "bigoted rednecks."

For some in rural communities, this becomes a self-fulfilling prophecy, where such behavior is expected and promoted as the norm. Rural people are also affected by how the media portrays rural life, and things like country music exacerbate the situation by promoting this myth. Living up to the myth becomes a way of life.

Rural America is deeply affected by both myths and simply cannot live up to either one. As many rural communities bounce back and forth between the two myths, forming a narrative somewhere in the middle is difficult to do. Without a straightforward and unifying narrative, many communities struggle to develop a realistic identity.

The Impact of These Myths on the Rural Church

Both myths, the Mayberry myth and the modern media myth, have had a profound impact on rural churches today. Both present a distorted view of rural America and rural churches, causing people in the community, potential pastors, and church members themselves to have a flawed understanding of their community.

Few seminary graduates want to go and plant their lives as rural church pastors. Rural churches are good enough for "starter churches," to get experience and eventually move on to a larger, more urban church. Prospective pastors coming from the suburbs and trained in seminary do not want to be Andy and Barney's pastor, nor are they interested in leading a group of redneck Bubbas in rousing theological debates.

Rural churches are currently suffering a severe shortage of pastors. When the Jeffersonian yeoman ideal described our nation's view of rural life, rural churches raised up their own pastors. Baptists had "farmer pastors," men from the community who served their entire lives in one church. Methodists had circuit-riding pastors who covered multiple churches in a large field. And many Presbyterian churches had pastors serving multiple fields of churches (sometimes two or three churches simultaneously). As the twentieth-century view of rural areas morphed toward these two extremes, rural churches shifted away from raising up pastors from within their congregation to lead the church and became dependent on bringing in pastors from outside the community, often young and inexperienced, fresh from seminary.

As more people moved to cities and rural churches had fewer and fewer resources, hiring a pastor fresh from seminary became increasingly difficult for rural churches. Compounding this issue is the reluctance of seminary graduates to serve for three to four years in remote areas, with limited opportunities for advancement or recognition.

The Rise of "Urbanormativity"

Along with the myths, the rise of "urbanormativity" has infiltrated rural life. Rural sociologists Fulkerson and Thomas describe the growing influence of urban culture upon rural areas by coining the word "urbanormativity." This term means "normal" life has come to imply urban.[19] Thus, urban implies moving forward and progressing and is assumed to be the ideal; anything deviating from this is considered backward and undesirable. This has also infiltrated the church culture. Students at the seminary are taught church leadership and ministry from the context of the urban church. Because rural churches operate differently, they are often perceived as outdated and rustic. When urbanormativity infiltrates the church, it marginalizes the rural church. What Fulkerson and Thomas state regarding culture is actual in the church as well:

> Once urbanormativity captures a culture, it has the effect of rendering urbanites the normal and natural members of society, while rustics are taken as marginal. This creates a cultural hierarchy that comes with a set of privileges for those who can claim an urbane identity while punishing and depriving the rural rustic.[20]

This is seen at almost every pastor's conference where the main speakers come from large urban churches, and the "rural speaker" is relegated to the small back room at the end of a forgotten hallway. Fulkerson and Thomas further argue, "In an urban society, rural has come to be devalued, located at the bottom of the cultural hierarchy."[21] Tragically, this is often the case in urbanized church culture. Rural churches are characterized as legalistic, judgmental, and resistant to change. To accept a call to pastor a rural church is seen as ecclesiastical career suicide.

19. Fulkerson and Thomas, *Urbanormativity*, 2.
20. Fulkerson and Thomas, *Urbanormativity*, 3.
21. Fulkerson and Thomas, *Urbanormativity*, 4.

Urbanormativity has not only infiltrated the broader culture but has also influenced the church.

Conclusion

Truthfully, rural is notoriously difficult to define and even more difficult to describe. Trying to generalize about rural communities across the nation—from commercial fishermen in Maine, to tourist areas like Gatlinburg, Tennessee, to American Indians living on a reservation in Montana—makes it impossible to capture the essence of rural America in a single phrase or a universal description.

The reality is that the broad negative generalizations made by the media today are both true and false. Are there, like Obama inferred, racist rednecks running around with assault weapons in the name of God still in rural America? Yes, in certain places they can be found. However, this broad generalization does not accurately describe the entirety of rural America but rather only a small minority of rural people who are vocal and receive considerable press. Conversely, is life in rural areas slower, and are people friendlier, willing to help a neighbor out in a crisis? Yes, in some places, that stereotype still holds—but not in every case, and not all rural people in one rural setting.

The problem with these stereotypes, both positive and negative, is their profound impact on how rural America is perceived by most people today. Broad generalizations, accompanied by a few carefully selected video clips, can significantly alter a nation's perception of rural areas, either positively or negatively. Sadly, today, negative stereotypes of rural America are more prevalent than ever in the media, painting rural America as white, racist, tradition-bound, and Christian.

For well-educated seminary students, this picture of rural America, along with the limited opportunities for success in ministry (often closely tied to numbers), makes serving in rural areas less appealing. The suburbs are the place to go for a young seminary graduate. This is where the people are, this is where the money is, this is where diversity is greater. The ideal of pastoring a little country parish where the pastor knows everyone in the church and in the community by name, where the pastor has coffee every morning at the local diner, and where life is more community-oriented holds little appeal to the up-and-coming seminary graduate.

The rural mystique promoted by Thomas Jefferson and promoted throughout the 1800s is quickly giving way to seeing rural America as left behind in the forward progress of society. For many, the rural ideal is an anachronism where urban folk drive out to look at and then return to the conveniences of urban life. As a result, an accurate picture of rural America becomes more difficult to discern from the characterizations made from both ends of the spectrum.

Ultimately, rural America is more complex than what is presented in the media. It is a mixture of positive and negative attributes, varying from one rural setting to the next. The way the media presents rural America today has a profound impact on the people living in rural areas, the church in rural communities, and those considering a career in ministry.

It may be a good thing to remove some of the nostalgic myth of rural America as being predominantly Christian. The lostness of rural America makes the villages and small towns dotting North America mission fields once again.

The goal here is to move past "sound byte" stereotypes and see rural America for what it actually is: a complex mixture of the good and bad found in the two stereotypes, and just as complex as urban or suburban America. The same problems and similar opportunities that describe urban America also apply to rural America. Also, serving in a rural church is a lifetime lifestyle that offers ministry opportunities.

Part 2

The Changing Rural Church

4

The Changing Church in Rural Communities

THE FALSE PERCEPTION OF rural people presented in the previous chapter also distorts the view of the rural church. When people describe the character of the rural church, they often use terms focusing on its stability and stagnant ministry. For some, the image is positive. They see the rural church as a fortress resisting the secularization and liberalization of large urban churches, untouched by a feel-good, consumer-driven culture that, in their minds, permeates seeker-driven mega churches. The rural church remains grounded in the theological and biblical foundation of gospel-centered ministry.

For others, the image is quite different. They view the rural church as a place where tradition and legalism overshadow biblical truth. The congregation stubbornly resists any change or adaptation to a modern message, showing that the church is stuck in the past and disconnected from the present.

In reality, just as there are elements of truth in each of these perspectives, there are also misconceptions. The first fails to recognize the changes that are occurring in the rural culture and church. The second is because it fails to recognize the spiritual vitality within the rural congregation.

Both perspectives overlook the reality that the church has not only changed in the past, but it continues to be influenced by the cultural changes occurring in society in general, and in rural communities in particular. Not only is rural culture and society undergoing radical shifts but so, too, is the ministry and focus of the rural church. The broader societal changes are affecting the rural ministry, both positively and negatively. The rural church is not the same as it was one hundred years ago or even ten years ago.

The Changing Model

As was already pointed out, the Industrial Revolution not only had a profound impact on the culture and nature of rural communities. It also changed the perception of the church itself. Before the Industrial Revolution, success was grounded in stability and sustainability. The farmer aimed to provide for his family and sustain his livelihood. Success on the farm was measured by sustainability rather than growth. It was sufficient when the farm provided for the family's needs and had a little excess to sell to the local market, allowing them to purchase what could not be raised, grown, or made. However, the Industrial Revolution changed the perception. When Ford developed the assembly line for mass production, the definition of success underwent a transformation.

Now, success is measured by productivity, growth, market sensitivity, and the growth and profitability of a business. This change infiltrated perceptions of what the church should be. The mantra of church leaders became, "If your church is not growing (numerically), then it is dying." Effective growth can be achieved by becoming market-driven. Thus, an effective church leader articulates a clear vision for the church, establishes well-thought-out goals and objectives, produces growth and productivity, and maintains positive "customer" satisfaction.

Willow Creek and Saddleback became the new models as people flocked to their leadership conferences to try to replicate their "success." Successful pastors lead large, rapidly growing churches, gaining national influence and recognition. Leaders are visionaries to rally people to their vision for the church. The mantra at church leadership conferences became, "If there is no vision, the people perish." However, this was a misquote of the vision in Proverbs, which referred to a revelatory truth rather than corporate goals. But this matters little in the age of the corporate church. When numbers became the measure of success, truth became secondary.

The consequence of this obsession with growth, numbers, and recognition changed the church's mission from "go to the ends of the earth" to "go to the cities, young man." The masses take priority over the individual, and the mission is no longer to reach every individual in remote communities; the mission has become one of prioritizing and serving the largest number of people. In this new mission, the rural church became neglected as the priority shifted to the growing urban church, which became the model of church health. However, as John Adams points out, "God sent the Messiah to a people and a nation that was radically unstrategic."[1]

The Great Commission establishes the church's mandate. The task is not to gain prestige or influence; it is to take the gospel to every nook and cranny of the world to proclaim the gospel to every single person on the planet. Christ did not come to save the masses; he came to save individuals. The Great Commission is a mission of going, not building large churches. The church is not a business to develop but a mission to expand.

The emergence of a new leadership paradigm has significantly impacted the understanding of the church's mission. Instead of viewing the church as a community, it became an organization to run. In the organizational structure, efficiency and innovation became the new buzzwords of church health. As White and Yeats point out,

> Effective organizations work in a manner in which they were designed. They consistently produce results that align with the organization's aims, goals, and mission. In the process, effective organizations attain the greatest amount of production because their structures and organization work toward the stated goals of the whole.[2]

Efficiency for the church is defined by attracting the largest crowds. Productivity takes precedence over people. The mission of the church is no longer the development of people but the development of effective programs.[3]

Within the business model, the pastor's ministry was also redefined. Instead of a pastor being a proclaimer of truth, the pastor became

1. See John Adams, "Is Rural Ministry a Priority for God?," cited in Daman and Clark, *God of Small Places*, 11.

2. White and Yeats, *Franchising McChurch*, 23.

3. For an in-depth evaluation of the church growth movement and its effect upon the small church, see Vaters, *De-Sizing the Church.*

a professional CEO responsible for keeping the church's organizational structure moving forward. In this model, the shepherd metaphor of the pastor has become archaic and old-fashioned. The primary responsibility of the pastor was not shepherding the people but "casting vision, maintaining mission focus, and modeling risk so the sheep will be excited and challenged to resist the enemy."[4]

In 1995, Leith Anderson argued the church of the future would place a premium on performance rather than on credentials. Therefore, Anderson argues that we need to shift our theological training to offer two tracks: one for academic studies for those who choose academic scholarship (the theologians) and the other for practical training and ministry development (the pastors), thus implying that these are mutually exclusive.[5] He concludes, "We will need comparatively few graduate schools of theology and comparatively more professional schools of ministry."[6] In other words, pastoral programs should place greater emphasis on "practical theology" than on languages and biblical and systematic theology. One would be better equipped with an MBA than a ThM. Ultimately, truth becomes minimized (we do not want to offend people), and methodology is centralized (we want to be effective). *How* we do church has become more important than *what* the church is.

This approach had a devastating effect on the rural church. In a world where size is often equated with health, the small church was viewed as a failure due to its lack of numerical growth and its perpetual smallness. Borden argues this when he writes,

> In North America, most small congregations are small and remain that way because they are spiritually and organizationally dysfunctional. Many large congregations have grown significantly as a result of pursuing organizational health, and in many cases, spiritual health as well. If the small congregation is truly healthy, they will not remain small but will grow and reproduce in one way or another.[7]

In the eyes of many, the small and rural church became a model of what is wrong with the church; its focus on community and relationships, rather than programs and numbers, was stifling its opportunity to grow

4. Borden, *Hit the Bullseye*, 22–23.
5. Anderson, *Church for the 21st Century*, 46–47.
6. Anderson, *Church for the 21st Century*, 47.
7. Borden, *Hit the Bullseye*, 59.

numerically. Consequently, small church pastors and congregations become discouraged, wondering if the glory of God has departed, leaving them to flounder in the turmoil of spiritual upheaval without any hope of experiencing God's blessing within the church.

For denominational leaders, the answer for rural communities was not to establish missionary outposts to reach the community. It was to develop "Walmart churches." Leith Anderson referred to Walmart churches as "the most promising prospect for rural Americans in the twenty-first century."[8] These churches

> will serve regional rural markets; churches that are friendly, carry lots of programs, are customer-driven rather than institution-driven; churches that transcend the deep traditions of small communities and give permission to worship without alienating family histories and relationships.[9]

That is not to say that plans, objectives, programs, and visions are unimportant; they are indeed helpful. But they are only effective in a predictable world.

When Amazon first broke onto the national scene, the shopping mall had a firm hold on consumers. In 1986, North America had approximately 25,000 malls scattered throughout every city.[10] The malls were more than just a shopping experience; they were social centers where young people would gather and meet. When Amazon first started selling books, it was not considered a threat to the retail market. The mantra of many was, "If I can't see it and touch it, I will not buy it. Who wants to buy online when you cannot see the product?" As Amazon jumped into the online sales business, few thought it would endanger the malls' popularity. Today, Amazon is the top online retailer in the United States and has replaced Walmart as the world's largest company by sales.[11] Now the attitude of shoppers is, "If I cannot order from the convenience of my home and have it delivered to my doorstep, I will not buy it. Who wants to go to the store when you can get it delivered to your house?" Malls and shopping centers are struggling to compete with the convenience of online shopping. In the volatile world of the internet, malls have become obsolete. Today, fewer than 5 percent of malls remain in the

8. Anderson, *Church for the 21st Century*, 58.

9. Anderson, *Church for the 21st Century*, 59–60.

10. Capital One Shopping Research, "Mall Closure Statistics," para. 2.

11. Selyukh, "Amazon Dethrones Walmart," para. 2.

United States, and the number is likely to decrease further.[12] Not only has Amazon taken over the retail market but Instagram, X, TikTok, and other digital social platforms have replaced the mall as a social center.[13]

The same volatility that affected shopping centers is also affecting the church. People no longer view the church as a necessary "third place." The church is losing its role as a gathering place for people in the community. Instead, the church is increasingly being marginalized. Recently, Pew Research indicated that in the near future, Christians will fall below 50 percent of the population for the first time in US history.[14] As late as 1972, 90 percent of Americans classified themselves as Christians. In 2020, the number dropped to 64 percent In this postmodern, post-Christian world, dynamic worship and felt-needs programs are no longer appealing. People will not drive across town to attend a church, much less drive fifty miles to attend a Walmart church. The church of the future cannot assume that "if we build it, they will come." Not only is the church no longer viewed as a social hub, but it is also no longer regarded as a center of faith and community.

The Changing Message

Not only has there been a shift from developing a community of believers to running a business, but a seismic shift in the church's message has also occurred. In a consumer-driven church, the consumer now determines the message. In a consumer-driven church, denouncing unpopular sins has become a common practice. However, the church becomes complacent about the sins we engage in. It is easier and safer to condemn homosexuality than it is gossip and greed. We want a church to condemn the sins of the world but not confront the sins in our own lives.

In an editorial by *The Guardian*, the writers warn that the boom occurring from market-driven Christianity is now beginning to falter. They conclude,

> A religion that is responsive to the pressures of the market will end up profoundly fractured, with each denomination finding most hateful to God the sins that least tempt its members, while those sins that are the most popular become redefined and even

12. Capital One Shopping Research, "Mall Closure Statistics," para. 2.
13. Johnson, "From Mall Madness to Sadness," para. 9.
14. Pew Research Center, "Modeling the Future Religion," chart 1.

> sanctified. In the end, a market-driven approach to religions gives rise to a market-driven approach to truth, and this development ultimately eviscerated conservative Christianity in the U.S. and left it the possession of hypocrites and hucksters.[15]

Not only are these writers correct in their assumptions, but they are also writing from the perspective of outsiders. When the church becomes driven by the market, it becomes driven either by legalism or liberalism, depending on the demands of the consumers. Instead of being a broker of truth, the church becomes a broker of the local culture.

As culture shifted from being governed by a Judeo-Christian ethic, there was a shift in how the church communicated the message of the gospel and the gospel itself. While the church growth movement reminded the church of the importance of evangelism, its focus on numerical growth rather than spiritual transformation shifted the church's emphasis from truth to the arts. The way to attract people was to make worship an experience rather than an affirmation of God's nature and supremacy. Dynamic, contemporary music and drama became the church's central focus. Preaching was directed toward practical messages addressing felt needs rather than inward transformation. Entertainment, rather than proclamation, became central. Worship became an "experience" appealing to the emotions rather than an exhortation challenging the soul to stand in humility before the holy God. Doctrinal affirmation was replaced by personal affirmation. The result was a "weaker community, weaker theological acuity, weaker biblical knowledge, and little understanding or appreciation of the historic liturgies of the church."[16] In an entertainment, consumer-driven church, felt needs became primary; truth became secondary. What we believe is not nearly as important as what we experience.

However, the quest for the visual experience leads to the blurring of reality and imagination. People are more likely to form their understanding of the life and teaching of Christ by watching *The Chosen* than they are through a careful study of the gospel message. In the past, truth was determined by what was written; then, truth was determined by what one experienced; now, truth is governed by what is visualized. Instead of conforming beliefs, doctrines, and lives to the truth of the Bible, people began to conform the Bible and the doctrines of their church to their own

15. Guardian, "Guardian View of American Christianity," para. 1.

16. Austin, "How the Church Growth Movement," para. 19.

personal narratives and experiences. This results in a vacuum of truth. The truth is no longer affirmed. Instead, the truth is questioned because it does not conform to one's perspective. Moving forward, the church faces the challenge of adapting how to communicate the gospel without changing the message of the gospel.

The Changing Mission

In both the Great Commission and the church mandate of Acts 1:8, the mission of the church was simple and straightforward: to make disciples of all nations by being a witness for Christ in every community and place where people live throughout the world. The task of the church was to be the visible representation of Christ to proclaim the hope and redemptive work of Christ to a spiritual blinded world and advance the kingdom of Christ in the world. This mission was singular in focus and universal in scope. However, in recent years, the church's mission has become refocused. Instead of transforming the world through the proclamation of the gospel, the church's ministry has adapted to fit the local context. In the political world, the church became a political action group. In the world of consumerism, the message of the church became one of "self-fulfillment" rather than radical transformation. In a secular world, the church became marginalized. The church was no longer the place to connect with God through the proclamation of Christ, which was transcultural; the church became an expression of the culture.

The Political Church

Throughout the history of our country, the power to transform people and society was through the proclamation of the gospel. However, in the development of our country, the church played a significant role in shaping the nation's political identity. As a result, the church gained political influence as a key player in shaping public opinion and voting patterns. However, in recent years, as our culture has become more secular, the nation is turning its back on its Christian identity. In this new environment, the church has sought to regain its political influence to stem the moral and spiritual decline in our society.

Consequently, especially in rural churches, Christian nationalism began to take shape. Paul Miller, in his critique of Christian nationalism, defines Christian nationalism as

> the belief that humanity is divisible into mutually distinct, internally coherent cultural groups defined by shared traits like ethnicity, language, religion, or culture; that these groups should each have their governments; that one of the purposes of government is to promote and protect a nation's cultural identity; and that sovereign nations with strong cultures provide meaning and purpose for human beings.[17]

He goes on to point out,

> Christian nationalism believes that America's predominant culture was, and substantially still is, Anglo-Protestant. We must sustain our Anglo-Protestant culture, and our Anglo-Protestant culture was the essential precondition for the American experience in liberty, and American democracy would become unsustainable without it. God blesses nations who honor him with symbolic gestures of reverence, and our Anglo-Protestant culture honors him.[18]

Stephen Wolfe, a proponent of Christian nationalism, takes it a step further when he argues that "Christian nationalism is the totality of national action, consisting of civil laws and social customs, conducted by a Christian nation as a Christian nation, in order to procure for itself both earthly and heavenly good in Christ."[19] The key point is that Christian nationalism is not just the belief that Christians should have a positive influence on society by promoting biblical values, but it also posits that Christians have a moral and divine mandate to gain dominion over society through political engagement. As the church adopted politics as a means of influencing society, it adapted its approach to achieve personal and cultural transformation. Instead of transforming culture through the proclamation of the gospel and applying biblical theology to political issues,[20] the church turned to political engagement as a means of making our nation "Christian."

17. Miller, *Religion of American Greatness*, 31.

18. Miller, *Religion of American Greatness*, 59.

19. Wolfe, *Case for Christian Nationalism*, 181.

20. For a balanced perspective of the church's involvement in political issues, see Matthew Wigton, "Engaging the Political Parish," in Horn and McConnell, *Return to the Parish*, 61–77.

However, the foray into the political arena is not without its costs. Politics has always been a dirty game that results in division and hostility. When the church and Christianity become involved in the political arena by aligning itself with a political party, it becomes defined by its political ideology rather than the gospel. This is not only true of the perception of the church by people outside the church, but it is also true of people's perception within the church. What party one votes for has become the new litmus test of orthodoxy for many people in rural churches. Christians can judge people by the political party to which they belong. Churches legitimize one party by demonizing the other. Instead of being ministers of reconciliation, the church became contributors to the political division threatening the stability of our nation. When the church gained its political voice, it lost its prophetic voice. The method for influencing and redeeming our culture shifted from the proclamation of the gospel to the election of the right political candidate or party.

The Consumer Church

As our culture embraced consumerism both economically and culturally, the Baby Boomers became increasingly concerned with enjoying life rather than transforming it. As a result, they stopped going to church. As Skye Jethani pointed out, "The culture had changed—secular values, youth culture, and entertainment had taken root and the small, simple churches could not compete with the gravitational pull of malls, multiplexes, and rock concerts."[21] Consumerism infiltrated and altered the ministry's focus. The way to achieve growth was to develop a ministry catering to the consumer demands of people. The atmosphere became more important than the message. To attract people, messages became short homilies. Instead of Sunday school rooms, churches put in coffee bars and even restaurants to provide a "full-service" ministry. The way to attract people was by having more robust coffee than robust sermons. Ford rightfully describes the result of the consumer church:

> The problem is not recognizing the importance of the individual. The problem is the glorification of the individual. When the individual self is glorified over the greater good of the community, rights begin to take precedence over responsibility, isolated pursuits replace the struggle for the common good, desires are

21. Jethani, *How Churches Became Cruise Ships*, 113.

> twisted to resemble needs, and the imitation is presented as the real thing.[22]

In the end, the church becomes narcissistic, where people have an inflated sense of their self-importance. They judge the church by how well "it ministers to my needs." The church no longer prioritizes what is best for the community but instead focuses on what is best for the individual and their desires. Instead of calling people to a life of self-sacrifice, we cater to their self-demands.

The Convenient Church

When COVID-19 threatened to overwhelm the nation's medical infrastructure, the world was brought to a sudden halt as government mandates sought to slow down the spread of the pandemic by restricting community gatherings. In a scope of one week, churches (including rural churches) were forced to do what they had never considered: to go virtual with their services. Throughout the land, churches embraced the internet as a means of connecting with the people and disseminating the Sunday service. The result was the rise of the internet church. While the digital church had already gained popularity since the early 2000s, COVID-19 brought the digital church into the mainstream. Facebook Live, YouTube, Zoom, and a host of other internet platforms became the gathering places for the church.

Since the COVID-19 pandemic, Lifeway Research has found that 45 percent of Americans have watched a service online.[23] According to Pew Research, in 2023, about a quarter of US adults regularly watch religious services online.[24] Now, the Meta Church, combined with VRChat, has become the latest trend. No longer do people attend a church because of the community it offers; they attend because of the convenience it provides. This is not just an urban phenomenon. Instead of attending a local church, rural residents can sit in the comfort of their own home and watch their favorite preacher.

22. Ford, *Transforming Church*, 32.
23. Deaton, "Rise of the Digital Church," para. 5.
24. Pew Research Center, "Online Religious Services," para. 1.

The Socialized Church

With a focus on social action, some churches, in an effort to connect with the world, became agents for social change rather than agents for spiritual transformation. As the society shifted away from traditional Christian values and became hostile to the church, some churches became focused on "an evolving synchronization with the secular elite culture, particularly on matters of race, immigration, and the Me Too movement—aligning more closely with progressive culture and political positions."[25] To try to appeal to the broader culture, the socialized church sought to become a champion of social issues. For example, while holding to traditional teaching on sexuality, instead of focusing on condemning the views contradicting biblical teaching, they sought to be more appealing by emphasizing how the church "should be a welcoming place for all and how the church failed to properly treat those who struggled with their sexual identity. To remain relevant, the social church emphasized social justice as the means for cultural transformation."[26] In contrast to the political church, which sought to transform culture through political action, the social church aims to advance the gospel through social action. While the church should be engaged in addressing issues of poverty, racism, and violence within the culture, it should not become a replacement for the gospel as the means of transforming our culture.

Reorienting Our Focus

The crisis in our culture is not cultural, moral, social, or political; it's doctrinal and spiritual.[27] In God's redemptive program, it is a spiritual transformation that changes people, not a political or social reformation.[28] When Paul wrote to Timothy to address moral and spiritual decline, he did not call him to become politically involved or socially engaged; he challenged him to preach the gospel (2 Tim 4:2–5). Because the battle is "not against flesh and blood, but against the rulers, against the authorities, against the cosmic forces over this present darkness, against the spiritual forces of evil in heavenly places" (Eph 6:12), we need spiritual methods rather than social-political methods. The power to change culture is

25. Renn, *Life in the Negative World*, 36.
26. Renn, *Life in the Negative World*, 36.
27. Lutzer, *No Reason to Hide*, 49.
28. Lutzer, *No Reason to Hide*, 83.

found in the power of the gospel (Eph 6:13–20). In the future, if the rural church is going to have an impact, it will need to refocus its methods on how it seeks to change people by calling them to advance the gospel and to live and serve one another in a community of faith.

As society becomes more secular, relevance comes not from the church's programs but from the gospel message. The more the church strives to appease the culture, the more it will alienate itself from the broader society, and the more it will lose its voice within society. This is not to say the church should not be involved in seeking to influence our society through our political/social engagement. As Christians, we should strive to speak publicly about the nation's moral and ethical issues.[29] Throughout the Old Testament and New Testament, the prophets sought to influence society by providing biblical teaching on current issues and calling political leaders to uphold the moral compass by condemning sin. However, a significant difference exists between speaking to culture and becoming an expression of our culture and the arm of a politician. If the church is to have a voice, it must stand above the public arena and call the nation back to God's moral standard. The church influences the moral foundation of society not by endorsing political parties, promoting social change, or adapting methods to make the church more appealing. The church influences the world by confronting people prophetically with the voice of God's word. When the church becomes driven by the desire to be appealing to our culture, then we will no longer be free to confront people with the clarion call to biblical morality.

In our rapidly changing world, where morality is as shifting as the whims of people, the church cannot afford to be driven by politics, the market, or social concerns. To minister effectively in the changing world, the church needs to be a community rather than a business, a prophetic voice rather than a political voice, and an agent for spiritual transformation, not just social transformation. For this to happen, the church needs to focus on developing a community of disciples who proclaim the gospel to the world rather than a business catering to the spiritual market and the political and social winds. The church needs to refocus on the gospel as the foundation for transformation, and the measure of success is not the size of the church but the message it conveys.

29. Grudem, *Politics According to the Bible*, 68–69.

The Changing Ministry

The church is not only facing the challenges of the changes in the rural community and the rural church in terms of its message and mission; rural communities are experiencing a dramatic shift demographically and spiritually, affecting how the church will effectively minister. In the past, the rural church was the center of community life as people identified with the local church (even if they did not regularly attend). The church was a place where people attended funerals, where weddings were held, and where people would turn in times of personal crisis. Evangelism involved being present in the community and being a welcoming place for people to come.

Rural communities are experiencing dynamic changes. The nature and makeup of the community have shifted from traditional characteristics, with a focus on the church and family, to a more culturally diverse community. Wilkinson writes,

> A useful approach to understanding the contemporary situation is to recognize that the community in rural areas is in flux and not necessarily in transition. Transition would imply a more or less orderly change from one stable form to another, from "traditional" to "modern." Rural areas today do not contain stable or traditional communities, and the cross-cutting forces in the present trends do not add up to a coherent process of transition.[30]

In the future, the church will have to rethink its ministry. In the past, people attended church because it was considered the "proper thing to do." This is no longer the case. It is easy to mistake political and moral conservatism with spiritual transformation. The reality is far different. Rural communities are not just becoming the new ghetto; they are becoming the new mission field. This requires a new approach to ministry and community engagement. We cannot assume people will come because the church doors are open.

In the past, denominational leaders sought to regionalize churches. The idea was that a regional church with multiple programs would draw people. However, when people no longer see the importance of attending church or identify with it, they will not drive to nearby towns to worship. As the church moves forward, it must recognize that the most critical aspect of missions is the church's presence within the local setting. People

30. Pigg, *Future of Rural America*, 73.

and the local community cannot be reached in absentia. If the church is to fulfill the mandate of the Great Commission, it must reaffirm the importance of the local church. This also means that the local church needs to start thinking missionally. Rural communities are now a mission field.

As the church undergoes radical transformation and change, it is easy to yearn for a return to the past to preserve what once was. Wisdom comes from recognizing the aspects of ministry that cannot change, as well as what needs to change to be more effective in the future. In a rapidly changing world, the church must acknowledge that it cannot replicate the past and it cannot control or predict the future. Instead, the church will need to develop ministries that respond to each specific community so it can impact the world with the gospel of Christ. Effective ministry in a changing church requires the church to discern and defend what cannot be changed (our message and mission) and adapt its ministry in the areas that can and must change to remain effective in the future (our methods). To adjust, the church needs to recognize that not only is culture changing but, as we will see in the next chapter, we're in the midst of a radical shift in the spiritual perception of people and how they view the world.

5

The Changing Spiritual Worldview of Rural Communities

It seems almost cliché to say that we live in a time that is experiencing rapid change. It seems almost every day we hear stories in the news of technological, medical, and social changes that will revolutionize our lives. No generation has experienced as much change as those alive today.

For example, I grew up in Southern Middle Tennessee in a county where Appalachia and Southern culture mixed. When I was growing up, my hometown was definitely rural and somewhat isolated. I lived one and a half hours from Nashville but went there only five or six times in my childhood. Going to Nashville was an exotic journey to what felt like a foreign land.

The rapid change that has taken place in the twentieth and twenty-first centuries can best be illustrated by the lives of my grandfather, my dad, and me. My grandfather was born in 1907. He used to regale the family with stories of seeing the first car in the county, watching the county pave the first road, and seeing an airplane for the first time.

My dad, now eighty-eight years old, tells stories of walking to town, a six-mile journey, once a month to watch movies and to see the newsreels. He also talks about seeing his first television and gathering around the radio to listen to Lum and Abner, which came on after the noon news.

As for me, I remember the first color television I ever saw. The first thing I remember seeing in color was Super Bowl IV, where the Kansas

City Chiefs defeated the Minnesota Vikings. We went to the house of my dad's friend, and the purple uniforms of Minnesota and the red uniforms of Kansas City were sensory overload. The next day, Dad went out and bought a color TV. The first time we got a push-button phone and wondered what the "number" key (also called "pound sign" or "hashtag," depending on your age) and the "star" key could possibly be used for, and watching the first man walk on the moon.

Even now, my daughters (ages thirty-seven and thirty-one as of this writing) are beginning to gather stories of the rapidly changing landscape in which they live. They can tell of connecting to the internet using a dial-up connection, life before smartphones, and the rise and fall of video rental stores.

The truth is, over the last one hundred years, our world has experienced some of the most massive changes in the history of the world. These changes have affected every part of our lives, including church life. We now live in a radically different world from when my grandfather was young.

Washington Irving told a story that sheds light on where we are as the church in North America today.

Rip Van Winkle: The Changing Worldview of Rural Communities

In 1819, Washington Irving published a book in which he provided thirty-four essays and short stories. The best-known stories from this book are "The Legend of Sleepy Hollow" and "Rip Van Winkle."

In the story of Rip Van Winkle, the main character is an affable but lazy farmer with an overbearing wife. One day, he heads to the woods to hunt and escape his wife's sharp tongue. Deep in the woods, he encounters a group of dwarfs that offer him their special grog. Having drunk his fill, he went to sleep under a tree. When he wakes up, he returns to the town to discover he has been asleep for the last twenty years. During that time, his wife died, and his unruly children grew up. Most importantly, he went to sleep in a British colony and woke up in the United States of America.[1]

Is it possible that among all the changes that have happened over the last fifty years, the church could go to sleep in 1975 to wake up fifty years later? When I visit many rural churches, they often look the same as they

1. Irving, *Rip Van Winkle*, 45.

did fifty years ago. The carpet and paint are the same color; the pulpit and pews have remained the same. Furthermore, they are still using the same piano, the same hymn books, singing the same songs. The sermon is preached in the same format, three points all starting with the same letter, and a closing story meant to invoke a response to the invitation. In many ways, these churches look and act the same as they did fifty years ago.

If one of these slumbering churches were to awaken, they would find the world has radically shifted. Many things may still look the same, but the world has moved on. Just as Rip Van Winkle discovered he no longer lived in a British colony, the church today no longer lives within the safety of the worldview called Christendom, prevalent in many rural areas in the 1970s.

The rural church today lives in a world with two competing worldviews. However, many churches are simply unaware of this clash between two cultures. They are, in essence, still sleeping.

Christendom

I grew up where the worldview was thoroughly within the purview of Christendom. What do I mean when I say Christendom? Merriam-Webster defines Christendom as "the part of the world in which Christianity prevails."[2] When I was a young (1960s and 1970s), decisions made by the school board, the local government, and by local businesses were based on a Judeo-Christian worldview. It was incomprehensible to think of making a decision that might go against biblical values.

Another example: a business owner in my hometown in 1975 was unofficially required to go to a church. No one in my hometown in 1975 was going to buy furniture from a heathen (or an atheist or a communist). Thus, every businessman in town belonged to a church, whether they lived by Christian standards in their business dealings or not.

Pastors in the 1970s were able to relate to their community based on these assumed Christian standards. They could preach sermons addressing the community from a Christian foundation. Even in talking to the most adamant reprobate in town, the pastor could witness using "Four Spiritual Laws" and know the "sinner" would have a basic understanding of these "laws."

2. Merriam-Webster, "Christendom."

Pluralism

The once powerful hold of Christendom in my county has slowly melted away until my county today lives in a new world order called *pluralism*. Merriam-Webster defines pluralism as "the holding of two or more offices or positions at the same time."[3] Today in my county, two worldviews compete for the same space.

This can be illustrated by two examples. First, when I was a child, my county had a strict set of Blue Laws in place. No business could be open on Sunday! Then they revised the Blue Laws to allow grocery stores and convenience stores to be open on Sunday but not sell alcohol. Once again, they revised the Blue Laws so stores could sell liquor after 12:00 p.m. Today, any vestige of Blue Laws is long gone. Stores are open on Sunday and can sell liquor at any time of the day.

The second example would be sports in my county. When I was in school, the school sports programs like Little League Baseball, high school football, and basketball developed their schedules around local church activities (and deer season). Today, all sports programs in my county make their schedule first, and the church adapts to their schedule.

Secularism

The second worldview competing with Christendom today is called *secularism*. Secularism can be defined as "indifference to or rejection of religion and religious considerations."[4] Secularists are not necessarily opposed to Christendom; they are merely indifferent to Christendom and to the church in general. They simply have no interest in Christian ideas or in the church.

This means two opposing world orders are prevalent in my home county; one based on Christian values and one indifferent to Christian values. The truth is, to the dismay of local churches, secularism seems to be winning. No longer are school board decisions based on Christian values, city council decisions based on church beliefs, nor are store owners required to be members of a local church. Schools no longer allow Christian organizations to come on campus, and schools no longer have daily scripture readings.

3. Merriam-Webster, "Pluralism."
4. Merriam-Webster, "Secularism."

Many in my county bemoan the demise of Christendom, blaming the diminished influence on the influx of "foreigners" who have come into my county to retire next to the TVA Lake. You know the kind of people I'm talking about; they are from somewhere up north, like Michigan, Indiana, New York, or *Nashville*. These "outsiders" have moved into the county and have changed everything, so the old-timers say.

Christendom waning in my home county had little to do with the "outsiders" coming in. Rather, rising secularism has been prevalent in practically every rural county in North America. After fifty years, some rural churches have awoken to find themselves in a pluralistic society. Furthermore, they find themselves in large part unable to deal with the new world order.

Postmodernism

When the idea of postmodernism and secularism comes up, they are often discussed in much the same way as the age-old question of which came first, the chicken or the egg? Did postmodernism contribute to the rise of secularism, or did the rise of secularism contribute to the current prevalent view of postmodernism? The answer is impossible to discern as to which came first. What can be discerned is that they are in a symbiotic relationship, where each one contributes to the other.

Whereas secularism was fairly simple to define, postmodernism is a nebulous term that is extremely difficult to define. Britannica offers a concise attempt to define postmodernism:

> Postmodernism is a late 20th-century movement characterized by broad skepticism, subjectivism, or relativism; a general suspicion of reason; and an acute sensitivity to the role of ideology in asserting and maintaining political and economic power. It is a philosophical movement that impacted the arts and critical thinking throughout the latter half of the 20th century.[5]

Thus, for the postmodernist, logic simply cannot account for everything in the natural world. As a result of this thinking, a debate about scientific research expands into a debate about Western culture in general.[6] Rational thought is closely tied to Western thought, coming from

5. Duignan, "Postmodernism."

6. Goldman, *Science Wars*, 253.

the Enlightenment, and is not to be seen as definitive. A summary of the main tenets of postmodernism includes the following:

1. Social Constructivism: Meaning, morality, and truth don't exist objectively and are solely constructed by society.
2. Cultural Determinism: Individuals are shaped by cultural forces.
3. Rejection of Individual Identity: People exist as members of groups (collective).
4. Rejection of Humanism: The idea of misplacing creativity, priority, and autonomy of human beings; there is no universal humanity because different cultures indicate different realities.
5. Denial of the Transcendent: There are no absolutes.
6. Rejection of Reason: Reason and the impulse to objectify truth mask cultural power.[7]

Postmodernism has influenced every part of society and has had a profound impact on rural areas as well. Postmodernism has ushered in a secular worldview where decisions are no longer based on a larger community ethic (such as Christendom) but are now based on what one perceives as right for themselves.

The highly individualistic nature of postmodernism has had a profound effect on the church today. The transcendent truths of the Bible are no longer universally held by the majority. When truth becomes an individual choice, Scripture is relegated to mere suggestions that can be accepted or rejected as one decides for themselves.

Deconstruction is more than just wrestling with one's faith. It is a fundamental questioning of the basic tenets of orthodox faith and rejecting absolute truths. Several famous Christian leaders who have gone through this process have walked away from their faith due to this process—like Joshua Harris, author of *I Kissed Dating Goodbye*, revealed that after deconstructing his faith, he no longer considers himself to be a Christian and has divorced his wife.

Similarly, Kevin Max from DC Talk deconstructed his faith, yet he maintains a belief in the "Universal Christ," although he does not explain what that means. Max describes himself as "anti-war, pro-peace, anti-hate, pro-live, pro-LGBTQIA, pro-BLM, pro-open-mindedness, anti-narrow-mindedness, pro-utopia, anti-white nationalist agenda,

7. Roy, "Major Tenets of Postmodernism," para. 1.

pro-equality, pro-vax, pro-music, anti-1%rs, pro-poor, pro-misfit-pro-Jesus, etc.,"[8] all while contending that he has a belief in Jesus.

Postmodern views reach even the most rural communities in North America, as the internet makes access to postmodern views available to even the most remote areas of North America today. Since postmodernism has no absolute beliefs, more and more people in churches are looking at how to build their faith as a buffet, where one picks and chooses what to believe and what to reject. Establishing a faith is merely a matter of personal preferences. To espouse eternal, immutable truths from Scripture is now seen as imperialistic, imposing one's belief on another.

The effects of postmodern thought on the local church have been profound. The first effect of postmodernism is relativism, coming from a super-individualistic mindset, where each person does what is right in their own mind. Thus, truth is relative to each person, and their version of truth takes priority over church doctrine or even the Bible itself. Most pastors today have entered into a counseling session where someone says, "I know the Bible (or the church) says what I want to do is wrong, but I just believe this is what God wants me to do." Their feelings take priority over everything else.

As relativism entered the church, its deleterious impact on the prophetic cannot be denied. If right and wrong are left to the individual to decide, then what authority does the church have to tell someone they are sinning against a holy God? Scripture is replete with prophets who speak against the social norms of the day, espousing a transcendent truth and a call to repentance.

From a postmodernist perspective, there can be no call to repent, because there is nothing to repent from. People are no longer sinners in need of a savior. Everyone is merely working out their own salvation on their own terms. Tom T. Hall epitomized postmodern Christian thought when he sang,

> Well, me and Jesus got our own thing goin'
> Me and Jesus got it all worked out
> Me and Jesus got our own thing goin'
> We don't need anybody to tell us what it's all about

Once the prophetic voice is eliminated, so, too, is any sense of a community ethic. The Judeo-Christian mores that have long been the defining glue holding rural communities together dissolve into a hundred

8. Goins-Phillips, "DC Talk's Kevin Max," para. 7.

different theologies, as each person is now free to choose their own theology. With Christendom only a memory and, as a postmodern mindset settles into rural America, rural churches are giving way to a hyper-individualism that destroys any sense of community. Each person hearing a sermon is free to interpret the sermon as they see fit, or to even reject it by saying, "What the preacher said, what the Bible says, simply does not apply to me." The end result is sixty-five people attending a rural church participating in parallel worship but not becoming one body in Christ.

For the pastor, the ultimate dilemma is how to make disciples in this postmodern age. In our postmodern world, the pastor no longer holds authority, even from Scripture, to tell someone what they are doing is wrong. Even worse, a pastor today may face tremendous opposition if he were to call someone's actions sin. In such a situation, a pastor has no way to call for repentance, for no one has anything to repent from. A person can only repent for breaking their own rules, which is dismissed as a mistake.

Thus, disciple-making becomes, at best, a form of self-help rather than an iron-on-iron sharpening of one's faith against the hard truths of the Bible. The goal of discipleship is to become better at being true to oneself. Discipleship becomes an individual effort apart from the community of believers: "After all, they do not believe the same as me and I am on a different journey than they are traveling."

Conclusion

It is easy to think things never change in rural America. The town square looks the same, and the stately old houses on First Street in 2025 look much like they did in 1925. The family names of the founding fathers are the same family names as those of the current leaders. The little country church built in 1925 still looks the same one hundred years later. The pews are the same, the board holding the hymn numbers is the same, and the piano has been in the same place for generations.

For all the "sameness" in rural America, the truth is, things have changed even in the remotest parts of America and in the most idyllic rural church. As a result of this change, rural North America now lives in a pluralistic world where the rule of Christendom has waned to the point that Christian values are becoming marginalized. And despite what many rural churches secretly wish for, the world is not going back to 1975.

As the rural church today wakes from its slumber, the question remains: What does the rural church do to survive in a landscape vastly different from 1975? Ultimately, the church has two options: retreat into a shell of "us vs. them," or adapt to the rapidly changing world to engage a new generation with the gospel. For many in rural North America, this loss of identity has led to a form of "rural rage" that has bled into the rural church, as we will see in the next chapter.

6

The Paralysis of Fear in a Changing World

Growing up on a farm, one lives with darkness. When night comes, walking outside the light of the house is to encounter a world where darkness reigned supreme. There are no streetlights to keep the darkness at bay.

As a child, there was something unsettling and disturbing about darkness. During the day, the fields and the forest were our playground. It was a place of wonder and excitement that invited exploration. It was common for us to leave the house after breakfast, come back for a quick lunch, and then not return until supper. The day would be spent exploring each nook and cranny of the land. We would fish the streams, make forts in the trees, and explore the forests, all without fear.

However, when the sun set and the light faded, the world of wonder became a world of uncertainty and fear. When we would sleep outside in the backyard, the noises of the night became foreboding and threatening. A squirrel scurrying in the grass became a terrifying grizzly bear searching for its next meal of foolish children camping outside. It did not matter that a grizzly bear sighting had not occurred anywhere in the region. Their mere existence on the planet was proof enough of the threat. The dogs fighting over a bone became a pack of wolves attacking and prowling in the night. The cry of a coyote was the cry of witches practicing their evil incantations. Nothing was more terrifying for a child than darkness. For the darkness concealed the unknown, and the unknown was petrifying.

Adults continue to fear the dark. Not the dark of a moonless night but the darkness of a world of uncertainty. We fear what we cannot control. We fear the loss of Christendom and the onslaught of postmodernism. We fear the future as it increasingly becomes foreboding and uncertain. While our lives are currently safe and secure, we have no assurance that this will continue into the future.

The Pitfall of Fear

Fear not only affects us, but it also affects the church. As the country around us changes, the church can become gripped by fear. Church members fear the future, including the decline in attendance and the potential abandonment of the church by young people. When fear grips the church, it incapacitates the church from fulfilling the great commission and being a powerful force to transform the world. This is especially true as the church enters the realm of uncertainty.

A rapidly changing world requires courage, not anxiety. Change is a threatening experience for people, as it confronts them with the unknown, which brings anxiety and apprehension. Walrath observes, "People have difficulty giving up these old ways, even when they apparently don't work because they *seem right*."[1] We find comfort and security in the familiar. For most people, the safest course of action is to continue doing what they have done in the past, what they know, and what has proven successful in the past. However, as culture becomes increasingly secular and the world changes, the church is shrinking in fear rather than moving forth in confidence in God's work. To understand why, it is essential first to understand how fear has gripped the culture and the church today.

The Culture of Fear

Sociologists are now describing our culture as a culture of fear. The phrase first began to appear on the literary landscape in the late 1990s, when two authors Frank Furedi and Barry Glassner each wrote a book with the same title: *Culture of Fear*. Since then, the phrase has become prevalent

1. Walrath, *Leading Churches Through Change*, 56.

in the national discourse as culture has become increasingly preoccupied with threats to safety and existence.

We have become fixated on what we should fear. Some things are seen as existential threats, such as global warming, pandemics, and weapons of mass destruction. Other things are seen as a threat to our health and safety: crime, our diet, and the attack of terrorists. We fear what we perceive to be a threat to our way of life: the geopolitical world, the political leaders of the nation, and the instability of the economy. However, even more alarming is the fact that we now fear those closest to us. We fear our neighbors because they voted for a different party. We fear our schools because they are indoctrinating our children. We fear our doctors because we believe the pharmaceutical companies are manipulating them. Furedi points out, "Fear itself has become politicized to a point where debate is rarely about whether or not we should be fearful, but about who or what we should fear."[2]

In our culture of fear, even the ordinary becomes a threat. We fear that the water we drink might have been contaminated by a foreign object, so we only drink bottled water. However, we fear bottled water because it might be contaminated by the leaching chemicals used in the plastic. In this world, even the most mundane and tedious aspects of life bring fear and require vigilant monitoring, for behind the mundane lurk unknown risks and dangers.[3] In 2016, *Time* magazine published an article entitled "Why Americans Are More Afraid Than They Used to Be." In 2023, they published another article, "Why Americans Are Uniquely Afraid to Grow Old." Everything is to be feared, even age itself.

Fear feeds itself. The more one fears, the more one becomes entangled in fear. Fears today are being "cultivated through the Media and are less and less the outcome of direct experience."[4] In other words, the more society embraces fear, the more it finds to fear, both real and imaginary. In the age of mass media, we become afraid, not of the actual threats we face in our lives but of the perceived threats experienced by others. If it happened to them, then it might happen to us. So, we fear the threat of a terrorist attack, even though we face more risk driving our car to church (1 in 95) than being killed or harmed by a lurking terrorist in our midst (1 in 4.5 million). We are afraid not because we face a real potential risk

2. Furedi, *How Fear Works*, 2.
3. Furedi, "Only Thing We Have," 3.
4. Furedi, "Only Thing We Have," 3.

but because it has happened somewhere else. If it happened to someone else, it could happen to us.

"The secure person lives in a reliable world—the word 'secure' means 'untroubled by feelings of fear, doubt or vulnerability'—while the insecure person lives in a world that at any time can turn against him, where the basis of existence at any time can be pulled out from under his feet."[5] As the media bombards us with the tragedies that occur elsewhere, we start to see the threats to us. As a result, we now live in a world where it seems nothing is secure and everything becomes a threat.

Fear becomes contagious. When someone else experiences fear, it can spread to others. We become fearful because others are fearful. In the culture of fear, our most significant threats are not what is a reality but what is perceived. As Svendsen points out, "There is a shift between possibility and reality—and as long as one is in the realm of possibility, all disasters are within reach."[6]

When governed by fear, we base our decisions on risk assessment rather than benefit assessment. This paralyzes the church from making positive changes. Instead of focusing on potential benefits, we focus on the worst possible outcome, which leads to a crisis of causality in which uncertainty becomes the driving force. When confronted with a need for change in the church, instead of basing our evaluation on the potential benefits, we often focus solely on the potential detrimental outcomes. We sacrifice the good on the altar of the unknown. We would rather do nothing than take a risk.

Married to the culture of fear is the culture of vulnerability. Because there is no control over what threatens us, it affects how we understand ourselves. When we face uncontrollable and uncertain threats, we develop a perspective that risk is no longer about the possibility of something adversely affecting us; it is part of our identity. In our culture, everyone is "vulnerable and at risk." Whole subgroups are now identified as "at risk" by government agencies. Furedi points out,

> In the late 1980s, the word 'vulnerable' started being used to describe people's intrinsic identities. Vulnerability was no longer seen as something that springs from specific circumstances, such as poverty; rather, it was considered an inherent condition of an

5. Svendsen, *Philosophy of Fear*, 12.
6. Svendsen, *Philosophy of Fear*, 17.

> individual. Vulnerability is a state of mind, an identity, rather than a description of your relationship to a specific threat.[7]

This leads to an inability to accept responsibility and a failure to take risks. The conclusion is that when the church is declining, it is not because the church is failing to adapt its ministry to a changing world; rather, it is because the church is governed by forces outside its control. Instead of examining how a church can be more effective in change, it reverts to the default in which effectiveness is based on stability.

Fear and the Church

Not only does fear creep into the perception people have of themselves, but it also creeps into the perception of the church. Denominational leaders often view small and rural churches as being "at risk and vulnerable." Due to its small size, its existence is perceived as being at risk. As a result, it becomes identified by this vulnerability. Instead of seeing its security based on God's sovereign work, people view its sustainability as determined by the number of people in the pews and the amount of money in the account—the culture of vulnerability gives rise to a culture of paralysis. The unknown becomes a threat and then becomes normalized, so people live in fear.

We not only see a world filled with physical threats, but we also see a world filled with spiritual threats. The church believes its freedom and very existence are at stake, and the world is fraught with dangers. The shutdown of the church during COVID-19 was viewed as a tool of manipulation to shut down the church. The well-being and future of democracy and our society are threatened by the newly elected party. We can only avoid the impending moral and spiritual collapse by electing the right candidate.

The church has embraced the culture of fear. It sees the world and people outside as a threat rather than as the focus of evangelism. When people are perceived as a threat, they can be seen as an enemy to be avoided. The only way to protect the church from the world is to isolate the church from the world.

7. Furedi, "Only Thing We Have," 7.

Fear Leads to a Preoccupation with Safety

Israel was gripped by fear. When they left Egypt under the leadership of Moses, they entered a world of the unknown. Even though they had groaned under the weight of slavery, the uncertainty of what lay ahead made them fearful. This fear was overwhelming as they stood on the borders of the promised land. To take possession of the land, they would encounter hostile armies. When the spies returned from their excursion into the land, they not only reported on the land's productivity but also on the threat posed by the armies. As a result, the people responded in fear. They grumbled against Moses and demanded a new leader take them back to the familiarity of Egypt, even though it would involve a return to slavery (Num 13–14). When faced with the uncertain and the unknown, it is easy to succumb to a paralysis of fear. As a result, a church can become preoccupied with safety and security. It is also easy to become suspicious of others and their motives. It is even possible to suspect anyone who promotes change within the church.

A culture of fear worships safety and security. As culture becomes increasingly uncertain and the unknown becomes more prevalent, it is easy to become preoccupied with what is safe. As Furedi points out, "Safety is more highly valued than any other condition in the culture of fear, acquiring the status of a moral good that trumps all others."[8] The question is no longer "Is it right?" but "Is it safe?" Bader-Saye rightly points out, "We thus lead timid lives, fearing the risks of bold gestures. Instead of being courageous, we are content to be safe. Instead of being hopeful, we make virtues of cynicism and irony, which keep us at a safe distance from risky commitments."[9] He goes on to point out that "suspicion becomes a virtue in the culture of fear."[10]

In *The Lion, the Witch and the Wardrobe*, when Susan found out Aslan was a lion, her first question was, "Is he—quite safe?" However, Mr. Beaver pointed out that she was asking the wrong question. The question is not "Is He safe?" but "Is He good?"[11] The church faces the same challenge today. As it navigates change, the most common question asked is not "Will it advance the kingdom of Christ?" but rather "Is this a threat to our stability and sustainability?"

8. Furedi, *How Fear Works*, 207.
9. Bader-Saye, *Following Jesus*, 39.
10. Bader-Saye, *Following Jesus*, 41.
11. Lewis, *Lion, the Witch*, 91.

The worship of safety and security can hamstring the rural church. In a world of volatility, the fear of the unknown can lead back to the slavery of Egypt. The church becomes more concerned about safety than ministry. However, God did not call the early Christians to a life of safety; he called them to the opposite. They were to take the gospel and assault the gates of hell. This would cost them everything, including their lives. In Matt 16:24–26, Christ makes it clear to the disciples that advancing the kingdom would not be a safe endeavor. It required a willingness to give up everything. Change inherently involves risk, and only when we are willing to risk everything to advance the kingdom of God will we have an impact.

Fear Undermines Trust

What Svendsen says about fear and society is equally valid for the church. "Fear normally leads to seeking to establish a distance between oneself and that which is feared. A fear culture can, therefore, undermine the trust many philosophers, theologians, and sociologists consider to be one of the most basic characteristics of human relations."[12] He goes on to point out, "A fear culture is no trust culture—and that has major consequences on how people relate to each other. Trust can be described as a 'social glue' that keeps human beings together."[13] This is true not only of society, but it is also of the church and our relationship with God. When we are governed by fear, we no longer trust people, and we begin to question God. We question people's wisdom, motives, and agenda when they propose something that, in our perception, may involve risk. Fear drives a wedge between people, creating distrust and fragmentation within the community.

Fear can paralyze a congregation. In Deut 20, Moses outlines the principles to govern the nation as it engages in battle against its enemies. Moses reminds the people to trust in God as they face their enemies. They are not to fear, for God is present with them, and he will fight the battle for them. However, having warned the people of the dangers of fear, the leaders are instructed that if there is any man who is afraid, he is to be sent home "lest he make the heart of his fellows melt like his own" (v. 8).

12. Svendsen, *Philosophy of Fear*, 92.

13. Svendsen, *Philosophy of Fear*, 101.

Fear breeds fear. When people become fearful of the future and the challenges it presents, it can incapacitate God's people from acting. In 1 Sam 28, Saul became afraid due to the uncertainty of the battle. Rather than turn to God in faith, Saul turned to a witch to find out what the future would hold. In the end, it cost him his life.

Fear undermines faith. When life becomes marked by uncertainty, it is easy to become apprehensive of the unknown that lies ahead. This can weaken a congregation so they are unwilling to take any risks for fear it might hurt the church, even as the church dies a slow (but familiar) death.

When the church becomes preoccupied with safety and sees others as a risk, it leads to isolation. The church starts to see the world as a threat. Instead of seeing people as prisoners of war who are captured by the enemy and in need of deliverance, it is easy to see them as the enemy itself. It is easy to rewrite Paul's words to read, "We wrestle against flesh and blood" (Eph 6:12). Developing a fortress mentality is easy to do, in which protecting the church from the world is prioritized, rather than engaging the world through the gospel. A church can strive to isolate and protect itself from those who are not part of the church. Strangers are often perceived as individuals who threaten the health and stability of the church, rather than those who need to be rescued.

The Cause of Fear

In the physical world, we become fearful of what we perceive as a threat to our physical well-being. But what about the spiritual world? Why do we become afraid when we serve an infinitely powerful God who promises to be present with us and triumph through us?

Fear Arises When We Lose Sight of God

It is not a coincidence that the rise of the culture of fear corresponds to the decline of the fear of God as the foundation by which the church views the world. In the past, the fear of God was seen as a positive virtue to be celebrated and valued. A proper fear of God served to provide stability and give boldness to the church to proclaim the gospel. God was to be feared because he is holy and just, and he governs the universe. In previous generations, the fear of God was more than just a religious attitude; it was a framework by which the world was understood. His control over the events was recognized. The fear of God was not just a moral perspective governing conduct. The fear of God was a moral code guiding the events of life.

When one's outlook is guided by an understanding of God's control over the universe, fear becomes concrete and specific. One only feared what was a real threat. However, once society abandoned God, fear became more abstract. Since chance, rather than a personal God, governs the world, life becomes uncertain and unpredictable. There are no guarantees of the outcome. Therefore, fear is now spread to what is potential. Furedi points out, "In the absence of a compelling moral code that can guide people's lives, the tempting to moralize fear appeals have proved irresistible."[14] A popular saying attributed to John Wesley states, "If I had 300 men who feared nothing but God, hated nothing but sin, and were determined to know nothing among men by Jesus Christ and Him crucified, I would set the world on fire."[15] However, in today's culture of fear, it is easy to fear everything but God and desire everything except God. When God is no longer in control, bringing stability and security, then life is lived in the dark, where everything is uncertain and a threat.

The way for finite man to comprehend an infinite God is to make him finite. Instead of trusting in God's sovereignty over the universe and one's life, God can now be manipulated and controlled to conform to each person's perspectives and desires. The smaller God becomes, the greater the threat is to personal and corporate existence. To fear the unknown of tomorrow is to reject that God controls and determines tomorrow. People want a God who is loving and gracious, but not a God who is sovereign and powerful. However, a powerless God leads to uncertainty. As society turns against God and the church, it is easy to become fearful that God has lost control. Instead of God protecting the church, the well-being of the church and, by extension, our very lives are threatened. Rather than trusting that "the gates of hell shall not prevail against it," the church fears it cannot prevent the onslaught of the world.

14. Furedi, *How Fear Works*, 128.

15. This statement is attributed to John Wesley, although there is no direct statement found in any of his writings. AZ Quotes, "John Wesley Quotes."

Volatility, Fear, and Isolation

A predictable world is a safe world, one in which people not only know how to act but also can understand the outcomes of their actions. However, when life becomes unpredictable and the result is uncertain, it becomes marked by risks and apprehension. Volatility and uncertainty produce a systematically distorted picture of the world. It is easy to find comfort and security in a world of stability and familiarity. People fear what they cannot control. This is especially true as culture becomes more hostile to the Christian faith.

This nation was founded upon a Judeo-Christian ethic. However, as the previous chapter demonstrated, over the past decade, culture has increasingly adopted the postmodernist worldview. This new world feels as if Christianity is not just under attack but the church's very existence is threatened. In response, the church isolates itself from the world. The Great Commission becomes the great surrender. Instead of being a force to transform the world, it becomes a fortress to protect ourselves from the world. In fear, we overlook Jesus' prayer that we are to be sent into the world (John 17:14–19).

Change Creates Fear

In a rapidly changing world, we long for stability and familiarity. However, with change comes uncertainty. Ingrained within us is a powerful desire for stability. We want a world that is predictable, for a predictable world is understandable and controllable. However, a world of exponential change is unpredictable and uncontrollable.

The world we face tomorrow is unknown, and with the unknown comes fear. As Walrath points out, "Change is a threatening experience. This is especially true for weaker congregations, for whom most changes in the last several decades have been negative."[16] Rural churches have long been perceived as struggling churches, whose existence is often tenuous at best. The narrative today is that a church that is not growing is dying and a healthy church is large. Consequently, the rural church fears change, perceiving it as a threat to its existence.

16. Walrath, *Leading Churches Through Change*, 122.

Change Brings a Feeling of Loss

People fear that change will bring a loss of connection with previous generations, whose memories remain in the walls and pews of the church. These relationships are woven into the fabric of the traditions and heritage that comprise the church. When new people join the community and the church, they bring different values that conflict with those of the traditional rural residents. As the writers of *Leading Through Change* point out, "The newcomers' arrival also causes considerable conflict with others, particularly the long-term residents. These conflicts stem from a different way of thinking, a different cultural orientation, even a different vocabulary."[17] The potential for conflict is especially true when it is perceived that changes will bring a sense of spiritual loss. Fear further compounds the apprehension people feel in a changing world. Consequently, people revert to what they have done in the past without realizing their fear of change and desire for stability are the very things undermining ministry. The greatest threat to the church is not the changes it is facing but rather the refusal to adapt to the new world in which we live. As Furedi points out, when confronted with a changing world, instead of seeking the latest ministry opportunities, we continually anticipate the worst possible outcomes.[18] This is especially true within the rural church. We fear change because we become focused on the worst possible outcome.

The Effects of Fear

When Paul arrived in Corinth, his ministry seemed to have hit the wall of indifference and rejection. He had been driven out of one Macedonian city after another. When he arrived in Athens and engaged the philosophers on Mars Hill, he was met with apathy. Facing the prospect of failure and opposition, fear began to have a stranglehold on his faith. Paul would later write of his struggles, "For we do not want you to be unaware, brethren, of the affliction we experienced in Asia. For we were so utterly burdened beyond our strength that we despaired of life itself" (2 Cor 1:8). He would also state that when he came to Corinth, he came "in weakness and in fear and much trembling" (1 Cor 2:3). This fear became so powerful that it began to paralyze Paul in ministry. So great was his

17. Wells et al., *Leading Through Change*, 25.

18. Furedi, "Only Thing We Have," 6.

fear that Jesus himself appeared to Paul to encourage him by exhorting, "Do not be afraid, but go on speaking and do not be silent, for I am with you, and no one will attack you to harm you, for I have many in this city who are my people" (Acts 18:9–10). Ministry is inherently risky, and so fear can undermine one's faith and hinder their ministry. Instead of being driven by faith, Christians must not become driven by fear that distorts and undermines one's testimony.

Psychologists identify four distinct responses that people exhibit when confronted with a threat that evokes overwhelming fear: fight, flight, freeze, or fawn. These same characteristics are evident in the church's response to the fear we experience due to the changing culture.

Fear and Fight

The first response is to fight. When confronted with the uncertainty of a radically changing world, people tend to go on the defensive, often condemning those perceived as a threat. Instead of loving one's enemies, the goal is to defeat them. One can only imagine the fear of the disciples when a gang of armed soldiers came to arrest Jesus in the garden. They knew they would not be invited to the next community potluck. It was a life-and-death event. Peter's immediate response was to pull out a sword and fight back (John 18:1–11).

While an actual sword may not be brandished today, often the response to changes occurring in the world today is to pull out the proverbial sword. Those promoting changes are seen as enemies to be defeated. Thus, some speak of the cultural changes occurring as a cultural war, one in which Christians must engage. This was typified by the Religious Right and Moral Majority movement of the '70s and early '80s. As already demonstrated, for some, this not only involves active engagement in culture today by defending the Christian worldview but it also consists in promoting a revolution involving a "forcible reclamation of civil power by the people in order to transfer that power on just and more suitable political arrangements."[19] The result is to see people as the enemy rather than people in need of deliverance.

19. Wolfe, *Case for Christian Nationalism*, 326.

Fear and Flight

A second response to fear is flight. The fight-or-flight response stems from the belief that the imminent danger cannot be overcome; therefore, it must be avoided by fleeing. As Svendsen points out,

> Flight need not be understood spatially, that is, it is not necessarily a question of running away; it can just as well consist of creating a barrier between oneself and the object, such as protecting oneself with one's arm or hiding behind a door. The crucial thing is that in some way or another, one tries to position oneself where one is invulnerable.[20]

For churches, this is manifested by the fortress mentality that seeks to isolate itself from the world by hiding behind the church doors. People tend to avoid what they fear, and when the fear is for the world, people will isolate themselves from it. The way to protect the church from the negative impact of the world is to disengage from it. This leads rural churches to become reluctant to embrace new arrivals in the community because their urban values are seen as a threat. Instead of welcoming them, they receive a cold shoulder from the church. Yet God does not call the church to disengage and isolate from the world or to associate only with fellow Christians. Like the Pharisees of Jesus' day, we see the sinner as someone to avoid. But Christ did the opposite; rather than avoiding them, he went out of his way to engage them (Matt 9:13; Luke 7:34; Mark 2:15). God calls the church to go into the world. He calls Christians to be vulnerable, but in that vulnerability, God's protective hand (John 17:16) can be felt. When the church isolates itself from the world, the Great Commission is nullified, which calls us to take the gospel into the world.

Fear and Freeze

The third typical response to danger and fear is to freeze. Freeze is a response where someone is unable to physically or mentally react to the threat, and as a result, they become immobile and unable to move. A church can freeze when it stops proclaiming the gospel. Instead, it merely tries to maintain the past. The church fears change, so it reverts to traditional methods. Instead of being gospel-driven, the church becomes tradition-driven, where keeping the traditions of the church (which

20. Svendson, *Philosophy of Fear*, 31.

bring safety and continuity) is more important than fulfilling the Great Commission. The mantra becomes the status quo rather than "Onward, Christian Soldiers."

When the early church was confronted with the radical shift from the old covenant to the new covenant, it created tension and even division within the church. In response, some sought to move forward by embracing the past. While accepting Jesus as the Messiah, they still wanted to maintain the status quo. In Acts 11, even some of the apostles were responding to the salvation of the gentiles by wanting them to conform to the rituals and practices of the old covenant. While they affirmed Christ was the Messiah and accepted the salvation he offered, they still wanted to maintain the past (Acts 11:1–2).

Many churches respond by freezing today. Within the rural church, some desire to maintain the traditions and practices of the past. The answer to the changing culture is to revert to the way the church has always been. In the end, the church denies the reality of the changes occurring in culture and instead attempts to maintain the way things have been done in the past, even though this approach is slowly leading to the church's demise.

Fear and Fawn

A fourth response to fear is the fawn response. This response occurs when people seek to appease those who are threatening them. According to Pete Walker, a psychotherapist who specializes in trauma, fawning is a response to a threat that involves becoming more appealing to the danger by mirroring or merging with those who pose a threat.[21] This can happen in the church as the church seeks to appease culture by minimizing the radical nature of following Christ. In other words, the best way to gain a following is to no longer make demands upon the people. Renn describes the current movement by some churches away from confronting our culture to appeasement by stating,

> Rather than denouncing secular culture, they sought to confidently meet that culture on its terms in a pluralistic public square. They believed that Christianity could still be articulated compellingly and something to offer in that environment, even

21. Clayton, "What Is Fawning Trauma Response,?" para. 2.

> as they wanted to challenge aspects of the culture that conflicted with Christian teaching.[22]

Instead of discovering new ways to convey the gospel and call people to change, it seeks to appease people by denying and/or avoiding anything that might be offensive.

As the moral foundation of the world is dramatically shifting and is in direct conflict with the church's moral teachings, instead of engaging with culture, many churches capitulate to it. Instead of confronting culture, the goal is to adapt messages to be more acceptable to it. Os Guinness describes this danger when he writes, "What remains of traditional beliefs and practices is altered to fit in with the new assumption. It is translated into the language and expectations of the new assumptions, which become the controlling assumptions."[23] Instead of confronting our culture by exposing sin (Eph 4:8–14), many churches redefine and reinterpret the Bible to make it acceptable to culture. Paul warns Timothy of the danger of his message being driven by appeasing the culture rather than confronting the culture when he warns, "For the time will come when they will not endure sound teaching; but having itching ears they will accumulate for themselves teachers to suit their own passions" (2 Tim 4:3). In fawning, instead of confronting culture, the message is adapted to the culture. This overlooks the fact that the gospel will always be inherently offensive (Rom 1). When a church seeks to remove the offense of the gospel, it distorts the gospel. In fawning, the church undermines the radical transformation God desires to accomplish.

Responding in Faith Rather Than Fear

In a radically shifting world that is becoming more hostile to biblical truth, Christians are not to live in fear but in faith. This involves trusting God and responding in obedience despite our fear. In a changing culture, rather than responding with fight, flight, freeze, or fawn, the church is called to respond in faith, no longer fearing the changes in the culture but seeing opportunities to address our culture in fresh ways.

In many ways, we are living in a time that reflects the culture confronting the early church. John Ritner reminds us, "Christianity began in first-century Rome in a pluralistic culture, where it flourished on the

22. Renn, *Life in the Negative World*, 28.

23. Guinness, *Dining with the Devil*, 57.

fringes of society. In that place of marginalization, existing as a minority movement gospel spread like wildfire."[24] However, as our culture pushes the churches to the margins, we must recognize that the need is even greater for the church to become more engaged in outreach.

We are not called to a life of fear, but a life grounded in the moral certainty of God's word and the sovereignty of God overseeing the affairs of the world. When God called Ezekiel to be a prophet, the nation of Israel was already taken into captivity, and the southern tribe of Judah was rapidly descending into spiritual and political turmoil. The people had rejected God and embraced the moral and spiritual corruption of the surrounding nations. Yet when God called Ezekiel to be his prophetic voice to the people, he warned Ezekiel, "And you, son of man, be not afraid of them, nor be afraid of their words, though briers and thorns are with you and you sin on scorpions. Be not afraid of their words, nor be dismayed at their looks, for they are a rebellious house" (Ezek 2:6–7). It was a time when being a prophet of God would be costly and dangerous. Yet God calls him not to shrink back in fear but boldly proclaim the message God was proclaiming through him (2:5). The task of the prophet was not to say what people wanted to hear; it was to declare what God told them to proclaim so that even if they rejected his message, they would know that a prophet was among them.

The stability and security of the church are not based upon the number of people in the pews, the popularity we enjoy with the community, or the absence of persecution. Our security is grounded in our faith in a God who governs all the affairs of the universe and is using the church to proclaim his message. Although our world is changing and the methods by which we engage with it are evolving, our mission and message remain unchanged. Because of faith, instead of shrinking back in fear, we can be confident, for we know that God is in control. Thus, the sage writes, "The wicked flee when no one pursues, but the righteous are bold as a lion" (Prov 28:1).

Conclusion

The greatest challenge before the church is not the changing culture around us. The greatest challenge the church faces today is to recognize our need for change. We lament what is happening in the broader culture

24. Ritner, *Positively Irritating*, xix.

and pray for God to change our nation. The reality is the church needs to change. The change is not in its message or mission but in its culture and methods. We need to recognize that the greatest threat to the church is the church itself, by either capitulating to our culture or withdrawing from it. Historically, the church has focused primarily on its internal matters. Our ministry and mission were to serve others and invite people to join us in this service. However, in a post-Christian world, the church must recognize that it is not to be internally focused, but externally mission-driven. To achieve this, we need to transform the church's culture from one that is passive and self-serving to a missional focus that reengages the community with the gospel. With this goal in mind, we now turn to examine how the church can shift from a passive congregation to a dynamic, mission-driven force for the kingdom of Christ.

Part 3

Establishing a Theological Foundation for Rural Ministry

7

Building on Truth

A Message-Driven Mission

FARMERS TAKE PRIDE IN how straight the rows of grain are and how straight they drive the tractor and combine. When they drive by a field of their neighbors, they will cast their eye upon the tracks or the rows of grain to see how straight they are. If the lines are crooked or the tracks are wavering, they will mutter "rookie driver" under their breath as they chuckle. But the greatest faux pas is when those seeding grain, spraying weeds, or driving a combine leave a noticeable skip. Throughout the rest of the year, these skips will be a source of embarrassment and ribbing from their neighbors. If you leave a noticeable skip, you can be sure that someone will mention it to you the next time you attend a community gathering.

When I learned to drive a tractor, one of the most important lessons was not only how to safely operate the machine; it was how to ensure your tracks are straight. The key to driving straight is maintaining proper focus. You need to focus on an immovable object and then drive straight toward it. In our technologically driven world, tractors are equipped with GPS, allowing farmers to keep their lines perfectly straight. While the salesmen market the GPS-driven tractors from the standpoint of efficiency and avoiding unnecessary waste of chemicals and seeds, I suspect that the real reason farmers gravitate towards them is that they can have straighter tracks in the field without leaving the dreaded "skips."

In a volatile, chaotic world, the struggle is to maintain the center and direction of the church. With conflicting worldviews, the church can quickly stray from its focus. We live in a world where people, including the church, have embraced consumerism. As a result, we start to lead the church on a crooked path. Ford and Singleton point out that much of today's culture, including the church, is driven to use organizations, services, or entities to satisfy personal needs. The result is a culture of narcissism where everything is viewed, including the church, as a means to personal happiness rather than personal transformation.[1] Worship is no longer about standing in awe before the Almighty God; it is about the experiences that we have. Instead of being confronted with a holy God exalted in heaven, people today want a service that entertains.

Today, the church faces the challenge of maintaining relevance and influence in a post-Christian world. As we have repeatedly pointed out, society and culture are undergoing significant changes, and the approaches taken in the past will become increasingly irrelevant in the future. However, the most critical decisions regarding change are not determining what needs to be changed but determining what cannot and must not change. Change is beneficial when it is necessary and well-defined, but change can be destructive when it is haphazard and arbitrary. In a world of volatile change, change must have a central point—a reference point that remains unchanging and enables us to stay on course in our spiritual journey.

The Centrality of the Message

The crisis confronting the church in a changing world today is just not the changes in culture or the changing morality people embrace. It is the abandonment of truth as the foundation of the church and the basis for living. In a changing world, the church will need to adapt its methods and ministry to remain relevant. Still, the most essential foundation for relevancy remains grounded in the unchanging message. When the church loses sight of the message, it no longer has anything to say to culture. The church may have the right mission and programs, but if it has the wrong message, it is building a house upon the sand that will crumble in the face of adversity and opposition.

The temptation is to seek modern solutions to contemporary problems. Instead, we should seek ancient solutions to contemporary issues. For all the changes faced in culture today, the underlying problems are not new but go back to the very beginning of time. From the start in the

1. Ford and Singleton, *Attentive Church Leadership*, 123.

garden of Eden, the greatest threat confronting people is the rejection of God's message. Satan's temptation was not to embrace a new lifestyle or new forms of worship; it was to deny the truthfulness and relevance of God's words: "Did God actually say. . . . You surely will not die!" (Gen 3:1–5). Throughout history, Satan's tactic has remained the same: attack the credibility and veracity of the message of God. When the church is no longer governed by the message, when our message and mission conform to the latest fad, so that we rely on methodology rather than theology to define our spiritual vitality, we start to drive crooked in the field.

In 1993, David Wells warned that the church was wavering in the practice of the faith. He cautioned that the message and doctrines of our faith were no longer determining how we live:

> It is not that the elements of the evangelical credo have vanished; they have not. The fact that they have professed, however, does not necessarily mean that the structure of the historical Protestant faith is still intact. The reason, quite simply, is that while these items of belief are professed, they are increasingly removed from the center of evangelical life where they defined what that life was. They are now relegated to the periphery, where their power to define what evangelical life should be is lost. It is an evangelical practice rather than an evangelical profession that reveals the change.[2]

Tragically, twenty years later, many evangelicals have not only abandoned the practice of our faith but have also abandoned the profession of our faith. Research suggests that only half of evangelical pastors possess a biblical worldview.[3]

To minister effectively in a changing world, the church today needs to recognize that the message *is* the mission. Without the message and the communication of the truth of the Bible, the church no longer has a mission. In the Great Commission, Christ set forth the universal task of the church throughout all ages. The mission was not to develop vision strategies or establish programs and buildings. The mission was simple: to make disciples who live in obedience to Christ's teachings. The mission was to proclaim the message of Christ to every community and person in the world.

2. Wells, *No Place for Truth*, 18.

3. See Barna, "American Worldview Inventory 2022."

To understand the church and maintain relevance in a changing world, the church must start with the unchanging message it is called to proclaim. Missiologist Donald Smith pointed out,

> It is the Word that shows us God's purpose, that gives understanding of the cosmic conflict and our role in it. It is the Word that draws us outward, away from ourselves, so that we can introduce all men to God's new family and race through the wonder of the new birth. The living Word in us gives us not only a Message but the authority and courage to fully and faithfully proclaim that Message.[4]

Yet it is this message that tragically becomes secondary. In a complex world, the tendency is to seek modern solutions to contemporary problems. However, we often overlook that it is only through embracing these ancient words that solutions to the challenges can be found.

The Relevance of Our Message

As seen in the previous chapter on the changing spirituality of our nation, the focus has shifted in recent years from the message to the method. Pragmatism (what works) rather than proclamation has become the driving force. In a changing world, the emergent church movement viewed the message of Scripture as outdated and culturally out of touch with the modern world. To fulfill our mission, we needed not only to change how we communicated the message but also to change the message itself. For some, the message was a product of a previous culture disconnected from the present reality. The evolutionary theory of science became the evolutionary theory of epistemology. Just as organisms evolve into new species, so, too, must truth evolve into a new message.

In the age of moral relativism, the Bible is relevant only in that it gives a starting point for discussing modern problems. Thus, Brian McLaren argued that holding to the view that the Bible is absolute truth and unchanging is to embrace "conceptual idolatry." He writes,

> This evolutionary approach also helps us understand one reason for the absolute refusal of the Jewish people to tolerate idols: idols freeze one's understanding of God in stone as it was. This approach also warns us about the danger of another kind of idolatry, to which we today are more susceptible. Although few

4. Radmacher, *Celebrating the Word*, 94–95.

> of us today are tempted to freeze our understanding of God in graven images; we may too quickly freeze our understanding in printed images, rigid conceptual idols not chiseled in wood or stone but printed on paper in books, housed not in temples but in seminaries and denominational headquarters, worshiped not through ancient ceremonies and rituals but through contemporary sermons and songs.[5]

For McLaren, the Bible is not relevant as the source of unchanging truth; instead, it is merely a point of discussion and departure from which to form a contemporary view of God. Biblical truths must be deconstructed and reinterpreted to speak to modern culture. Derek Vreeland writes, "The quest for inerrancy puts too much pressure on the Bible. The Bible itself is an ancient collection of books. It is simply unfair to force this ancient collection of books to answer modern questions."[6] Instead of human reason being formed by the Bible, the Bible must be formed by human reason.

In contrast, Paul reminds Timothy that the message of the Scripture remains central to answer the needs of humanity: "All Scripture is breathed out by God and profitable for teaching, for reproof, for correction, and for training in righteousness, that the man of God may be complete, equipped for every good work" (2 Tim 3:16–17). The Scriptures provide all that is needed to change people and build the church. When Paul wrote to Timothy, his protégé who would become his successor, he did not outline his methodology or the style of worship he was to employ. He did not challenge Timothy to disconnect the Bible from its Jewish roots to make it more palatable to a Greek culture. For Paul, relevance was not found in our organizational systems and cutting-edge ministries. The significance of the Bible lies in its message itself. Paul did not challenge Timothy to develop a dynamic vision statement or even a clearly defined mission statement; he challenged him with a message statement. Throughout his letters to Timothy, Paul reminded Timothy that his ministry was to be centered and driven by the message.

The Bible is relevant because it originated in the mind of an infinite and omniscient God, who sees the total history of humanity—past, present, and future—in a single vision. Because he sees the beginning and the end (Isa 46:9–10), he can write a message that is always relevant to all individuals. The Bible provides the metanarrative for humanity. As

5. McLaren, *New Kind of Christianity*, 110.

6. Vreeland, "Why Biblical Inerrancy Doesn't Work," para. 13.

Erickson points out regarding the message of Scripture, "It is a universal explanation, and in two respects. It is universal or all-inclusive in the sense of encompassing everything, including all aspects or elements of reality. It is also universal in the sense that it is a narrative that claims to be valid for absolutely all members of the human race."[7] The Christian faith is first and foremost a "content-oriented religion"[8] in which life is viewed through the lens of Scripture rather than the Scripture being governed by the lens of experience.

Both in society and within the church, our view of leadership is often grounded in the leader being a visionary, so that the words "leadership" and "visionary" have become synonymous. A visionary leader is "someone who has a clear mental image of a better future, and who can communicate and implement that vision."[9] Thus, the pastor sets the organizational direction of the ministry and then rallies people to that vision.

To support the need for a clear vision, people often quote Prov 29:18 as a basis for the quest for a vision and direction for the church, assuming that it is possible to look into the future to see what the church must become. However, is it possible to project a vision for the future when the future is governed by intense unpredictability and instability? It is impossible to predict what cannot be controlled. The answer lies in Prov 29:18, but not in the way it was often used. The vision that the sage is pointing to is the vision of revelatory truth. In other words, the sage is saying that "where there is no revelation from God, the people perish." The word "perish" literally means to be turned loose or free from restraint. It is used in Exod 32:25 to refer to the people being spiritually "out of control" in their pursuit of idolatry. In other words, when moral truth does not originate from God, as revealed in his law, moral chaos results.

The uncertainty of today must take us back to the certainty of the Scriptures. The Bible serves as the point of reference, providing the necessary guidance for the church in the past, present, and future. It is relevant because the moral law of God remains unchanged. At the heart of the Christian message is the calling of God *to be* rather than *to do*. To be effective in the future, a vision is needed, not of the future but of the past, that which is found in the revealed word of God.

The greatest hindrance to the church is not adhering to an outdated biblical message that it is antiquated and irrelevant; it is the failure to

7. Erickson, *Postmodern World*, 67.

8. Erickson, *Postmodern World*, 71.

9. Barna, *Power of Vision*, 28.

derive its life and teaching from the unchanging message of the Bible. This is what Paul warned Timothy would happen and what he must guard against (2 Tim 4:1–5). For Paul, the message does not need to be demythologized; it needs to be proclaimed unashamedly (v. 2).

The Message Determines the Mission of the Church

In the current view of the church, the mission of the church is often separated from its message. Tod Bolsinger writes that the mission of the church must govern everything. This mission

> is not just about becoming more like Christ as an end in itself. In a post-Christendom world that has become a mission field right outside the sanctuary door, the Christian community is about gathering, forming a people, a spiritual transformation is both individual and corporate growth, so that they—together—participate in Christ's mission to establish the kingdom of God "on earth as it is in heaven."[10]

However, this can only be achieved through the proclamation of the unchanging gospel. What brings about spiritual transformation, both individually and corporately, is the proclaimed message, rather than the implementing programs or leadership functions. When the message is distorted, the mission becomes misguided. The message is not superficial but goes to the core of the church. A church that has the wrong message becomes a force for evil rather than righteousness. The stakes cannot be higher. Christ warns that a church with the wrong message, even though it is doing the right things, leads people down the pathway to hell (Matt 7:21–23).

The mission of the church is not just driven by the message; the message *is* the mission. Throughout Scripture, when God called people to a mission, the mission was to communicate the word of God. God's mission to Isaiah was simple: "Go and say to this people" (Isa 6:9). In Jer 1, God calls and commissions Jeremiah. The calling was to be his spokesman to the nations. In response, Jeremiah expressed reluctance because of his age. Commentators suggest Jeremiah was approximately seventeen years old. In a culture that equated wisdom with age, Jeremiah felt a sense of inadequacy. He lacked the training to be a dynamic orator who could expound the law of God. However, God makes it clear that the message of

10. Bolsinger, *Canoeing the Mountains*, 39.

his ministry was not based on his skill, charisma, or leadership qualities. Instead, the success of his ministry was based on his faithfulness to speak the words God had commanded him (Jer 1:7–8). The calling of Ezekiel was likewise a calling to proclaim a message. The success of Ezekiel was not based on the results of his message or even the influence and renown that he would attain. The success of his message was attributed to his faithfulness in communicating God's word to the people (Ezek 2).

The Message Defines the Health of the Church

When defining church health, the focus is often on the church's ministry and its impact on the community. Kevin Ford, in his book *Transforming Church*, identifies five key indicators of a healthy church:

1. A healthy sense of community
2. An alignment between their operating culture and their clear sense of identity
3. Shared leadership within the congregation
4. A clearly defined ministry that ministers and glorifies God in the neighborhoods, workplaces, social circles, and schools
5. A willingness to embrace change in their ministry[11]

The fault does not lie in what he says but in what he does not say. A church can possess all these characteristics, but if it conveys the wrong message, it will lead people astray. A church that distorts, rejects, or redefines the message is an unhealthy church, regardless of its goals, dynamic programs, or clear sense of identity. At its core, it fails to be the church. This was the case of the churches in the book of Revelation. They were churches that would be held up as models today. However, the churches of Pergamum and Thyatira allowed false teachers to infiltrate the church. The churches of Sardis and Laodicea were organizationally vibrant but spiritually bankrupt. They had all the outward ministries and characteristics that made other churches envious. But in the end, they were condemned because their message was incomplete or distorted.

When Paul arrived in Corinth, he entered a city with a distinct culture, one characterized by its immorality and marked by an openly hostile attitude toward the gospel. In the face of this challenging task,

11. Ford, *Transforming Church*, 9–12.

Christ did not give him a strategic plan. He did not give him a new program to implement. He gave him a simple task: "Do not be afraid, but go on speaking and do not be silent" (Acts 18:9). The mission he gave Paul was to proclaim the gospel. Later, as Paul looked back upon his ministry, he would reflect that his success in establishing a church in Corinth was not based upon strategic planning or utilizing the latest program. Paul only came with one purpose: "For I decided to know nothing among you except Jesus Christ and him crucified. And I was with you in weakness and in fear and much trembling, and my speech and my message were not in plausible words of wisdom, but in demonstration of the Spirit and of power" (1 Cor 2:3–5). It is no wonder Paul gives Timothy the same mandate. When setting forth his mandate for Timothy, he did not challenge Timothy to develop programs and build effective strategies. He gave him a straightforward command: "Preach the word" (2 Tim 4:2). In Eph 4:11–16, Paul reminds the church at Ephesus that the goal of ministry and the nature of spiritual maturity is found in obedience to the truth. A church can only be healthy when it is gospel-centered, gospel-driven, and gospel-transformed.

The Message is the Foundation for Ministry

The message must drive the ministry so that the goal of everything done in the church is centered on the proclamation of the gospel of Christ, for the gospel itself is relevant and transformative. As Witmer points out,

> The Gospel of Jesus Christ is a big gospel in at least four ways. It's big in terms of its importance; it's the most urgently needed news anyone could ever hear (Romans 10:13–15). It's big in terms of its power; it's the power of God for salvation (Romans 1:16). It's big in terms of its effects: remaking not just individual people but the entire cosmos through Jesus Christ (Matthew 24:14; Colossians 1:5). Finally, the Gospel is big in terms of its centrality; it's the central of the Christian life, not just one more thing for Christians to know in addition to other things.[12]

In a changing world, the greatest threat to the church is not irrelevance or outdated programs or worship but theological and biblical ignorance and distortion. Without the foundation of its message (which includes its theological teaching), the church is doomed from the outset.

12. Witmer, *Big Gospel in Small Places*, 67.

The starting point and underpinning for ministry are the message of God's word. Without a solid theological and biblical base for its ministry, the church no longer has a mission.

The activities of the ministry must be governed by the message preached. In defining church health and ministry, it starts with the message proclaimed. A contextualized message means that the gospel message establishes the mission and ministry of the church. As Zane Pratt rightly points out,

> What we do is shaped by what we believe is true. This is the point at which theology intersects with missiology. Whether mission strategists realize it or not, the answers they provide to our two foundational questions—"What is our mission?" and "How do we do it?"—accurately reflect what they believe is true and what they value as important. Theology shapes mission, and missiology reveals theology.[13]

A church can survive and be reasonably successful spiritually without a clear understanding of its vision or having well-defined programs, but it cannot survive shoddy or incorrect theology. Without a foundation of biblical theology, the church is reduced to a social organization that operates programs rather than developing a ministry that challenges the hearts and minds of people with biblical truth.[14] David Wells points out, "In the past, the doing of theology encompassed three essential aspects: 1: A confessional element, 2: a reflection on this confession, and 3: the cultivation of a set of virtues that are grounded in the first two."[15] However, he warns today that the therapeutic age has supplanted confession, preaching is psychologized, and the meaning of the Christian faith has become privatized so that our theology is gutted and reflection is reduced mainly to thought about one's self.[16] Regele rightly warns, "There are few things worse than an inordinate amount of zeal and a dangerously minimal amount of Biblical theology."[17] When Christ states, "Upon this rock I will build my church" (Matt 16:18), he was not referring to a program but a confession of faith grounded in the message of the supremacy of Christ.

13. See Pratt, *How Theology Drives Missions*, para. 9.

14. For further discussion see Daman, *Shepherding the Small Church*; Daman, *Leading the Small Church.*

15. Wells, *No Place for Truth*, 100.

16. Wells, *No Place for Truth*, 101.

17. Regele, *Death of the Church*, 39.

The Contextualization of Our Message

While the message must be the driving force of ministry, how the message is communicated requires contextualization. This is not "demythologizing" the text to conform to the modern morality and the modern concept of God. Instead, it involves communicating the text authoritatively to bring clarity and direction to the confrontation with and formation of our contemporary morality. Contextualization is "the attempt to communicate the message of the person, works, Word, and will of God in a way that is faithful to God's revelation, especially as put forth in the teaching of the Holy Scripture, and that is meaningful to respondents in their respective cultural and existential contexts."[18] Paul recognizes contextualizing the message when he writes that he became all things to all men. Contextualizing the message involves communicating it in a way that is relevant to the people and the challenges they face in their lives, rather than changing the message to make it more acceptable to our culture. It conveys a clear and understandable message. When Christ spoke to the rural people of Galilee, he spoke in parables they could understand. Contextualization is bridging the gap between the ancient world of the Bible and the modern world of today.

First, a contextualized message involves connecting the biblical message to the lives of the people. It is not just bridging the language and cultural gap between the biblical world and the modern world; it is also bridging the spiritual and moral gap. Our task is to connect the Bible to the current moral and spiritual debates dividing the country. The Bible is not meant to be communicated as a dead, sterile, and irrelevant message with no connection to the modern world or the problems of today. Instead, the church must convey the message by bridging the words of Scripture to the world in which we live. Eckhard Schnabel points to Paul's contextualization of the message:

> Since faith in Jesus Christ was, for Paul, not a matter of theoretical or theological insight only, but a set of convictions that could influence the behavior of the converts in everyday life, it . . . included pointers to the consequences of faith in Christ for those who accepted his message.[19]

18. Plummer and Terry, *Paul's Missionary Methods*, 96.

19. Schnabel, *Paul the Missionary*, 189.

We are to connect the gospel to the lives of people. The goal is for the gospel to be relevant in the lives and circumstances of people today. For people to receive the gospel, they need to see the application of the message to their lives and circumstances. Tim Keller refers to this as theological vision: "The middle space between doctrine and practice—the space where we reflect deeply on our theology and our culture to understand how both of them can shape our ministry."[20] In bringing the gospel to rural communities, we must recognize that the gospel is relevant to the people of rural areas.

Second, a contextualized message motivates rural ministry. As Stephen Witmer points out,

> If we believe that the Gospel informs everything, shouldn't we expect it to speak into the many aspects of small-place culture, supporting some and subverting others? Shouldn't we look to the Gospel to be shaped as small-place ministers? This is the best possible source for developing and deepening a God-oriented theological vision for small place ministry.[21]

It is the message of the gospel that leads to the church's mission in rural communities. The message confronts us with the necessity of the church's presence in rural communities, not just because of its responsibility to minister to the community's social needs but also because of the need to proclaim the redemptive hope of Christ to the remotest parts of the world.

Third, a contextualized message embraces and values the local culture as we seek to communicate the gospel in the language, culture, and world that people face. The gospel is not transmitted in a spiritual or cultural vacuum. Instead, the gospel is connected to the challenges people face in their lives and the cultural perspectives they hold.

Pastors often criticize rural churches for their unwillingness to change and their adherence to tradition. However, they fail to recognize that rural communities value stability and tradition, for it not only connects them to the past, but it also gives a sense of stability and meaning in the present. The challenge for missionaries who go to a different country is to avoid ethnocentrism, which views people in other countries as spiritually inferior.

20. Witmer, *Big Gospel in Small Places*, 63.

21. Witmer, *Big Gospel in Small Places*, 69.

We can also fall prey to "culturocentrism," in which rural churches and people are viewed as inferior because they do not embrace the fast-paced, vision-driven, dynamic worship of urban churches. Often, the goal is to force the rural church to mirror the suburban church. Instead, the goal should be to adapt forms and methods to the local community in order to communicate the transcultural message of salvation effectively. Not only is the goal to use the local language as the first step in communicating the gospel, but it must also include adapting worship, leadership styles, programs, and even preaching styles to fit the local context.[22]

In bringing the gospel to the local community, the requirements remain unchanged, and the content of the gospel is not adulterated; however, the gospel is communicated in a way that connects with the lives of the people. A contextualized message directs us to a different matrix, where effectiveness is measured by our ability to communicate the gospel in a manner that is relevant to the spiritual needs of the people we serve and delivered in a way that is sensitive to the local community's culture.

Paul understood the importance of contextualizing his message when he writes that he becomes all things to all men so that he might by all means save some (1 Cor 9:19–23). To the Jews, he couched his message in the language of the law; to the Greeks in Athens, he adapted his message to the philosophers debating at the Areopagus. To effectively communicate the gospel, one must understand the language, struggles, and perspectives of the local community. We need to understand and value the culture of the local community and church, embracing the aspects of the culture that affirm the gospel while also challenging those aspects that undermine it. Before we can confront others with the need to change, we must first understand the individuals we are facing. The first step in communicating the gospel is to value the people for who they are and the culture they embrace.

Fourth, a contextualized message that embraces the language of the people is especially critical, as our culture has largely abandoned the Judeo-Christian ethic. In our present world, people speak an entirely different language. A missionary entering a region where the gospel has never been shared recognizes the cultural gap between the biblical text and the local culture, which necessitates rethinking how to communicate the gospel effectively. The same is true today. In the past, we were taught how to share the gospel in a world where a common knowledge of the

22. Plummer and Terry, *Paul's Missionary Methods*, 198.

Bible existed. This is an assumption we can no longer make. Not only are many people ignorant of the Bible but they also hold many different views that contradict the Bible.

Conclusion

As our culture becomes embroiled in moral and spiritual chaos, we need to return to the certainty of the unchanging message of Scripture. However, we need to recognize that how we communicate the message to a changing world will require new approaches and new forms of communication. We will need to develop new strategies and new methods for engaging our community with the gospel.

8

Building on Purpose

A Mission-Driven Ministry

I (JEFF) WENT TO seminary and started my ministry career in the middle of the church growth movement era. I was thoroughly indoctrinated and completely invested in the ideas of this movement. Like many others of that era, I believed "if the church is not growing, it is dying." I desperately wanted the churches I started to grow! If asked, I would have said church growth meant the expansion of the kingdom and more people coming to Christ. If I were truly honest, I felt the growth of the churches I served was a reflection of me personally and the success or failure of my ministry. (This is very difficult to write!)

When I transitioned from starting churches to overseeing church starts, I began to train others in church-starting and church growth methods. After all, a church start will not survive if it does not grow. So, armed with my "successes," I taught others the keys to growing a new church.

The first thing a new church needed, according to my training, was a mission statement![1] During my week-long training on church planting, I spent hours helping new planters refine their mission statements to be precise and memorable.

Looking back on that training, I can say most of what I taught was actually very good. However, the emphasis on a mission statement may

1. I understand the difference between mission statements and vision statements. For this chapter, I am going to combine my discussion of the two into one phrase: mission statements.

have been overrated. Most mission statements simply were not that memorable. They were made with great care by the church planter. Yet, when the church planter presented the mission statement to the core group, their verbal assent did not necessarily mean they had bought into the statement as the driving passion for the church. Ultimately, few people in the church could repeat the mission statement, and it soon fell to the wayside.

So, was making a mission statement a bust? Not entirely. For many church planters, it helped hone their purpose for planting the church in their setting. However, working so diligently to develop a pithy mission statement might have been a distraction and wasted too much time. (I will come back to the mission statement concept later.)

My struggle with the church growth movement stemmed from how success was measured and how that conflicted with the values of many of the smaller, rural churches I was serving. The very name—church growth movement—instills a vision that every church should grow numerically. This idea may have some legitimacy in a suburb where a church is surrounded by forty thousand people. However, if the church is in an eastern Montana town of 350 people, the possibility of growing year after year is practically impossible. Non-growing churches are labeled by the church growth movement as plateaued or declining churches, both very negative terms. But in a town of 350 people, having 50 in worship year after year may be better categorized as *stable* church; or for a town in central Kansas that went from 2,500 people to 1,800 people over a fifteen-year period and maintained a church of 120 people during that same time, a church like this may be better categorized as stable or even *growing* in a declining community.

When the focus becomes solely on numerical church growth, several issues arise. Since I come from a church-planting background, let me illustrate by sharing a question I ask at the beginning of any church-planting or church growth seminar I am asked to lead. At the very beginning of each training on church planting, I ask the students to provide a biblical passage that commands us to start churches. Likewise, I often ask participants at seminars I lead on rural ministry to provide the biblical basis for growing a church. The answer to both inquiries is that no single text exists in Scripture commanding Christians to start a church or to grow a church.

I contend that both church-starting and church growth are byproducts of effective evangelism and disciple-making. When new Christians are born into the kingdom, they *want* to worship together, learn together, and be discipled as a family. They want to attend church and share their conversion experience with friends and family. Personally, I never cared about hearing sermons until I became a believer. Then, I loved hearing sermons.

The question now arises about what shall be the focus: starting and growing a church, or on evangelism and discipleship, leaving the results to God? One of these is popular today, and one of these is biblical.

The danger of starting with church planting or church growth as the focus is that the mission becomes muddled. Putting these two things first means a planter or a pastor might be willing to compromise to get more people in the seats. Usually, this is not a moral compromise or a blatant biblical compromise. However, I have seen churches take angry, disruptive church members from other churches simply because these believers were faithful to come and were faithful to give. In the long run, many of these angry, disruptive souls were more of a problem than an asset to the church.

When you are a church planter just starting out or a pastor in a small village church, it is difficult not to be excited when a new family begins attending church, even if they are under church discipline from another church. When the focus is on growing the church rather than on growing the kingdom, the mission of the church becomes confused with the goal of growing the church. Thus, the mission of the church becomes compromised.

Starting with evangelism and discipleship means planning becomes more difficult. People tend to respond more positively to outreach events, clever advertising, and well-crafted worship services than when the church focuses solely on discipleship. Planning events and developing clever worship services is easier than spending hours, weeks, and months discipling a new believer into a well-grounded, self-feeding Christian.

Ultimately, it is possible to worship the church, with its history, traditions, and memories, rather than worship the God who does not live in buildings made by man (Acts 7:48). Many good Christian church leaders have spent sleepless nights worrying over the survival of their church and how to grow their church rather than weeping over the harvest field going unharvested. The focus on the church has distracted the church from the mission God gave the church to go and make disciples and teach them to obey all things Jesus has commanded.

A Biblical Understanding of the Mission of the Church

The Task

While many clever and well-designed mission statements abound within the church world, I think the simplest and most concise statement concerning the mission of every New Testament church can be found in Scripture. The Great Commission found in Matt 28:19 puts the task of every Christian and every church in the most succinct terms: "Go therefore and make disciples of all nations." Mark 16:15 restates the primary task of all Christians and every church in similar terms: "Go into all the world and proclaim the gospel to all creation." Acts 1:8 states the same idea in yet another way when it says, "You will be my witnesses in Jerusalem, in all Judea and Samaria, and to the ends of the earth."

Many more biblical texts exist concerning the primary task of believers to share their faith. Most revolve around the three main themes found in the above texts: preaching the gospel to all creation, being witnesses to the ends of the earth, and making disciples who make disciples. The biblical evidence is overwhelming. Christians are called to preach the good news and make disciples of new believers, even to the uttermost parts of the world.[2]

Ultimately, every mission statement developed by a church planter or a church leadership team comes down to one simple task: Go and make disciples of all nations! Obedience to this task becomes the test for every activity of the church. "Does this activity help make disciples?" If not, then the church does not need to waste time on activities that distract from its main task.

If the mission of the church is to make disciples, then the church must quit focusing on survival or growth as the answer to its problems. The church's survival and growth are entirely in God's hands. He promised to protect the church, build the church, and grow the church. Christians are to go and make disciples. The beauty of having a mission focused on making disciples is that it is relatively low-cost, and any believer who has been discipled can, in turn, disciple others.

2. I understand Christians are also encouraged to gather for worship, minister to each other's needs as well as minister to the needs of those in need outside the church, and be a prophetic voice in society. As great as all these ministries are, all of these ministries are part of how the church goes about "making disciples."

The Scope

If the mission of the church is to make disciples, what is the scope of that task? Just how far is a church required to go in making disciples? In Scripture, three texts stand out as commissioning Christians to evangelize. These texts formed the basis for missionary activity for two millennia and drive churches and mission organizations today.

Matthew 28:18–20

Matthew 28 is called the Great Commission for a reason. It outlines in clear terms what the church is to do until Jesus returns, and it defines the scope of this task in unambiguous language. The word "all" occurs four times in Matt 28:18–20. The Greek root for "all" in this text is *pas* (πᾶς), which simply means "all" in over 1,200 uses in the New Testament.[3]

What are the "alls" in the Great Commission? First, Jesus says he has "all authority." This means that when he gives a command, it is not a suggestion and cannot be superseded by circumstances, limited finances, or other ministries. "All authority" in Matt 28:18 means that what Jesus is about to say next is of paramount importance and must be obeyed completely.

The second "all" in this text is the command to make disciples of "all nations" (πάντα τὰ ἔθνη).[4] Jesus does not exempt nations because they are difficult to get to, because they hate Christians, because a villainous dictator leads them, or because it is too expensive to go to that nation. No place on earth is beyond or exempt from the Great Commission!

"All nations" speaks directly to the scope of Jesus' commission for every church in all ages. The church must not be content until the Gospel reaches every nation and every people group. This is why in mission circles, the phrase "unfinished task" is used. While significant progress has been made over the last two hundred years, much work remains to be done to make disciples of all nations.

Jesus states the third "all" as "teaching them to observe *all* that I have commanded you" (Matt 28:20).[5] Not only is the church to go to all nations, but the church must also teach all of Jesus' commands. Often, the temptation is to teach the parts of the Bible that match well with the

3. πᾶς; Strong, *Strong's Greek Dictionary*, 3956.

4. *Panta ta ethne*: *panta* is from the root word "pas" (πᾶς).

5. Emphasis is mine.

culture of a given place. When teaching the whole truth of the gospel results in people walking away from Jesus, the temptation is to compromise to make the gospel more appealing.[6] The truth is, the gospel, by its very nature, is confrontational. It confronts people with their sinfulness, their helplessness, and the need to submit to Jesus as Lord. The most challenging thing for a new believer anywhere is to say, "I'd rather have Jesus than financial success, than family acceptance, and/or my very life."

The fourth "all" in this text is a promise that Jesus makes to be with those going to all nations. He promises to be with them "always, even to the end of the age" (Matt 28:20). This promise means that as the church goes into places where it will face terrible opposition, persecution, and even the possibility of martyrdom, Jesus is walking with the missionaries. Even as they travel down through the valley of the shadow of death, he will never leave or abandon his people as they are on a mission for him.

Acts 1:8

This text lays out specifically where the church is to go by providing very specific locations. "But you will receive power when the Holy Spirit has come upon you, and you will be my witnesses in Jerusalem, *all* Judea and Samaria, and to the end of the earth."[7] Very seldom have I encountered a Christian who quotes this verse correctly. Almost everyone omits the word "all" that modifies Judea, Samaria, and the ends of the earth.

From the standpoint of scope, the church is tasked with being a witness of Jesus in all places outside of Jerusalem. Why is Jerusalem exempt from the modifier "all"? No sufficient answer addresses this exclusion. The remaining locations, "all Judea and Samaria, and to the ends of the earth," are regional, including cities as well as great swaths of rural areas. Looking at these locations in Acts 1:8, it is clear that the further one goes away from Jerusalem, the less Jewish it becomes and the more rural it becomes. The phrase "ends of the earth" comes from the Greek words *eschatos ge* (ἔσχατος γῆ), which literally means "the remotest parts of the earth" or "the least important ends of the earth."

A pertinent question concerning this text is whether Luke intended for these locations to be sequential or simultaneous. Ed Stetzer answered

6. This is the temptation that comes when the focus is on starting a church or growing a church instead of on making disciples.

7. Emphasis is mine.

this question by stating, "Christians have tended to adopt a 'Jerusalem *before* Judea, Samaria, and to the ends of the earth' interpretation of Acts 1:8."[8] He refutes sequentialism for Acts 1:8 when he states,

> The only concentric advancement of the disciples' witness, however, occurs in the first ten chapters of Acts. After the Holy Spirit descended on the household of Cornelius, the movement of the Gospel became simultaneous: both local and international.[9]

Mission Frontiers takes an even stronger stance by stating,

> The strongest argument that this verse was NEVER understood by the early Church as being sequential is the behavior of the early Church itself. If the early Church had taken this verse to mean that they would FIRST reach Jerusalem and then move on, then the Church would likely still be in Jerusalem today. So, how did they know when to send out their first missionary teams? When the Holy Spirit told them to do so. They prayed, He spoke, they obeyed. It would have been ridiculous to argue with the Holy Spirit that Antioch had not yet been reached and therefore they could not move on to another place.[10]

Acts 1:8 makes it clear that the mission of the church is to be witnesses in all places, even to the ends of the earth, simultaneously. No place is exempt, and no place should be waiting for the gospel.

Mark 16:15

The last commission text is found in Mark 16:15, where Jesus says, "Go into all the world and preach the gospel to the whole creation." In this brief text, the mission of the church cannot be more simply stated. Jesus commissions his followers to go into *all* the world and preach to *all* creation. Clearly, no exemption is to be made due to the strategic or un-strategic nature of a specific location. No place is exempted due to financial constraints. And no priority is stated or implied in the command. The gospel is to go to all places, to all people—no exceptions, no excuses.[11]

8. Barnett, *Discovering the Mission of God*, 112.
9. Barnett, *Discovering the Mission of God*, 585.
10. Arlund, "Acts 1:8 Sequentialism," para. 4. Emphasis is from the original text.
11. A random sampling of other Scriptures featuring "all" includes Matt 24:14: "This good news of the kingdom will be proclaimed in *all* the world as a testimony to all nations, and then the end will come"; 2 Pet 3:9: "The Lord does not delay his

The Focus

Going back to the beginning of this chapter where I spoke about the church growth movement, I have been able to see the good, the bad, and the far-reaching implications it has had on the church in North America today. I mentioned earlier my struggle with the church growth movement's fixation on numerical growth. Another issue I have with the church growth movement, particularly when working with rural churches, is its emphasis on the church rather than the kingdom.[12]

Everything about the church growth movement is focused on the church. After all, it is the bride of Christ and the gathering of believers. This truncated focus on the church leads to a couple of fallacious thoughts. The first error is believing that if the church is growing, the kingdom is growing. Sadly, many of the fastest and largest growing churches today are simply transferring believers from one church to another. If the focus is on growing a church, anyone who comes to the church is welcome. Numbers are more important than the mission or the ministry of the church. For the church growth movement, who is joining the church is of little interest as long as people are joining.

Many rural churches are under great stress due to limited finances, limited leadership, and limited hope to resolve either. The natural tendency, and the second fallacy of being church-centered instead of harvest-field-centered, is the desire to protect the church to ensure its legacy for the next generation. A church fighting for survival often does the one thing that will ensure its demise: it turns inward and focuses on the church rather than the harvest field. Thus, the focus shifts to finding people who can help the church rather than finding people who need help from the church.

---

promise, as some understand delay, but is patient with you, not wanting any to perish but *all* to come to repentance"; and Luke 2:10: "But the angel said to them, "Don't be afraid, for look, I proclaim to you good news of great joy that will be for *all* the people." (Emphasis added.)

12. As I proceed, please know I am not opposed to churches growing, nor do I want to diminish Jesus' great love for his bride. I hold both ideas in high esteem! What I want to focus on is developing a biblical understanding of the task of every Christian, and if you have been indoctrinated in church growth ideas, what I am about to say may be difficult to follow. I just ask that you take the time to examine Scriptures to see if what I say is true.

Harvest-Field-Focused

When any ministry, especially a church, loses its focus, problems tend to arise quickly. The solution is to refocus the church on the task at hand. A return to a scriptural focus is needed.

Matthew 9:36–38 provides a recentering for the mission of the church. These few verses provide a clear understanding of the rural church today and the solution to many of its problems. What follows is a brief walk-through of this text to help refocus the rural church on its primary task.

Verse 36 starts with what is the most overlooked part of this text. Jesus *saw* the crowds. Too often, it is easy not to see the people immediately surrounding the church. It is easy to drive by houses and farms but never see the people. The ESV says Jesus saw the crowds as "harassed and helpless, like sheep without a shepherd." The idea is that our neighbors are unlikely to be able to come to our church and start teaching Sunday school next month. They are coming into our church weary and worn out, harassed and helpless, needing help!

Then Jesus gives a promise and a problem. The promise is that the harvest is abundant. If we are willing to seek to serve the harassed and helpless, the weary and worn out, we will have an abundant crop. Weary and worn-out people will flock to a church offering hope.

Jesus states that the problem is a lack of workers. Ministry to the harassed and helpless is hard, messy work. It takes hours, weeks, and months of work to disciple them. Then, after a couple of years of investing in them, they might be able to serve the church in some capacity. The problem is few church members are willing to be that kind of worker, one who invests years of their life into someone who is harassed and helpless, needing help. To regain our focus, we must embrace the long, hard, and messy task of making disciples.

Verse 38 explains that the work of Christians is in the harvest field, not in the church. Jesus made two promises about the church in Matt 16:18. First, he states that he will build the church. We cannot build or grow a church. We can buy programs, implement new ministries, and do the best we can to conjure up visitors. The church is built on Jesus alone, and he does as he pleases with his church. Second, he promises that even the gates of hell itself will not overpower his church. Honestly, if Jesus sees his job as protecting the church, he does not need us meddling in his work.

Every small rural church belongs to Jesus. He established it, and he will protect it. He needs no people inside the church fortress bearing arms against the onslaught of social ills assaulting his church. He can defend every church without anyone's help.

If church members are not to spend their time defending the church and protecting its legacy, what are they supposed to do? Matthew 9:38 states, "Therefore, pray earnestly to the Lord of the harvest to send out laborers into his harvest." Oddly, this text does not say to pray for more workers in the church. How many times have I visited a small rural church struggling to keep its doors open, only to hear the church members say they are earnestly praying for God to send them workers for the church? In verse 38, Jesus admonishes his disciples to pray for more workers in the harvest field. When I ask the struggling church what they are doing to reach their community for Christ, the answer is usually not much of any significance.

The time is long past when harassed and helpless people turn to the church for help. The mission before the church today is to develop ways the church can enter the harvest field and minister to the hurting crowds all around them, who are not even considering attending church to address their problems. The one sole problem with the hurting and harassed all around us is that they need Jesus. To address this issue, the church must first go into the field and begin ministering to them where they are.

Conclusion

Here is where this becomes difficult for many. The focus of the mission is not on the church but on the harvest field. Church members must ensure they are not worshiping the church but the One it is based on. It is easy to make traditions or to make the building holy and become defenders of things God has not called us to defend. Jesus is the protector of the church. We are to be field workers in the harvest.

The goal must transition from growing or protecting the church to working in the harvest field. Christians are to engage their neighbors, friends, and community members in a way that ministers to their harassed and helpless situations. We need to see the crowds of people living around us, have compassion for them, and then serve them in the name of Jesus. People are attracted to this kind of ministry. I have yet to have someone come to me and say, “Last night I was at the local bar having a couple of beers with my friends, and I said, ‘I hear the church down the road has a great preacher, I think I will go hear him tomorrow.’” Nor have I ever heard anyone in a rural setting say that they heard the nearby church has excellent music, a great children’s program, or a great light show, and they plan to go to church next Sunday to experience it for themselves. To refocus on our task is to quit focusing on the church and return to a focus on being in the harvest field.

This means a fundamental shift in the role of the pastor and the role of parishioners. The pastor must transition from being the one hired to do the ministry to becoming the one who equips the saints for the work of ministry (Eph 4:12). The pastor becomes the overseer of those who do the ministry, rather than being the one who does the ministry. Thus, parishioners must realize they are the ones called to work in the harvest field, alongside their pastor. Parishioners cannot be like Moses and say, “Here am I, Lord, send Aaron.” No place in the Bible is there an allowance for church members to hire someone to go in their place. Each Christian must recognize their role in working in the harvest field.

The mission is very clear: Go and make disciples of all nations. The scope is wide. We cannot be satisfied with our work until everyone has an opportunity to hear the gospel presented to them in a clear and contextually relevant way. The focus must be on the harvest field, not on the church itself. God can do great things through a church aligned with these biblical principles!

Part 4

Reshaping Ministry Philosophy for a Post-Christian Era

9

Retooling the Mission in a Post-Christian World

Missionary Mandate or Missiological Myth

A POPULAR CURRENT MISSIOLOGICAL strategy is to focus on reaching cities first, then moving out to rural and remote areas. Tim Keller advocated for this in his e-book *Why God Made Cities,* where he stated, "We believe ministry in the center of global cities is the highest priority for the church in the twenty-first century."[1] For Keller, reaching the cities first was the primary task of mission organizations.

The goal of this chapter is to examine the missiological theory of "urban first" in light of two basic questions.[2] First, does "urban first" have substantial scriptural support? Any solid mission strategy must be rooted in solid biblical exegesis.

Second, since this theory claims to be rooted not only in the New Testament but in the early church as well, does this theory match the realities of the early church up to the time of Constantine? Did the early church missionaries solely focus on urban areas and ignore rural areas,

1. Keller, *Why God Made Cities*, 27.

2. This book is not a direct refutation of Keller's e-book *Why God Made Cities.* He is most often quoted in this book because he sums up the idea of "urban first" succinctly.

as Keller asserts in his statement, "The early Christian missionaries in the Roman Empire did not go to the countryside"?[3]

The rural church today must be able to see its role within the biblical missiological mandate. How the rural church fits within God's strategy for reaching the world will determine its priorities and its value within the kingdom of God. Are rural churches a primary tool for reaching all people with the gospel, or are they simply an outpost on the edge of the Great Commission? The answer to this question has a significant impact on the role of the rural church and the Great Commission.

Scriptural Review

Jesus as the Missionary Model

For modern missiologists looking to develop a biblical foundation of missions, the natural tendency is to turn to the book of Acts and to study the life of Paul, the premier missionary in the New Testament. However, the logical starting point in any study of missions should be Jesus himself. How did Jesus spread the good news of the kingdom of God? When Jesus was on the earth, where did he take the gospel? After all, Jesus is the only model the disciples had. Should he not be the gold standard for everything we do in his name?

A quick review of Jesus' missiological strategy finds him going to what seem to be very un-strategic places to speak to un-strategic people. With only three years to complete the task, Jesus bypasses the masses, focusing instead on small towns, villages, and farming communities. In the Gospels, Jesus spends the preponderance of his ministry in rural areas outside of Jerusalem. A word study of where Jesus served and where he sent his disciples paints a clear picture of Jesus' value for rural people and their overwhelming response to his teaching.

Komē

If "urban first" was Jesus' strategy, it seems odd for him to spend the preponderance of his time preaching, teaching, and healing people in small

3. Keller, *Why God Made Cities*, 27.

remote villages. These small communities seem to be where Jesus was drawn to serve. The Greek word for village is *komē*.[4] The size of a village can best be described as follows:

> In biblical times, villages were small settlements that played a significant role in the social and economic life of ancient Israel and the surrounding regions. Unlike cities, which were often fortified and served as administrative and religious centers, villages were typically unfortified and primarily focused on agriculture and local trade.[5]

Examples of selected texts demonstrating how Jesus ministered in villages include the following:

1. Matt 9:35: Jesus taught in the villages.
2. Mark 8:23: Jesus healed a blind man in a village.
3. Luke 9:6: Jesus sent his disciples into villages.
4. Luke 9:52–56: Jesus stayed in villages—the first one rejected him.
5. Luke 10:38: Martha, Mary, and Lazarus lived in a village.
6. Luke 17:11: Jesus healed ten lepers in a village.
7. Luke 24:13: Emmaus was a village.

On twenty-six separate occasions, Jesus ministered or sent the disciples into villages to minister. His focus on village ministry was greater than on any other place in the four Gospels. Villages were where Jesus spent most of his time, taught most of his lessons, performed most of his miracles, and conducted most of his training with the disciples.

Topos

Topos is a Greek word used to define an area marked off for a place or dwelling.[6] Most often, this word was translated as "place," an area smaller than a village but still a named entity. Often, this word was used for where farmers gathered to spend the night in or near their fields. A *topos* seldom had any businesses. Instead, it was merely a place where farmers banded together to spend the night and protect their crops. Each morning, they

4. κώμη; Arndt and Gingrich, *Greek-English Lexicon*, 461.
5. Bible Hub, "Village," para. 1.
6. Kittel and Friedrich, *Theological Dictionary*, 8, 188.

would leave their *topos*, their "place," to go out to their individual farm plots. Examples of Jesus ministering in "places" include the following:

1. Matt 14:35: Jesus prayed in a place called Gethsemane.
2. Mark 6:7–13: Jesus sent the seventy out to minister in places.
3. Mark 6:33–35: Jesus taught in a desolate place.
4. Luke 4:37: Jesus' reputation went out to every place.
5. Luke 10:1: Jesus sent the disciples to places where he himself was about to go.

Jesus ministered, prayed, and taught in and sent his disciples to "places." In Luke 10:1, Jesus sent the disciples to places where "he himself was about to go." These small remote locations where farmers gathered were not too small for Jesus.

Chora

Another word used to describe where Jesus ministered is *chora*, which means "the rural region surrounding a city or village, the country."[7] A *chora* was the open land between two villages, often translated as "field" or "region." *Choras* were so remote that they did not have names.

Remarkably, Jesus' ministry often included serving in open rural areas too remote to have a name. These places were significant in Jesus' ministry.

1. Matt 8:28: Jesus drove demons from two men in the area of the Gadarenes.
2. Mark 1:5: Jesus was baptized in a rural area of Judea.
3. Mark 6:55: Jesus healed many people in the countryside.
4. John 4:35: Jesus stated that the fields (countryside) were white to harvest.

7. χώρα; Arndt and Gingrich, *Greek-English Lexicon*, 889.

Agros

Another word commonly used of Jesus' ministry was *agros*, which means "land, field, countryside."[8] *Agros* was a Greek term used in connection with farming. It was the Greek word from which we get today's word "agriculture." Jesus went out from the villages and places and ministered in the farm areas. Examples of where Jesus went and where his message was carried include the following:

1. Mark 5:14: Jesus spoke, and all who heard went into the countryside to tell what they had heard.
2. Mark 6:56: Jesus entered villages, cities, and the countryside.
3. Luke 8:34: Jesus' words were reported in the countryside.

"All" in the Great Commission Texts

In Scripture, three texts stand out as commissioning Christians to evangelize the world. These texts have formed the basis for missionary activity for two millennia and drive churches and mission organizations today.

As we pointed out in the last chapter, but again need to emphasize, these three texts have one word in common: the word "all." These texts not only give us the mandate but also set the scope of our mission. Each of these three texts uses the same Greek word "πᾶς," or *pas* in transliterated English. This word is not complicated, nor does it have a secondary or secret meaning. The Greek word *pas* simply means "all" or "every."[9]

The main text serving as the lynchpin for missions is found in Matt 28:18–20:

> And Jesus came and said to them, "All authority in heaven and on earth has been given to me. Go therefore and make disciples of all nations, baptizing them in the name of the Father and of the Son and of the Holy Spirit, teaching them to observe all that I have commanded you. And behold, I am with you always, to the end of the age."

No nation is exempt from this Great Commission. No exemption is made from this command due to opposition, persecution, or financial

8. ἀγρός; Arndt and Gingrich, *Greek-English Lexicon*, 13.
9. πᾶς; Arndt and Gingrich, *Greek-English Lexicon*, 631.

cost. One place must not be prioritized to the exclusion of another place. The mandate of Scripture is to go to all nations!

The second commission text is found in Acts 1:8. It states, "But you will receive power when the Holy Spirit has come on you, and you will be my witnesses in Jerusalem, in *all* Judea and Samaria, and to the ends of the earth."[10] As we pointed out in the last chapter, the focus is not sequential but simultaneous.

The last commission text is found in Mark 16:15, where Jesus says, "Go into *all* the world and preach the gospel to *all* creation."[11] Clearly, no exemption is made due to the strategic or un-strategic nature of a specific location. The gospel is to go to all nations, all places, and to all people.

Keller's statement that reaching "world cities" must be the highest priority encounters an issue when confronted with the scriptural command to go to all nations and preach the gospel to all creation.[12] To prioritize one place over another means to prioritize one set of people over the marginalization of another. This simply does not resonate with Jesus' command to go to all nations. Indeed, Jesus' example was not to prioritize world cities.

Paul's Missionary Methods

Did Paul have an exclusively urban strategy or a primarily urban strategy? The difference between "exclusively" and "primarily" is significant. Recent writing, such as Keller's, seems to support Paul's mission strategy as being exclusively urban.

To be in line with the Scripture already examined, Paul's strategy must be seen as primarily urban. An exclusively urban missiological strategy by Paul would contradict the model given by Jesus and be contrary to Jesus' clear and compelling command to go into *all* the world, even to the remotest parts of the earth. Yet Keller states, "They went into the cities and only the cities to preach the Gospel. Why? Because they knew that the small towns and the countryside are places where people are more conservative. They're not as likely to adopt new religions. They're not as open to new ideas."[13]

10. Emphasis added.
11. Emphasis added.
12. Keller, *Why God*, 27.
13. Keller, *Why God Made Cities*, 29.

What evidence exists to indicate Paul included rural areas in his missionary strategy? In Acts 14:5–7, a plan was developed to stone Paul and Barnabas. Finding out about the plot, they fled "to Lystra and Derbe and to the surrounding countryside. There they continued preaching the gospel."[14] Driven from the city, Paul and Barnabas were undeterred in sharing the gospel, nor did they move on to the next major city. Instead, they fled first to Lystra, a small village, and then to Derbe, which W. M. Ramsay states, "Derbe has left no great mark on history."[15] From these small and seemingly insignificant towns in the Roman Empire, Paul went on to preach to the people in the surrounding countryside.

At the parting of Paul and Barnabas, Paul took Silas and traveled through Syria and Cilicia, strengthening the churches (Acts 15:41). Syria and Cilicia were regions primarily composed of small towns and villages. The implication in Acts was that Paul and Silas traveled throughout the countryside of Syria and Cilicia, where multiple churches already existed.

Examining Paul's missionary journeys raises several questions. What if Paul was not as strategic as the Western world thinks, and he merely targeted certain cities because these cities were where Jews lived?[16] Few Jews lived in rural areas outside of Israel. Thus, going to the cities made sense, not for strategic reasons but for logistical reasons. The greatest concentration of Jews would be in the cities near the synagogues. Additionally, traveling to the Jews in the city would be easier for Paul, as rural areas throughout the Roman Empire often had different languages or dialects. The Jews in a city would speak Hebrew, allowing Paul to share with them without needing to learn a new language or dialect. Thus, Paul's strategic movements may not have been based on the importance of a city within the Roman Empire but on the concentration of Jews and the common language of those to whom he spoke.

The second issue is twofold. First, if Paul's goal was to reach the most strategic cities of the Roman Empire, the cities designated as "world-class cities" with worldwide influence, why did he avoid some of the most globally strategic cities in the Roman world at that time? Paul never attempted to go to the great cities of North Africa, such as Alexandria, Cyrene, and Carthage. These cities would have been vitally strategic places to start churches. Within Europe, Paul avoids Byzantium, which later became

14. Surrounding countryside in Greek is *perichoros* (περίχωρος), which comes from the word *chora*.

15. Ramsay, *Cities of St. Paul*, 385; Balance, *Site of Derbe*, 147.

16. Witmer, *Big Gospel in Small Places*, 169.

Constantinople and is now present-day Istanbul. Additionally, the New Testament does not mention Paul visiting Aquileia, one of the largest and most significant cities of the time.

The second part of the same question is, if Paul's focus was on strategic cities, why did he intentionally go to uninfluential or non-strategic cities? In response to this question, Witmer states,

> Many of the cities where Paul preached were organized as poleis, or Greek city-states, and would have had limited influence beyond their own territories. Moreover, each city fostered its own identity; cities competed with one another and would therefore have resisted influence from other cities.[17]

Paul was indeed strategic in that he was determined to preach the gospel everywhere he went. He did not avoid places because they were small or insignificant or because they were not part of his strategy.

Also, it would be difficult to imagine Paul traveling great distances between provincial cities without preaching or teaching along the way. For Paul to traverse from one city to another, he had to walk through miles of countryside where he stayed in inns or homes, ate local food, and talked with local people. It is inconceivable to think Paul spent days and weeks walking through the countryside and avoided telling them about Jesus.

Ultimately, Paul's "strategy" was to go to provincial cities. Nowhere in his travels or writings, however, does Paul seem to be exclusively focused on provincial cities, on reaching world-class cities, or having a "city first" mentality. As Witmer so aptly states, "Paul never commanded anyone to focus on cities, nor did he explain why he himself was drawn to cities."[18] For Paul, cities were most likely the best and easiest place to find people who spoke his language and understood his culture.

Other Missionary Activity in the New Testament Era

While Paul was the premier missionary in the New Testament, he was not alone in taking the gospel into all the world. After the death of Stephen, the church was dispersed, and the gospel spread into the land of Judea and Samaria.

17. Witmer, *Big Gospel in Small Places*, 170.
18. Witmer, *Big Gospel in Small Places*, 172.

Acts 8:1–24 tells the story of the gospel spreading from Jerusalem to Samaria. As Philip began to preach in a Samaritan city, the church in Jerusalem took notice and sent Peter and John to see what was happening. Impressed with Philip's work among the Samaritans, Peter and John returned to Jerusalem, preaching in Samaritan villages (*komē*) along the way (Acts 8:25). The first endeavor at missions by the Jerusalem church was not to cities but to small villages of Samaritans.

In Acts 8:40, we see Philip preaching in all the towns until he came to Caesarea. Looking at maps of this journey, the only town of any size along Philip's path was Joppa. The other "towns" where he preached do not show up on any map and could be labeled as villages at best. Philip did not have an urban strategy focusing on major cities. It appears Philip employed no strategy other than to go where God sent him, which was a lonely desert road and a string of small, unimportant villages.

The dispersion of the church in Acts 8 and following resulted in the gospel going to regions of Phoenicia, the island of Cyprus, and to Antioch (Acts 11:19). Interestingly, the area of Phoenicia and the island of Cyprus are named, but no city is listed. Evidently, the gospel went to the region, not just to the cities within it.

Peter can be found in Acts 9:32–35 in the villages of Lydda and Sharon, where he healed a bedridden man. Neither of these two towns was an urban center. Peter does not seem to be following an urban model for missions.

Before Paul began his first missionary journey, the gospel had already spread throughout "all Judea, Galilee, and Samaria" (Acts 9:31). As Paul embarked on his second missionary journey, he and Silas traveled through the Syrian and Cilician countryside, strengthening existing churches (Acts 15:41). These two areas were not part of Paul's first missionary journey. If Paul was strengthening churches he did not start, then who planted these churches? No answer is given. Why would Paul and Silas go about strengthening churches in the countryside if the goal was to reach the cities? It is clear from Scripture that before Paul began his mission journeys, previous missionaries had traveled through the countryside proclaiming the gospel and starting churches. Paul saw it as essential to help strengthen these churches.

Historical Evidence

Many people today firmly believe the New Testament missionary endeavor was exclusively urban. Keller states this view in his e-book *Why God Made Cities*,

> Look at the New Testament. Historical research shows that the early Christian missionaries in the Roman Empire did not go to the countryside. They did not go to small towns. Paul was the best example of this. They went into the cities and only the cities to preach the Gospel.[19]

Keller is not alone in his presupposition that the early church was primarily urban. This commonly held belief among missiological circles is known as the "urban thesis of Christian origins" and has been widely accepted for the past sixty years.[20] The premise of this theory can be summed up by the statement, "Early Christianity was almost exclusively urban, spreading to the countryside in the fourth century only after Emperor Constantine's influence was sufficient to convert the conservative countryside."[21]

Closer scrutiny raises some questions about the veracity of this theory. Ample evidence available today shows rural Christianity was alive and well in Asia Minor, Egypt, North Africa, and Syria very early in Christian history.[22] Clement of Rome wrote in the mid-90s that the early apostles preached "throughout the countryside and in the cities," indicating that the gospel was not just confined to urban areas.[23] Furthermore, Witmer states, "In the early second century, the Roman governor Pliny said that Christianity had spread not just to the cities but to the 'villages and country districts.'"[24]

To further demonstrate how widespread Christianity was in the countryside very early in its history, Robin Jensen makes this statement concerning the early church in Italy:

> This examination of the spread of Christianity in Italy before Constantine qualifies the commonly accepted theory that

19. Keller, *Why God Made Cities*, 27.
20. Barth, "Vision for our Cities," 2.
21. Witmer, *Big Gospel in Small Places*, 171.
22. Robinson, *Who Were the First Christians?*, 152–75.
23. Clement, "Letter to the Corinthians," ch. 42.
24. Pliny quoted in Witmer, *Big Gospel in Small Places*, 172.

> Christian growth was initially and primarily an urban phenomenon. Among the Italian episcopates identified, no less than half were from small towns, some quite a distance from the coast. Modern studies on Christianization in northern Italy reveal a similar balance between urban and rural areas.[25]

Likewise, after examining the historical growth of the church, Robinson concludes,

> The weight of the evidence linking the urban and rural environments points to the likelihood of an early Christian presence in the countryside and a noticeable rustic complexion of the urban churches. If a rural and rustic element does not become a prominent factor in our reconstructions of early Christianity, we must revise almost every aspect of the urban portrait of the Christian movement.[26]

The preponderance of evidence for a large number of rural Christians in the Greco-Roman world suggests that Christianity had a greater impact in the rural world than previously thought. And that footprint would mean the early church had an urban *and* rural strategy.

Implications for Missions Today

The seemingly singular modern focus on urban strategies and reaching the cities for Christ has truncated a comprehensive mission strategy. The result of this narrow focus is evident in two missiological myths that must be addressed if the church today is to return to a mission strategy that encompasses *all* people. Each one of these offers some truth but must be measured against the total truth of Scripture.

Myth #1: Winning the Cities is Imperative to Reaching the World

Keller sums this up when he states, "As the city goes, that is how society goes. If you win the countryside and you ignore the cities, you've lost the culture. But if you win the city and you ignore the countryside, you've won the culture."[27] To further explain his case, Keller stated in an address to a

25. Tabbernee, *Early Christianity in Contexts*, 403.
26. Robinson, *Who Were the First Christians?*, 222.
27. Keller, *Why God Made Cities*, 34.

Lausanne conference in South Africa, "If you want human life as it is lived in this world to be shaped at all by Jesus Christ, we have to go to the city."[28]

The problem with Keller's statement is the idea that the church is to "win" the culture. Nowhere in Scripture is the church sent forth to convert the culture. There is a clear mandate to reach all people in all places.

Myth #2: We Must Go to Where the People Are

If the model for missions is driven solely by strategy and if the goal is to reach as many people as possible, then logically, missionaries should be sent to where the people are. The first priority would be to do whatever it takes to reach as many people as possible.

While this approach has merit, the question arises as to whether this approach is biblical. Repeatedly, Jesus is seen leaving the crowds, leaving the towns, and going to the people in rural areas. Philip was taken away from a fruitful ministry in Samaria to go to a remote desert road to witness to one person. Throughout Scripture, we see God calling some to cities and some to rural areas. To align with Scripture, the idea must transition from "going where the people are" to "going where God calls."

Conclusion

The question for mission organizations now becomes, "How can we be part of making sure everyone hears the gospel in a clear and culturally relevant way?" To be true to the biblical mandate, mission organizations cannot adopt a strategy that prioritizes one group over others while waiting to reach the others.

The ultimate goal of this chapter has been to help rethink our missiology and to see that Jesus' commission to the New Testament church was not sequential (city first) but comprehensive. Ultimately, the goal is that *all* may hear.

28. Overstreet, "Why God Loves Cities," para. 3.

10

Reimaging Ministry in a Post-Christian World

THE EVIDENCE IS ABUNDANT that we are moving into a new world concerning ministry. The days of maintaining ministries, promoting denominational programs, and being the center of the rural community are quickly waning for the rural church. Also, attractional ministries have less appeal than in previous generations. Few lost people are attracted to the rural church because of great preaching, great music, or even great children's programs.

This dilemma leads rural pastors to seek help from one of three areas. First, they seek help from their denomination. They attend denominational seminars, hoping that what they learn will translate into success in their rural setting. The problem is that most denominational seminar leaders come from successful, growing churches in the suburbs, and their seminars are not designed to be implemented in rural and remote settings.

Disillusioned, the rural pastor begins to look online for a program to purchase, guaranteeing to grow the church. Finding a program that fits the bill, the pastor convinces the church to spend $2,000 on this "surefire" answer to their problem of slowly declining attendance. However, the program is designed by larger churches and for churches with more resources than a country church possesses. The pastor works hard to sell the new program to his parishioners, only to become discouraged when the program becomes too cumbersome for a small church to administrate. Soon, the new program is stacked in the closet alongside the other failed programs.

Finally, in desperation, the rural pastor resigns himself to the belief that nothing will work at his church, and the best he can do is to care for church members as they slowly age and pass on. As the saints go home to glory one by one, the door to the church slowly creaks shut until one day, there are not enough saints left to keep this little church alive, and it becomes an antique store.

I know the scenario above sounds discouraging. However, it too often reflects the reality many rural churches face today. For the pastor who has not given up yet, the frantic search for the magic bullet or the secret sauce that will keep the doors open often leads to frustration and disillusionment.

Reality Check

Let me provide some cold, hard facts about where we are today. First, lost people in our communities have little interest in going to church today. For most non-church members, when life becomes difficult, and they need answers to questions concerning a troubled marriage, loss of a job, unruly children, or they begin to have deeper questions concerning spiritual issues, the natural tendency is to turn to Google for the answer, or now to AI. If Google or AI cannot provide the answer they want to hear, they turn to their friends, country music, or any source other than the church for help.

Most people who grew up in the world of Christendom were preloaded to turn to the church to answer spiritual questions and for assistance when life became difficult. The next generation(s) no longer sees the church as the source for help or sees Jesus' teachings as relevant to today's issues.

I often tell rural churches that no one sitting at the nearby bar on Saturday night turns to the person on their right and says, "I hear the church down the road has great music, I think I will go and try it out tomorrow." You can substitute "great music" with "great preaching" or great anything going on in the church. The truth is, very little a church does inside its walls makes a lost person want to visit the church. Attractional evangelism is largely ineffective in today's rapidly changing world.

Compounding this problem is the second fact that many lost people today did not grow up in the world of Christendom and have little to no biblical knowledge. What little knowledge they think they may have of the church comes from what they have seen in the media. Thus, much of what they have seen comes from news casts reporting abuse, racism, and sexism. They see a TV preacher riding in a gold-plated Rolls-Royce, living in a multimillion-dollar home, and see all pastors as charlatans and all organized religion wants is their money. Or they see where a pastor was arrested on child porn charges and assume all pastors are pedophiles.

So, if today's unchurched have little knowledge of Christianity, have little interest in going to church, and see canned approaches to evangelism and discipleship as inauthentic, what is a rural church with only a few overworked members and limited resources to do? Considering these rapidly changing times, is there any hope for the small rural church?

Back to the Basics

In 1960, the Philadelphia Eagles beat the Green Bay Packers 17 to 13 in a tightly contested playoff game for the NFL championship. The bitterness of that loss haunted the Packers. On the first day of camp in 1961, Vince Lombardi, the coach of the Packers, started camp with his now-famous "Gentlemen, this is a football" speech. The essence of his speech was that Green Bay must get back to the basics of sound, fundamental football. Each practice focused on the basics, such as proper footwork, proper placement of hands, etc. The players complained they already knew these things. Lombardi reminded them of the difference between knowing the basics and doing the basics.[1]

The result of their return to basics was a 37 to 0 victory over the New York Giants for the NFL championship the following year. Vince Lombardi would go on to win five more NFL championships and *never lose another playoff game!* The key to his success was not implementing some new program or strategy but getting back to the basics of sound football.

For the church to retool so it can minister in today's rapidly changing world, it must start by returning to the biblical foundations of ministry. Biblical foundations for ministry transcend time and culture and are not negotiable. Biblically based ministry has been proven to change lives in every setting, even in the face of overwhelming opposition. If the rural

1. Maraniss, *When Pride Still Mattered*, 305.

church today is to effectively minister in a secular world, it must return to its biblical roots!

Please do not hear me say returning to a biblically principled way of doing ministry guarantees success, i.e., numerical growth. Only God gives the increase. Christians are simply charged with the task of ministering in ways true to biblical principles. Through a biblically healthy ministry strategy, God can then do as he pleases. Remember, the goal of ministry is not to grow a church but to be faithful in our work and leave the results to God.

One other caveat needs to be made at this point. Returning to the basics of Christian ministry does not mean returning to ministry as it was done during the high tide of Christendom. The goal is not to return to 1955. The goal is to return to a biblically solid ministry model.

Jesus' Model for Ministry

When it comes to the missional mandate given by Jesus, almost every evangelical Christian knows the Great Commission found in Matt 28:18–20. Jesus' orders for his church are clear, and the mandate is simple to understand:

> All authority has been given to me in heaven and on earth. Go, therefore, and make disciples of all nations, baptizing them in the name of the Father and of the Son and of the Holy Spirit, teaching them to observe everything I have commanded you. And remember, I am with you always, to the end of the age.

These verses have been the marching orders for missionaries throughout the centuries since Jesus' ascension.

Just as Jesus provided a clear mission mandate, he modeled what the church should do once it arrived at Jerusalem, all Judea, Samaria, and the ends of the earth. For three years, Jesus provided a living example of how to do ministry for the church to follow.[2]

While Jesus' ministry method is clear and easy to understand, it is not easy to follow. In fact, his followers were often bewildered by Jesus' method of ministry. His strategy did not seem to make sense. As soon as he gathered a large crowd, he sent them away as he sought to seclude himself in some remote place. Every church growth consultant today

2. Just a brief reminder, missions is what we are called to do; ministry is how we are going to do the mission.

would have practically shouted at Jesus to "strike while the iron is hot." He needed to take advantage of his growing popularity.

Instead, Jesus did not try to turn the focus on himself. He did not seek to be a political voice in Jerusalem. He did not seek leadership within the Jewish Sanhedrin. In fact, when large crowds gathered around him, when people wanted him to march into Jerusalem and assume the role of a king, he retreated to the wilderness to pray and spend his time with just twelve people.

What was Jesus' ministry model? Craig Etheredge stated the problem of identifying Jesus' ministry model when he said,

> The attractional people point to how Jesus drew large crowds with his relevant teaching. The organic people point to Jesus' small group of twelve. The missional people point to Jesus' healing ministry and compassion for the poor. The social justice people point to Jesus' defense of those who couldn't defend themselves. The radical people point to Jesus' call to sacrifice and self-denial. Everybody claims Jesus as the poster child for their ministry model.[3]

The key to Jesus' ministry model seems to be his focus on making disciples. In the Gospels, Jesus starts his ministry by focusing on a few believers. In Matt 4, after the temptation, Jesus began to preach locally (v. 17) and began to call disciples (vv. 18–25). This same structure to Jesus' ministry is repeated in Mark 1. Jesus' first words in John are a call: "Come and you'll see," a call to follow him.

Oddly enough, Jesus did not filter down; he filtered up. The most popular model in the West today is to filter down. Start with the crowds, find the seekers, disciple new believers, and develop leaders who will then go out. Instead, we find Jesus starting with men who would one day be the leaders of Christianity. When Jesus first started, these men seemed to be the least likely leaders: uneducated, selfish, unable to understand even the basic parables Jesus taught, unable to replicate his miracles, and even denying him when under duress. Yet, Jesus could see in them the "not yet." They were going to be great leaders, but in Matt 4 and John 1, they were "not yet" there in understanding who Jesus was and why he came.

From those initial twelve followers came a band of about 120 or so dedicated followers of Jesus (Acts 1:15). These 120 or so believers were committed followers of Jesus. Included in this group were a host of

3. Etheredge, "Forgotten—Model Jesus," para. 1.

women such as Martha and Mary, Mary Magdalene, Joanna, and Susanna. Men who were part of this group include Matthias, Barsabbas, Joseph, Justus, and Bartholomew. It is evident that this group had an intimate knowledge of Jesus and his teachings. They followed Jesus closely and risked their lives by being together waiting for Pentecost.

Next, Jesus ministered to the large crowds that followed him. These are the crowds where he fed thousands, where he taught in parables, and where he healed many people. These crowds shouted as he entered Jerusalem, "Blessed is he who comes in the name of the Lord." But less than a week later, these same crowds are shouting, "Crucify him, Crucify him." While he taught large crowds, they were not necessarily his disciples. Many people were just following for food and healing, with the hope he might be the Messiah who would free Israel from the Roman chains of oppression; or they followed just to watch the show. This crowd was fickle, as they turned on him the minute things became difficult. In reality, Jesus spent the least amount of time with the crowds and the most amount of time with his twelve disciples.

Also, Jesus did not disciple the thousands that came to hear him preach or the hundreds that came to be healed. Rather than taking advantage of his popularity and leveraging his influence, Jesus focused on his small band of committed followers, dealing with such petty questions as, "Can my sons be on your right and left when you come into your Kingdom?" Or "Just who is my neighbor?" Or "How many times do I have to forgive someone?" Most leadership consultants today would argue that Jesus was wasting his time dealing with such petty issues among a small crowd of people rather than focusing on the crowds that wanted to follow him.

The foundation of Jesus' ministry strategy was not built on his personality, his public preaching, or his ability to do miracles. Rather, the foundation of his ministry strategy was built upon the selection and training of disciples to do the work of ministry. If he had built his ministry on himself and his ability to draw crowds after he ascended into heaven, his entire ministry would have crumbled. Although focusing on disciple-making was slower initially, by AD 313, Emperor Constantine granted Christianity legal status across the Roman Empire. The emphasis on disciples making disciples had a multiplying effect and has impacted the world for Christ, even to this day.

Jesus did not employ a discipleship program, nor did he lead a discipleship seminar. Jesus lived "life on life" with his disciples. He taught them as they walked along the way between towns. They listened to him teach in parables, and later, they asked him to explain the meaning of certain parables. His disciples did not learn about him; they learned *him* from living in his presence. Jesus prepared men to live as disciples and for all but two to die as uncompromised followers of Christ.[4]

Jesus' approach to ministry was not about preaching to great crowds, though he did; nor was it about leading social change, though his teaching would do that. Jesus' approach to ministry was all about two things: developing deep relationships with a few people and helping these people become disciples who made disciples.

Paul's Model for Ministry

Like Jesus, Paul was always surrounded by a group of people he was discipling and who could continue the ministry after Paul left or was thrown out of a town. His ministry team included but was not limited to Barnabas, Silas, Timothy, Luke, Priscilla and Aquila, Titus, John Mark, Epaphroditus, and Onesimus. His group was diverse, including Jews and Greeks, slaves and freemen, men and at least one woman.

Whereas Jesus stayed in one small area of the world, Paul traveled extensively around the Roman world preaching, teaching, training, correcting, and starting churches. Paul had advantages modern missionaries seldom have, such as being able to land in a town and preach immediately in the native tongue, having the protection of Roman citizenship, and he often went to where groups of Christians had already been formed.

Paul's model for discipling can be found in 2 Tim 2:2, where he presented a model he advocated for Timothy to follow. In this model, Paul gives Timothy, in a nutshell, how ministry is to be done. Here, Paul states, "What you have heard from me in the presence of many witnesses, commit to faithful men who will be able to teach others also."

Second Timothy 2:2 starts with Paul teaching, training, and mentoring Timothy in ministry. Timothy accompanied Paul on his second missionary journey. He was also with Paul in Ephesus during his third missionary journey. In these journeys, Timothy had an excellent opportunity to learn from Paul as he traveled around Asia Minor. And so, the disciple-making process moves from Paul to Timothy.

4. Judas died because of his betrayal, and tradition says John died of old age.

Timothy is then exhorted to share what he has learned from Paul with faithful men he is discipling. These men would then pass on to others what they learned to those they are discipling.

It is apparent that Paul adopted Jesus' model of developing relationships with a core group of missionary leaders, developing them into disciples as he lived "life on life" with them. What Paul shares with Timothy is how to multiply disciples in such a way as to see a movement of God. Jesus seems to have been focused on building a solid foundation with his twelve apostles. Paul seems to have been focused on how to now spread the gospel to the "ends of the earth."

With the help of the Holy Spirit, what starts off with a small group of devout disciples in Acts 2 quickly blossoms into a movement that spreads beyond the Roman Empire, and the key to this rapid expansion is the commitment to build relationships and disciple people who will disciple others.

Toward a New Way of Doing Ministry

As I stated at the beginning of this chapter, in our rapidly changing world, programs and attraction-focused ministry are no longer effective at reaching the lost in rural communities. Ministry must morph from trying to get the lost to "buy in" to our existing programs set up to function within the safety of the church walls. As the world becomes increasingly more hostile to Christians, we must quit worrying about how to repair our image and begin to focus on being the image of Christ in our world.

The focus must return to the fundamentals found in the life of Jesus and in the ministry of Paul. Christians must return to a ministry based on developing relationships with the goal of making disciples who make disciples. The truth is, many Christians today are not good at developing relationships with the lost. Several things have contributed to our declining relationship skills. First, we have isolated ourselves to just living among our Christian brothers and sisters. Many Christians don't want to develop relationships with the lost. After all, their worldview is so warped that we do not want to be near them.

Second, Jesus said that the lost are "harassed and helpless like sheep without a shepherd" (Matt 9:36). Many rural churches I work with ask me how to attract people who can come in and help their church. The truth is, Jesus promised an abundant harvest. However, the harvest will stumble into the church as harassed and helpless souls. The problem is that many small rural churches want people who help their church, not people they have to help. The future workers in rural churches today are currently harassed and helpless and in need of a Savior. They need someone willing to invest their lives in helping these people become solid disciples of Christ.

It is important to understand that the harassed and helpless are probably not coming into the church seeking a solution to their situation. The abundant harvest promised in Matt 9:37 remains out in the harvest field. Thus, the ministry of the church must focus not on maintaining the church but on getting workers into the harvest field, building relationships, and making disciples.

This leads to the second part of retooling rural ministry for the future. It must be based on making disciples that make disciples. Part of the church's leadership vacuum today comes from the fact that, for a number of years, the church has focused on making converts rather than on making disciples. Jesus' Great Commission to the church was to make disciples, men and women who can feed themselves (read the Bible, pray, witness, and minister), and then for these disciples to make disciples who can do the same. Just as he spent the last three years of his earthly life making disciples, so, too, are Christians to be about the work of making disciples.

The problem with powerful disciple-making is that you simply cannot buy a program for making disciples. Nor can you go to a seminar and receive training to be a disciple-maker. Ultimately, disciple-making involves living "life on life" with new believers. Remember, they come as harassed and helpless, like sheep without a shepherd. To transform them into godly warriors able to withstand the onslaught of Satan in their lives, they will need someone to walk with them, perhaps for years, helping them learn how to live as a discipled Christian.

Implications

If the task is to make disciples, what are some things the church must embrace to make this happen? First, the church must become harvest-field-focused rather than church-focused. The goal is not to grow the church but to serve in the harvest field. It seems obvious, but the harvest is not going to come from within the church but from out in the "real world." The promise given in Scripture is that if the church focuses on working outside its building in the harvest field, and if the church has compassion on the harassed and helpless, the harvest is abundant. The church will never lack for people if it focuses on the harassed and helpless of its communities.

Second, harvest-field work is not solely the work of the pastor or of just a select few within the church. Instead, harvest-field work is the work of everyone in the church. If a church truly desires to reach the lost in its community today, it must quit seeking programs and activities designed to bring people into the church and begin to work on how to get everyone out into the harvest field. Again, this does not require going to a seminar or purchasing notebooks for everyone. It may be as simple as developing relationships with your neighbor, with the parents of your child's classmates. It may involve going down to the local diner each morning and having a cup of coffee and talking with other locals, looking for an opportunity to pray with someone.

Doing harvest-field ministry is much like discipleship; it may involve a mature Christian teaming up with a newer Christian and showing them how to do ministry with lost people. The key is to get people to add Christ to what they are already doing.

It only takes twenty seconds of courage to share with someone that Jesus cares about them. I often ask church members to practice twenty seconds of insane courage to invite someone to church, ask someone what you can pray for in their life, put your arm around a hurting soul and cry with them. It is these kinds of actions that are harvest-field-oriented. It is these kinds of actions that cannot be "trained." They must be emulated.

With the present financial realities of many small rural churches, the pastor of a small church may be bi-vocational. The mistake many bi-vocational pastors make is to assume their goal is to grow the church to the point where they can become full-time in pastoral ministry. I encourage bi-vocational pastors to remain bi-vocational as long as possible. This provides multiple benefits to the pastor and to the church. First, being bi-vocational allows the pastor to be outside the church and in the harvest field where lost people live. It is easy for a pastor to become engrossed in church activities and to surround himself with church people, so that he never gets to the harvest field. However, he is to be the lead example to the church of how to serve in the harvest field, and being bi-vocational helps provide that example.

Second, by remaining bi-vocational, it helps the pastor's family financially while easing the financial burden on the church. With extra resources for his family, the bi-vocational pastor can stay longer at a church with limited resources. With extra resources, the church has the opportunity to hire another bi-vocational person, do much-needed updates on the building, or pay off debts, all while the pastor serves in the harvest field.

Conclusion

Many churches today are using ministry models from previous generations, and the results are limited. Attractional ministry programs are producing fewer results, requiring rural churches to rethink how they do ministry. Lost people today show little interest in coming to a church to participate in its programs.

Today, the church must move from program-based ministries focused on serving the church to focusing on harvest-field ministry that shows compassion for the harassed and helpless surrounding the church. Lost people, all people, are attracted to genuine love. It has been years since I heard someone say they started coming to a church because of some great program in the church. However, I have met several new church attenders who said they started coming to the church because someone in the church cared for them.

The church has long given mental assent to going out and serving people, but it keeps defaulting back to using programs focused on getting people into church. The problem is that the default of program-based ministry no longer works, and the mandate to return to the fields is stronger than ever before.

The task is simple: we are called to love the people surrounding our church and to meet them where they live! We can't program anyone into the kingdom, we cannot argue anyone into the kingdom, but we can love people into the kingdom, and that is our ministry mandate!

Part 5

Reshaping Strategies for Rural Ministry in a Post-Christian World

11

Creating Flexible, Responsive Ministries

WHEN WE LOOK BACK on life, we often find that the most significant, life-changing events hinge on what we considered to be an insignificant event at the time. While some life-changing decisions involve prayer, counsel, and careful thought, most of the decisions that change the course of our lives receive little thought. They were a response to an opportunity that presented itself.

After attending Bible college, I (Glenn) went to seminary to focus on biblical languages, intending to teach at a Bible college. Not only did I enjoy the research, but it also ran in my family. Both my cousin and uncle taught biblical languages in Bible college. My cousin was the instructor of biblical languages at the Bible college I attended. My uncle (Dr. Edward Goodrick) spent his career teaching Greek at Multnomah School of the Bible and was one of the authors of the NIV Exhaustive Concordance. As I was completing my double master's programs in Greek and Hebrew, I had a conversation with my uncle about the future. An off-handed comment he made would change the course of my life and ministry. In one of our conversations, he suggested that I pastor a church for a few years to gain some practical ministry experience that would help in my teaching. As a result of his recommendation, I accepted the call to a small rural church in eastern Montana.

I had not set out to be a pastor, and I never had any intention of becoming a writer on rural ministry. I was just a farm kid from Idaho who just wanted to teach biblical languages. However, a chance conversation and an offhand decision to serve a church in a small town in Montana would profoundly alter the entire direction of my life and career, leading me down a path I never envisioned.

The same is true of the church's ministry. When we look back over the years of ministry, many of our most significant results came from unplanned and unpredictable ministries we embraced at the time. After serving in the church in Washington for five years, we were given the opportunity to start a new ministry in another church on the brink of closure. We did not envision a multi-site ministry; it was an opportunity that arose out of necessity because a small congregation in a neighboring town was on the verge of closing. Not only did it reinvigorate the struggling congregation, but it was also instrumental in the spiritual growth of our church.

As we move into a volatile world, we face an unpredictable and uncertain future. The way we have done things in the past is no longer valid for the future. While our message and mission remain constant, the methods used to accomplish the mission and communicate the message will require adaptation. We no longer live in a world of incremental change. We live in a world of dramatic change that requires new ways of thinking and behaving.[1]

Moving Beyond a Vision in a Volatile World

For years, the mantra of organizational decision-making has been the importance of a clear and well-defined vision statement. From corporations to churches, we were told that to be effective leaders, we needed a written vision statement that described what the organization would be and accomplish. George Barna's book *The Power of Vision* became a Christian best-seller and sold over sixty thousand copies as church leaders embraced the importance of having a clear vision. Vision "is a clear mental image of a preferable future imparted by God to His chosen servant and is based upon an accurate understanding of God, self, and circumstances."[2]

1. Rendle, *Quietly Courageous*, 8.
2. Barna, *Power of Vision*, 28.

However, as we enter into a world of volatility, we no longer have a clear picture of what it will be. In recent years, the world has undergone a radical shift and continues to change at an unprecedented pace. In this world, rigid visions become a hindrance as they quickly become obsolete and irrelevant.

A vision of the future is based upon the assumption that the future is discernible and foreseeable; therefore, we can plan today what will be tomorrow. However, in today's world, the future is obscure and unknowable. We are drawn to vision statements and long-term planning because they give us a sense of familiarity and certitude. Inherent in our nature is the desire to avoid uncertainty and to embrace the predictable. In 1961, Daniel Ellsberg validated what has become known as the Ellsberg paradox. When given a choice between known probabilities and unknown probabilities, even when the expected outcome is the same, people tend to choose the option with known probabilities. People avoid uncertainty.[3] Uncertainty creates anxiety and makes it difficult to make decisions. Long-range planning is appealing because it gives a feeling of certainty, confidence, and control over our lives and events. As a result, we find ourselves drawn to the past. We embrace the nostalgia of the past because it gives us meaning and predictability in life. As Rendle points out, "When one is asked to lead with quiet courage in a situation in which no one can provide assurance about the right direction, it is far easier to turn back and play it safe in the familiar turf of nostalgia."[4] We strive to replicate the past, for it fits and conforms to our sense of competence and the skills we were taught in seminary. We celebrate nostalgia. Rendle goes on to argue,

> Nostalgia carries the temptation to work harder at what we already know how to do in order to recapture a time and strength that no longer exists. This temptation offers the rewards of feeling certain and secure in our efforts, as well as the satisfaction of getting tired from work familiar to our hands. Nostalgia does not ask how to be different for the future, which is much harder work.[5]

When we are uncertain about outcomes, we tend to avoid decision-making. Research has demonstrated that uncertainty is more paralyzing

3. Eikenberry, *Flexible Leadership*, 14.
4. Rendle, *Quietly Courageous*, 157.
5. Rendle, *Quietly Courageous*, 164.

than fear because we cannot see the end result.[6] However, in a volatile world, what we envision today may be invalid tomorrow. Vision requires the rules of the game to stay the same. But in a changing world, the game is constantly changing, so we need to be adaptable and flexible in our planning. Otherwise, we bring a football to a baseball game.

Embracing Change and Volatility

The first step in developing a ministry in a volatile world is to embrace the reality of change—change that is more than just superficial but is transformative. For the early church to move from the old covenant to the new covenant world, a complete and radical shift in their mindset was required. It was not just a matter of tweaking the old way of life and worship under the old covenant, with its rituals and sacrifices. Life under the old covenant was no longer valid under the new covenant. The change was not incremental but revolutionary, requiring a new way of thinking and acting.

The same is true today. As Rendle points out, "It is increasingly clear that the way ahead will not be mastered by cleverness, with which some leader or leaders will see something that is hidden from others. The way ahead will not be mastered by improvements on what we already know and what we already know how to do."[7] We have moved from a convergent culture to a divergent culture. In a convergent culture, the answers are the same, and there is only one correct answer for everyone. Preparing for ministry involved learning what worked well for others and then replicating it. In a divergent culture, the questions remain the same, but the solutions are multiple and defined by the circumstances and needs of each community.[8] Ministry will become more locally and culturally driven. Instead of being governed by traditions and methods, the church of the future will need to be more fluid and adaptable to the changes occurring in our culture and the local community.

6. Eikenberry, *Flexible Leadership*, 16.

7. Rendle, *Quietly Courageous*, 8.

8. Rendle, *Quietly Courageous*, 34.

Ministry in a Divergent World: Rethinking Ministry

In a divergent world, instead of looking for answers and methods that work elsewhere, we will need to respond to opportunities that arise that we did not anticipate. It requires the church to become more adaptable to the local context and the challenges it faces. As the church moves forward in our changing culture, it will need to embrace leadership that is not governed by plans and programs but by opportunities and flexibility. As pointed out in the previous chapter, to be effective, we need to minister to the needs of people outside the church. This requires adaptability as each individual and community faces unique challenges and needs.

In the past, most pastors were taught to do ministry based on a suburban/Christendom model. To attract new people, the church needed engaging ministries that offered a compelling reason for individuals to attend church. The belief was that people have an intrinsic desire to attend church; therefore, all the church had to do was remove the barriers and give people a reason to come.

Kevin Harney and Bob Bouwer, in their book *The U-Turn Church*, argue that one of the important aspects of a growing church is embracing the "wow" factor. To attract people, the church needs to have facilities, programs, and ministries that communicate that something outstanding has taken place. They compare a church to a restaurant, where people return to experience things they've determined are a "wow."[9]

The wow factor works only if people are looking for a restaurant to dine in. But if people do not want to eat at a restaurant, no amount of "wow" will attract them. The same is true of the church. A church can have the best programs, the most exciting worship, and the nicest facilities, but if people do not desire to come, all the "wow" will make little difference. To impact a world that is indifferent towards the church (and even hostile), we will need to rethink how we conduct our ministry.

Ministry in a Divergent World Requires Clarity

When everything seems to be changing rapidly, we often feel like explorers who are dropped in the wilderness without a compass or map and no clear direction on where to go. We need to make sense of the world. As Eikenberry points out, "Leaders need maps too—a way to give us context

9. Harney and Bouwer, *U-Turn Church*, 167.

and make sense of our situation. Because once we have that, while we may still feel worried, the other emotions may ease enough for us to feel less certain and be able to move forward."[10] We want to answer the question, "How do we make sense of the world so that we can act in it?"[11] The answer lies in our message and mission. The Scriptures provide us with clarity on why the world is changing so rapidly. It is changing because we are accelerating toward God's predetermined end, which he has already revealed.

From the formation of the church in Acts 2, the message and mission have remained the same, and they remain unchanged regardless of the cultural changes happening around us. While it may seem that the church is in a new world with no clarity or map, the reality is that Christ gave us both the compass (the message that guides every action) and the map (the mission that dictates the purpose in everything we do). The *what* and the *why* are both defined; what has changed is the *how*.

In this, we are in the same position as countless generations before us. Throughout history, significant social and spiritual upheavals have profoundly changed the world. The advent of the Dark Ages and the turmoil of the Reformation are two such events. The same is true for us today. We need to adapt our methods in a new world while keeping a firm focus on the two constants that cannot change: our message, grounded in the infallible Scriptures, and our mission, which seeks to call people to become disciples of Christ.

Ministry in a Divergent World Requires Adaptability

When Paul began his second missionary journey, his planned itinerary was to visit the churches he had established on his first missionary journey. However, when they arrived in Asia, they were prevented from continuing by the Holy Spirit, so they could not proclaim the gospel in Asia. The text does not inform us why or how Paul was forbidden from continuing with his plans. The only thing we know for sure is that Paul recognized it as the work of the Holy Spirit rather than external circumstances. Although the door was closed to continue to Troas, Paul received a vision from God to instead proceed to Macedonia. The result was the advancement of the church into Europe.

10. Eikenberry, *Flexible Leadership*, 24.

11. Eikenberry, *Flexible Leadership*, 24.

In a world increasingly hostile toward the church, the tendency is to circle the wagons and protect the church from the world. Engaging the world with the gospel is a risky business. It requires the church to put its financial security at risk and for people to face alienation from their family, neighbors, and coworkers (Matt 10:37). The church must be willing to put everything at risk to advance the gospel. It is one thing to engage culture when it is acceptable. It is quite another to accept rejection by our culture. Often, the church is open to change as long as no threat exists. But changes involve risk.

When Abraham left Ur to travel to an unknown destination, he risked losing everything he owned. When we encounter new opportunities with unknown results, we also face unknown risks. However, as Parrot writes,

> Without risk, there is no faith. And without faith, we would be foolish to take the risks to which God calls us. Although unique in their calling and setting, all of these leaders (in the Bible) shared a willingness to take enormous risks that were anchored in faith. Faith is our willingness to risk everything to trust God.[12]

The rural church often resists risk and fears it, for it pushes into the realm of the unknown and unpredictable, where the outcome is not only uncertain but also unpredictable. The fear is that change will put the church's future at risk, as we cannot always predict the outcome, whether it will be positive or negative. It goes against the fundamental desire for safety and security. However, Christ reminds us that faith and risk go hand in hand. Jesus states that what is true of each person is equally true of the church: "For whoever would save his life will lose it, but whoever loses his life for my sake will find it" (Matt 16:25). To be courageous as a church is to recognize that God calls us to live in the realm of risk, to be willing to sacrifice everything (whether our life or our church) for the advancement of the kingdom. Faith is recognizing that in our act of obedience, God assures us he is with us. The thing that should be feared most is not our culture or our security but being outside the will of God.

A divergent culture creates ambiguity. Parrott warns, "I am convinced that most people would rather live in mediocrity than grapple with a change that pushes them into uncertainty."[13] We desire predictability in the results of our actions, and when we are uncertain about the outcomes,

12. Parrott, *Opportunity Leadership*, 167.

13. Parrott, *Opportunity Leadership*, 54.

we avoid making a decision. We become paralyzed by the uncontrollable and unpredictable. Yet living by faith involves the willingness to react to opportunities when the future is unclear. When God called Abraham to leave the land of Ur, he did not give him a destination. He only told him to leave. Walking by faith means embracing the unknown, trusting that God governs the outcome. When Jeremiah accepted the calling to be a prophet, his vision was to lead the nation in a profound spiritual revival. However, God had other plans. When Jeremiah faced persecution and his message was rejected, he accused God of misguiding and deceiving him (Jer 20:7–10). Living by faith involves recognizing that the outcome may be dramatically different from our expectations, but that is okay, for it is the outcome God has determined. Aaron Renn rightfully warns, "Creating models for the evangelical church in the negative world will thus involve a large number of people exploring various parts of the landscape. It will involve a lot of trial and error. It will involve experimentation. It will involve false starts and the ability to adapt and adjust quickly."[14] In God's economy, it is not the result that is as important as it is the journey itself. It is when we step into the unknown that we learn to walk by faith.

Ministry in a Divergent World Requires Decentralization

A decentralized church seeks to engage with the lives of people outside the church by bringing the church's ministry into the community, rather than expecting the community to come to the church. As we shall see in chapter 13, effective ministry recognizes that we can only reach a community by being present within it. As people become increasingly indifferent to the church and choose not to attend, the church will need to move beyond its physical building. As it is pushed to the sidelines, the church will need to become less regionalized and more localized in each community.

However, this decentralization not only means taking ministry and the gospel outside the walls of the church, but it also means decentralizing the power and authority of the church. Organizational decentralization is the process of dispersing and delegating decision-making authority and administration to those individuals closer to the lower levels of the organization, away from the middle-level authority. In a more decentralized

14. Renn, *Life in the Negative World*, 46.

organization, the leadership delegates much of their decision-making authority to broaden the span of control with less rigid policies.[15] Paul reminds us that the task of church leadership is not to make decisions and govern ministries but to equip and empower the laity for ministry. This involves equipping them with skills and empowering them to make informed decisions. In doing so, the ministry extends beyond the church into the world. A decentralized church is one in which leaders equip and empower people to develop ministries in the community, rather than just within the church.

Ministry in a Divergent World Involves Flexibility

Growing up on the farm, you learn early that farm life requires flexibility and adaptability. At the start of the day, the crew gathers and reviews the tasks for the day. However, the day rarely goes as planned. Machinery breaks down, the weather changes suddenly, cattle knock down the fence, and new priorities emerge. Work on the farm requires constant flexibility. Not only must the farmer be flexible to adapt to changing situations, but he must also respond quickly to the evolving circumstances, challenges, and opportunities. The changing weather and shifting market conditions necessitate adjustments in crop rotation. Without the ability to adapt to the changing world, a farm will soon collapse.

As the church moves forward in a changing world, it must be flexible enough to adapt quickly to the challenges and opportunities that arise, thereby enabling the church to minister effectively in the community. Throughout his ministry, Paul made plans but recognized that ministry is more than just setting agendas and following them. Ministry requires flexibility to respond to the opportunities that arise. However, inflexibility can paralyze the ministry and blind the church to the unplanned and unanticipated possibilities.

In Acts 16, we see three different occasions when Paul responded to the unexpected. In verse 13, rather than going to the synagogue on the Sabbath as was his usual practice, he saw an opportunity where people gathered outside the gate. As a result, Lydia became the first convert in Europe. When going to a place of prayer, they encountered a slave-girl who was possessed. Rather than pass her by, they stopped to bring spiritual healing. When thrown into prison, instead of fleeing when the doors

15. Russell, "Great Commission," para. 3.

were opened, they remained to see what would happen. As a result, the jailer and his family were converted. The first converts in Europe did not come through a planned evangelistic program; they came as a result of Paul responding to the opportunities to share the gospel in the changing circumstances. The transformation of Europe did not begin with a planned evangelistic event at a local synagogue but with a gathering of people near the city gates and within the walls of a prison.

In the past, the church has been driven by plans, structures, and goals. Before a ministry was established, it was carefully researched and evaluated to ensure it aligned with the church's vision, goals, and direction. However, in a volatile world where the circumstances are rapidly changing, the church needs to be flexible and adaptable to the new opportunities that arise. This requires the ability to respond quickly and effectively. Fear leads to organizational paralysis. Flexible ministry is grounded in trust in God's sovereign plans and the ability to respond to the changing world in which we live. As we pointed out in chapter 6, fear can lead to organizational paralysis, where the church is hesitant to embrace change due to the uncertainty of the unknown. Faith, on the other hand, trusts in the sovereign God who is in control of both the present and the future. It is the willingness to embrace risk for the advancement of the kingdom rather than try to maintain the safety of the status quo.

Ministry in a Divergent Culture Requires Opportunistic Leadership

In a post-Christian world, people no longer desire to go to church. So, how do we effectively reach people with the gospel when people no longer see the need for church? The answer lies in becoming more fluid in our leadership and ministry by looking for and responding to opportunities for ministry. We need to move away from trying to control the narrative by establishing strategic planning with its goals and objectives. Goals, objectives, and strategic planning work well when the world is manageable and foreseeable. How do we lead and develop ministries in a world that is unpredictable and divergent? Roger Parrott, in his book *Opportunity Leadership*, gives the solution. The answer is to adopt opportunity-driven leadership and planning, rather than relying solely on strategic planning. He defines opportunity leadership as

> waiting in anticipation for God-given opportunities to develop that mesh seamlessly with our mission, gifting, and

> capacity—propelling us to destinations that are heavenly ordained. As a result, we become leaders who hone traits enabling us to become highly sensitive to the winds of God and create an organizational culture that allows us to respond to new opportunities with urgency, adeptness, and energy.[16]

Opportunity Leadership Involves Faith

It is grounded in the sovereign working of God. However, his work is often unpredictable and obscure. When we step out in faith to embrace an opportunity set before us, we must embrace the unknown and trust in God for the outcome, rather than relying on our wisdom and strength. Opportunity leadership begins with the awareness that the health, well-being, and security of the church are not based upon our ability or risk management but on God's sovereignty. To achieve God's purpose, sometimes we need to descend into the depths. Sometimes, before he can achieve his purpose, he must strip us of all pretenses of self-preservation. Instead of being driven by what is safe and what ensures the security of the church, we need to be driven by how to reach our community with the gospel.

The future of the church will not be based on the financial portfolio of the congregation but on the willingness to move outside the protective walls of the church to minister to people in the community. A safe church becomes an inward-focused church. However, God did not call us to pursue safety; he calls us to be willing to sacrifice everything to pursue the cause of the gospel (Matt 16:25). This not only means the church must place itself upon the altar of death to advance the kingdom, but also, the church must be willing to risk everything for the cause of Christ. Instead of stepping out in faith to embrace an opportunity that God brings, churches become willing to die a slow death. Embracing unplanned opportunities that arise moves from the realm of predictability to the realm of the unknown. However, instead of bringing a quick death, it brings new life.

16. Parrott, *Opportunity Leadership*, 19.

Opportunity Ministry Is Reactive: It Embraces Speed

We can never predict when opportunities will arise. They present themselves, and often, the window of opportunity is short-lived. Therefore, we must build within our ministry the ability to react with speed.[17] In the past, churches have focused on strategic planning and slow, incremental changes to minimize risks and control outcomes. Life was predictable, and programs provided safe outcomes. However, programs are no longer going to attract people. Instead, we must be able to respond quickly to opportunities that arise to minister to and engage the community. Instead of basing decisions on strategic planning or policies, the church needs to recognize and embrace the risk by responding quickly to opportunities to advance our mission. As the old proverb affirms, "Opportunity only knocks once."

Opportunity Leadership Embraces the Unknown

We fear the unpredictable. We resist change because "we have never done it that way before." If we have done it before, then we can predict the result. We desire predictability in the results of our plans and efforts, and when we are uncertain about the outcomes, we tend to avoid making decisions. Yet God calls us to embrace the unknown and the untried. To fulfill our mission, we must be willing to risk all to achieve God's purpose for the church and the world. When Christ called Peter to go to the house of Cornelius, it represented a radical departure from the traditional approach that had been followed for many generations. Jews did not engage with gentiles. Tradition! As Tevye states in the *Fiddler on the Roof*, "Because of our traditions, every one of us knows who he is and what God expects him to do. Without our traditions, our lives would be as shaky as . . . as . . . as a fiddler on the roof."[18] Yet God made it clear that to fulfill the Great Commission, the church was not to be governed by the past but responsive to the opportunities. Parrott rightly points out, "In capturing a new opportunity, the only thing you'll know for sure is how much you don't know. Those who wait to collect all the data and analyze all the angles don't provide leadership; they oversee bureaucracy."[19]

17. Parrott, *Opportunity Leadership*, 141.
18. Jewison, *Fiddler on the Roof*.
19. Parrott, *Opportunity Leadership*, 106.

Looking for New Opportunities in Rural Ministry

To develop an effective ministry in the future, we need to be willing to move beyond the traditional model. Opportunity leadership not only seeks opportunities for ministry outside the church but also explores new models of leadership and ministry within the church. "To move the adaptive leadership needle, you have to be willing and able to see the opportunities where you might have missed them before. Start by recognizing that these opportunities are present everywhere and every day in your life."[20]

We often confuse/equate mission and message with methods. When we equate the mission and message with the methods of ministry, we hinder the church by operating with methods that are no longer relevant. When the church sought to gain a foothold on the new frontier, it required circuit riders who traveled into unreached areas and established churches. New opportunities required new methods. As our culture evolves, we must acknowledge that the changing world necessitates adjustments to the process by which we convey our message and fulfill our mission in the world.

For the last hundred years, we have operated under the model of the church in which every church has a senior pastor who does all the preaching and oversees the programs and ministries. The pastor receives a full-time salary from the church. However, as the shortage of pastors continues to become a more pressing problem, there is a need to rethink the model.

Not only must the church move beyond the current structure, but it needs to move beyond the walls of the church. The church needs to recognize that it is not just the building, and that ministry is not limited to what is done within its walls but also extends beyond the walls of the building and into the fabric of community life. As the church develops a more versatile ministry, it needs to look for opportunities previously overlooked or rejected because they did not fit the former model of the church. This begins by recognizing that opportunities are everywhere and in everyday life. What Heifetz, Gashaw, and Linsky warn regarding businesses is equally valid for the church:

> Over time, the structures, culture, and defaults that make up an organizational system become deeply ingrained, self-reinforcing, and very difficult to reshape. That makes sense when things

20. Heifetz et al., *Practice of Adaptive Leadership*, 43.

> are going well. However, when something important changes, the system's tenacity can prevent it from adapting, from learning to thrive in the new context. Many organizations get trapped by their current ways of doing things, simply because these ways worked in the past.[21]

The church can confuse the mission and message with programs. As pointed out, the mission and message remain unchanged, but the church must adapt its ministry to a changing world by adjusting to the new context; otherwise, it will no longer effectively communicate its message or fulfill its mission in the world.

Conclusion

The pundits are right: "Insanity is doing the same thing over and over again and expecting a different result." As our culture becomes increasingly indifferent, and even hostile, towards Christianity, we can no longer develop ministry on the assumption that if we build it, they will come. While the mission and message remain unchanged, the church will need to develop new strategies, methods, and ministries to remain effective and relevant. This will require a shift from a maintenance mindset to a mission mindset, recognizing the need to seek opportunities to engage culture in the everyday aspects of life with the gospel of Christ. The smallness of the rural church is its most significant asset, for it is not encumbered by organizational structures, policies, and objectives. Therefore, it is well-positioned to do the one thing that will be essential for ministry in the future: adapting rapidly to the new opportunities that exist to connect the gospel to people's lives.

21. Heifetz et al., *Practice of Adaptive Leadership*, 51.

12

Fostering Innovation in Rural Churches

RECENTLY, WE WERE DRIVING through a small rural community, and it told a story repeated throughout the countryside. The population of this community was two hundred, roughly the same as it was in 1990. The average income is $24,500 per year, and 43 percent of the population lives in poverty. This is an improvement from a poverty rate of 65 percent in 2016.[1] The main street was once a bustling center but is now lined with boarded-up windows and decaying buildings. The park in town is well-kept but has few visitors. The remaining houses are old and showing the slow decline of neglect. The town has a small community church struggling to maintain a steady congregation, a consistent offering, and a pastor who is willing to stay. However, if the church closes, the nearest urban center is over an hour away, so the presence of the church is critical. However, with declining attendance and a lack of financial support, the church continues to live on the edge of survival. This is a story that could describe thousands of small churches and communities across North America.

Rural churches are facing not only a crisis in the broader changing culture surrounding them but also an internal crisis that threatens their stability, health, and sustainability. Throughout this book, we have been presenting the argument that the church must take the initiative to

1. Data Commons, "Washtucna."

advance the kingdom of God in rural communities. The harvest is becoming greater and greater as people turn to the false god of secularism for answers to life. Jesus, as he looked over the rural communities dotting the region around Galilee, reminds us that "the harvest is plentiful, but the workers are few" (Matt 9:37). The crisis of leadership in rural churches today is the same crisis of leadership Jesus saw in the rural communities of his day.

How will the gospel be advanced in rural communities when there are fewer churches, fewer pastors, and declining membership? Rural communities and cultures are facing a radical change, confronting the church with new challenges. However, the changes are not just cultural, moral, or external. They are not just changes in the world that surrounds the church. The changes are in the church itself. As we look to the future, at first glance, the future seems dark and foreboding.

The Decline of the Institutional Church

The age of the institutional church has passed. When we use the phrase "institutional church," it is essential to understand what this phrase means. We are not referring to the church Christ established in Scripture, which is both local and universal in scope and function. We are not referring to the church as the body of Christ and a community of believers who strive to advance the kingdom of Christ in the present world.

Instead, the "institutional church" refers to the church that has developed in Western culture. The institutional church is defined by its building, paid staff, professional worship leaders, and highly structured programs. The institutional church sees the pastor as a CEO and the church as a business. People are the consumers, and the success of the church is measured by growth in numbers, programs, and buildings. This growth could be achieved through effective marketing, strategic planning, engaging visions, and programs serving people's felt needs. In the institutional church, people come to be served and be ministered to rather than become involved in the ministry itself. The institutional church is led by dynamic leaders and passive followers.

However, in the New Testament, the church was not merely an organization; it was a living organism supernaturally driven and governed. As a spiritual entity, the church may possess organizational attributes, but these are not what give it life and vitality. Much of what is deemed necessary for the church as an organization—programs, financial stability, plans, and formal structures—is not essential for the church as a spiritual entity.

For the church to continue expanding in a post-Christian culture, it will need to move away from being a business to becoming a missional church. E. Glenn Wagner rightfully warns,

> I believe that the one problem underlying all others is that we have moved both pastors and churches from a community model to a corporation model. In some churches, the pastor serves as the primary preacher, while someone else handles the administrative side of things. In other churches, the pastor is the CEO, the boss, the chairman of the board. But in both cases, the pastor is a corporate officer, not a shepherd.[2]

In the corporate model, the church is viewed as a business, with people serving as its customers. Just as shopping malls have declined in a world of internet convenience, so the corporate church is becoming the dinosaur of Christendom.

As rural communities continue to adopt postmodernism, a greater need exists for the church to engage people with the gospel and expand its presence in rural communities. However, the rural church is in regression. Churches across the country are declining. The corporate church, with its emphasis on programs and multiple staff running dynamic ministries, has not led to a massive revival. Instead, the church has displayed a slow decay. In the past twenty years, a dramatic and rapid decrease in people's attendance at church has occurred. In one generation, membership plummeted from 70 percent to 47 percent.[3] As the country embraced secularism, the church is no longer seen as an essential part of people's lives. Therefore, it is not surprising that 67 percent of churches are experiencing decline, resulting in the median worship service attendance among US congregations declining from 137 in 2000 to 64 in 2020.[4] The American church is facing a pandemic of closures. Researcher and former president of LifeWay Christian Resources Thom Rainer predicts that fifteen thousand churches will close in 2025 alone.[5]

In a corporate model, closures are recommended, just as a franchise closes stores that are not turning a profit. Instead, we should only

2. Wagner, *Escape from Church, Inc.*, 21.
3. Jones, "U.S. Church Membership Falls Below," para. 1.
4. Earls, "Small Churches Continue Growing," para. 4.
5. Rainer, "Five Reasons Why," para. 10.

focus on those churches that are "successful." Bill Easum of The Effective Church Group recommends that those who serve struggling churches should leave. He writes, "From my 50+ years in active ministry, my guess is that 60–70% of pastors in the U.S. are pastoring churches that have no chance of long-term survival. All these pastors are doing is wasting time." He goes on to state, "So Folks, I'm pleading with you. If you are the pastor of a dying church and all you are doing is administering pastoral care, abandon that sinking ship and set sail to participate in authentic ministry that makes disciples."[6] Now, not only are rural churches declining, but pastors are being encouraged to abandon rural ministry. Many of these churches (if not most) will be in rural communities, where the closure of the church will mean that the community will no longer have a church presence. Urban centers are home to a plethora of churches. If one church closes, several other churches reside within a short driving distance. However, in many rural communities, when the church closes, there is often no other church for people to attend.

Along with the decline of the church, a significant shortage of pastors is looming. This trend is expected to continue as the number of people entering the ministry declines. Southwestern Baptist Seminary, once the largest seminary in the world, has experienced a nearly 30 percent decline in enrollment over the last twenty years.[7] Fifty-seven percent of seminaries accredited by the Association of Theological Schools have reported a consistent decline in enrollment since 2000. Not only is the number of pastors decreasing, but they are also aging, suggesting that the shortage of pastors will likely continue to intensify. The pipeline of individuals entering ministry is not keeping up with the current attrition rate of pastors retiring from ministry.

As we move forward into a post-Christian world, the church will need to become more pioneering. The era of the paid professional may be coming to a close. If so, how then do we build the church? The answer does not lie in trying to replicate the past but in embracing new strategies for the future.

As we examine rural ministry today, something is amiss; the current approach to rural ministry is struggling. Instead of churches advancing the gospel in rural communities, we are witnessing the slow decline of the church's presence. Often, the answer to this dilemma is simply to work

6. Easum, "Too Many Pastors Are Wasting," para. 2.

7. Orozco, "Theological Education and the Decline," para. 23.

harder. If the church can increase its recruitment of rural pastors, if it commits to working harder at its programs, if it can attract a younger pastor who can appeal to younger families, if it could raise more money, if . . . if . . . if.

A popular proverb states, "We cannot solve our problems with the same thinking we used when we created them."[8] This is especially true of the church. In our changing world, we revert to what worked in the past. When confronted with new challenges, we often return to the principles and methods that we used to establish the present ministry. However, in a changing world, not only are the previous methods obsolete but so are the assumptions and methods we used to create our present ministries. Our culture is changing at an unprecedented rate. Therefore, we need to cultivate a culture of adaptability and innovation, where we seek new answers and solutions to the challenge of reaching rural America.

The Call to an Innovative Approach to Ministry

One of the greatest hindrances to transforming ministry is "We've never done it that way before." Rural churches value traditions because they connect people to past generations who built the church. Rural churches are relationally driven, and a critical part of their traditions is the connection they provide to the former "heroes and saints" of the church. While these past connections are meaningful because they provide stability and identity, they can also become a hindrance when traditions overrule opportunities to advance the kingdom.

These highly valued traditions started when former generations broke from the status quo and started something new to connect with the world in which they lived. Many of today's traditions began with an innovator who embraced change and a new approach to ministry. In 1780, Robert Raikes saw the need for providing education for poor children, and so he started the first Sunday school that became an integral part of the rural church. *Innovation involves adapting the ministry to remain relevant and influential in a rapidly shifting culture.* Scott Cormode points out, "The problem comes when we feel obligated to stay connected to a past that was constructed for a world that no longer exists. We must

8. While this quote is widely attributed to Albert Einstein, there is no record of Einstein stating these words.

innovate because we can no longer rely on Christendom."[9] How we engage culture with the gospel of Christ requires changes as culture changes.

When we refer to innovation, we are not changing the unchanging message of the gospel or the core identity of the church. Instead, we are referring to the approach to ministry. In many ways, an innovative church is not innovative, but rather, it is returning to the nature of the church as designed in Scripture. It is stripping away the trappings we have added to our culture, altering our perspective of the church and our role as pastors. The essence of the church is organic rather than organizational, and spiritual rather than physical. The church is more than what we do; it is who we are. As Erickson points out, the church is

> the whole body of those who through Christ's death have been savingly reconciled to God and have received new life. It includes all such persons, whether in heaven or on earth. While it is universal in nature, it finds expression in local groups of believers which display the same qualities as does the body of Christ as a whole.[10]

The church encompasses all believers in all ages but can also be found in the gathering together of two people for the purpose of mutual edification. The church, by its very nature, is adaptive, as it strives to manifest Christ within the local context. The church is not the building, the programs, or the structures; it is people mutually encouraging one another to grow in faith and obedience in Christ and to advance his kingdom in the location in which they live.

The Nature of an Innovative Church

Innovation is the process by which the church identifies and understands its culture, equips the entire congregation for ministry, and develops new ways and methods to engage the community with the gospel of Christ, advancing Christ's kingdom within the local community. It recognizes that the gospel, while being universal in its scope, message, and application, must be communicated in a way that connects the gospel with people in a specific time, culture, and community. Innovation learns from the past but is not bound by it; instead, it embraces new ways and methods to engage the local community, advancing the gospel of Christ.

9. Cormode, *Innovative Church*, 29.

10. Erickson, *Christian Theology*, 1034.

Innovation is the process of retooling ministry in a vastly different culture. Cormode points out that presently, "The cultural toolkit available to contemporary Christians is constructed to support the task of a previous era, the era of Christendom."[11] The seeker-sensitive model, with its toolkit of dynamic worship, engaging services, and a dynamic personality, is rooted in a culture grounded in Christendom. But this toolkit is no longer effective. In a post-Christian world, we need to retool the ministry.

Retooling the church begins by viewing rural communities in a new light. It requires us to see rural communities not as Christian communities but as communities in need of the gospel. The Great Commission is to take the gospel to all people. It is not just a matter of having a church within the community; it is engaging the community with the message of the gospel in *a way that is meaningful and relevant to them.* The person who lives in a small rural town three doors down from the church is just as much in need of the gospel as the remotest, isolated tribe in the world or the masses in the urban center. We start by viewing rural communities as a mission field and recognizing the church as a missional institution. As we move forward, we need to change our perspective. The church does not exist solely for the benefit of those who attend; it also exists to benefit the community by sharing the gospel with them.

The Transforming Rural Church

From its inception, the church embraced innovation. The early church did not merely attempt to reform the old structures and methods that had become ingrained in the practice of the Jewish faith. Instead, it shifted radically to new forms and methods. It sought to adapt its method to the culture in which it was reaching. Paul embraced innovation by adapting both his message and method to the cultural context that he encountered. In 1 Cor 9:22–23, he writes, "I have become all things to all people, that by all means I might save some. I do it all for the sake of the gospel, that I may share with them in its blessings." In other words, Paul adapted his ministry to the local context so that, in all things, the gospel might be advanced. Rural communities are in desperate need of the gospel message and for a new approach to reach people in the community with the gospel. But this will require a fresh approach.

11. Cormode, *Innovative Church*, 34.

The Future Rural Church Will Need to Shift from Maintenance to Innovation

The rural church today is focused on maintaining the ministry as a place where people come—ministry based on getting people "in the door of the church." When asked where we go to church, we pointed to the local building, and evangelism is seen as "getting people to come to church." Our goal and objective for the church is to maintain its existing programs and services. To accomplish this, we look for what worked in other churches and implement their methods in our church. However, in the future, the church will need to be more adaptable to the specific location to develop a strategy for the particular community and context. What works in one community will not work in another.

The more the church struggles to exist and maintain its institution, the more it falls into the trap of prioritizing church maintenance over its mission. A maintenance approach to ministry strives to answer the question, "How can we keep our church alive?" However, our task is not to keep the church alive. The health and sustainability of the church is the work of God through us, not the work we do for God. Christ makes it clear that he builds the church, we do not (Matt 16:18). Paul likewise affirms this when he states, "So neither he who plants nor he who waters is anything, but only God who gives the growth" (1 Cor 3:7). When we hold fast to maintaining the church, we lose sight of our primary task, which is to advance the kingdom of God by striving to present the gospel in a culturally relevant way to everyone within our field of ministry. In a maintenance ministry, the goal is to maintain and operate the church's physical structures and organizational systems. In a transforming ministry, the goal is to proclaim the gospel in a way that connects the message to people's lives. As culture changes, so must methods in proclaiming the gospel. Innovation is not change simply for the sake of change, nor is it changing our message to make it more acceptable. Instead, it is adapting the message so that it connects the gospel with people's lives in a meaningful and transformative way.

The Future Rural Church Will Need a New Cultural Toolkit to Be Relevant

The apostle Paul was well-versed in the Jewish culture. He understood the traditionalism, the emphasis on rituals and regulations. In a Jewish culture, with its roots in the Old Testament law, the focus was upon lineage, ritual, and sacrifice. Paul could connect and challenge the Jews because he understood the value they placed on the past. Due to his background, he was well-positioned to confront the culture with the need for change. He could connect their reliance on circumcision, tribalism, and externalism (Phil 3:4–6), and challenge them with the failure of external tradition to bring about transformation. However, when he spoke to the philosophers in Athens, these issues were irrelevant. Their world was one of polytheism and philosophy. A different culture required different methods and a different approach to connect the gospel with their world (Acts 17:22–34). Both needed the salvation offered by the gospel, but connecting the gospel with the culture required a different approach.

In Christendom, the message of moral and political conservatism connected with people because they could identify with the language and outlook it presented. People understood the need for forgiveness and grace because they recognized their sinfulness and the need for salvation. In Christendom, sin is personal, God judges sin, and hell is real. However, in a post-Christian world, people see the world through the lens of social injustice, in which sin is societal. In a post-Christian world, we need a new set of tools to communicate the unchanging message of Christ. By starting with the reality of sin in society, we can then move on to the reality of sin in the personal realm and demonstrate that the redemptive work of Christ provides the answer for both.

This shift in perspective is also reflected in how people perceive the gospel and their own personal lives. The standard approach to applying the gospel today is grounded solely in people's spiritual issues. However, in today's world, many people view themselves as good, God as loving, and sin as injustice against people rather than an act of rebellion against God. They see no need for "salvation." However, the gospel is often presented today as only a spiritual issue and never touches upon the problems of daily life. The way we share the gospel needs to be recalibrated to connect it to everyday life. Only by showing the relevancy of the gospel to the struggles they face in their lives will they be able to connect it to their spiritual struggles with sin.[12]

12. Cormode, *Innovative Church*, 36.

The Rural Church in the Future Will Need to Embrace Intentional Change

As we embrace the need for innovation and change, we must also affirm caution. The call is not a challenge to embrace change for the sake of change but rather involves intentional and thoughtful change. In his book *Calling a Halt to Mindless Change*, John Macdonald warns against change driven by panic. He writes,

> There may well be a need for change, but in an era of uncertainty, management tends to be satisfied with the quick fix. Again, managers are vulnerable to the prowling gurus and consultants. They will demonstrate a need to get rid of the dirty bathwater that obscures vision, but it is all too easy to throw out some hidden babies in the process.[13]

The same could be said of the church. While recognizing the need for change and new approaches to ministry, we must also acknowledge the importance of thoughtful, intentional change. This comes through prayer, careful thought, and the affirmation of Scripture as the guiding point. Change in our structures and methods must be grounded in the foundation of our message and mission. While our changing culture highlights the need for innovation, our message and mission must remain the unwavering foundation that sets the parameters by which change is made. Before embracing innovation, we must define and maintain the clear values of Scripture and the mission Christ has given us. Change must not be haphazard; it must be intentional. The changes must lead to the fulfillment of our mission and align with our message, or we will merely create another "emperor in new clothing."

The Future Rural Church Will Require New Methods

During the COVID-19 pandemic, the church had to adopt new strategies and approaches to respond to the crisis. Literally, in a week's time, the rural church that never dreamed of having an online service was forced to embrace new methods of communicating. FaceTime has become a new tool for broadcasting the service to the community. Rural churches began using low-powered FM frequencies to broadcast their services over a newly formed local radio station. The events of COVID-19 not

13. Macdonald, *Calling a Halt*, 14.

only demonstrated that the rural church could adapt to new ideas and methods, but they also served to illustrate that as our culture becomes increasingly indifferent to the church, the church will need to adopt new ideas to engage people with the gospel. The question is no longer, "How do we get people to come to the church?" The question that confronts the church today is, "How do we get the church to go to the people?" How can the church expand its reach beyond its walls to engage people who may not attend the church?

Glenn Packiam challenges the church with the need to adapt our ministry:

> A successful church needs both stability and innovation. The core of a church—a steady congregation engaged in its spiritual life—provides a foundation for any new venture. Leaders should focus on nurturing this stable core to create a sense of security within the community. This stability, in turn, allows the church to explore an "innovative edge"—initiatives that push boundaries and try new approaches while preserving the essential elements of the faith. This balance ensures that innovation doesn't disrupt but rather enriches the church's mission.[14]

The apostles recognized the need for embracing new ideas if they were to advance the kingdom. In the past, the religious life of God's people centered on the nation of Israel, the temple, and the local synagogue. In many ways, the worship and spiritual life of the community in Jesus' day differed little from those of the preceding generations. However, in the book of Acts, the church was forced to rethink its whole ministry. No longer was the synagogue the center of religious life. The church was a gathering of people in homes (Rom 16:5; 1 Cor 16:19). The message was now proclaimed in the marketplace and places of commerce (Acts 17:17). Paul took the gospel to the places where people met to discuss religion and philosophy (Acts 17:19). Even a jail became a place of worship and evangelism. In many ways, Paul's method was less strategic and more opportunistic. Paul continually adapted his methods and message to the context in which he was. Today, we need to take the gospel to the local coffee shop, to the marketplace, to the community gatherings and events. Instead of looking for "evangelistic programs and methods" that are successful elsewhere and then trying to implement them in our local

14. Barna Group, "What Makes Innovation So Challenging," para. 5.

context, we will need to be creative and develop new methods and strategies that are an outgrowth of our local setting.

The Future Rural Church Will Prioritize Ministry Over Programs

We need to shift the focus from programs to ministry. When our focus is upon programs, our priority is on how we do ministry, rather than what we are to do in ministry and why. This is not to say programs are unimportant and useless. Programs are structures we develop to accomplish the ministry. The danger is not in the program itself; the danger is that the program begins to drive the ministry rather than the ministry driving the program. We become driven by the "how" rather than the "why." When we focus on "how," we focus on maintaining the past, on the structures that we have, and the methods we employ. The result is an inward focus by which we seek to preserve the past. The programs become the mission.

When we shift our focus to "why," the focus shifts outside the church walls and programs, allowing the mission to drive the programs, instead of asking, "How can we use our current programs to reach people?" The question becomes, "What do we need to do to reach people?" This not only involves a change in program focus but also a shift in priority. It involves an honest assessment of what we are doing within the church and why. Are we striving to maintain the organization of the church, or are we seeking to accomplish the mission of the church? We need to let go of the past to focus on the future.

The Future Rural Church Will Need New Strategies for Leadership

As churches struggle to find a pastor, they often start with the wrong question. They approach the problem with the question, "How can we recruit pastors for rural ministry to sustain rural ministry?" Instead, we should be asking, "How can we have a greater impact within rural communities with the leadership God provides?" This is an entirely different question. The first focuses on maintaining what we have; the second focuses on expanding it.

The biggest hindrance to the expansion of rural ministry is the financial burden of providing a full-time salary for the pastor and maintaining the church building. While we are not devaluing the importance of full-time pastors and the significance of the church building, we need to recognize that when these two things become the defining characteristics of the church, it can become a hindrance to the expansion of the church's ministry in rural communities.

When the biggest hurdle for expanding the ministry in rural communities is the financial burden of the building and the salary of the pastor, the question must transition from how to gain the funds for the ministry to how to eliminate the burden or reduce the burden these two issues have upon the ministry. This will necessitate new leadership strategies. However, in some ways, these are not new strategies but established methods used in the early church and are still employed throughout the world today. In the New Testament, many of the early church leaders were not "full-time paid professionals" but "bi-vocational" pastors. Paul, along with Priscilla and Aquila, supported their ministry by being bi-vocational.

Developing an Innovative Ministry

An Innovative Ministry Begins with Reevaluating the Role of the Pastor

The rural church in the future will need pastors who are equippers rather than managers and leaders. In the past, pastors served as professional "managers of the church." They set the direction and developed, oversaw, and ran the ministries. In the institutional church, the clergy were paid to perform the ministry. As a result, the church attracted a passive audience. Except for a few, the majority of people who came to the church came to be served. The adage became the norm in which 20 percent of the people performed 80 percent of the ministry. This approach worked well when the church operated as an organization, with its internal programs as the focus. Due to the common "Christian culture," one church quickly adopted what worked in another church.

As our culture changes, there will need to be a shift in the role of the pastor. With the rise of Church Inc.,[15] the focus of the pastor's role shifted increasingly to that of a leader and manager. If we examine the books on the role of the pastor today, the vast majority focus on the pastor as a leader who sets the direction of the church by establishing and overseeing

15. "Church, Inc." refers to the church as a business, where the focus shifts to numerical growth through marketing strategies and an emphasis upon the organizational structures rather than the organic nature of the church.

the programs of the church. The result is that the church is run by professional leaders who run the programs, while the congregation has become passive consumers who attend church to be served by the church staff.

In the future, the church will need pastors who are equippers rather than leaders. An equipping pastor is one who focuses not on leading the church and running its programs but on equipping the laity to lead and run the church's ministries. Instead of leading one church, the focus may shift to the itinerate pastor who trains and equips the laity to do the work of ministry, including the preaching and teaching ministries of the church.

The age of the professional pastor has created a lethargic congregation. Perhaps the reason the church is facing a shortage of pastors is not because of the failure of the church to send young people to seminary but the work of the Holy Spirit to awaken passive congregations who have become consumers rather than ministers. This focus on equipping rather than leading takes us back to the heart of the New Testament church. Paul writes that the task of the pastor was not to run the programs and develop the ministries but to equip the people for the work of ministry, including the proclamation of biblical truth (Eph 4:11–12). The church has defined discipleship as teaching people to be obedient followers of Jesus but not faithful servants and ministers within the church. Both are necessary for a healthy congregation. A disciple is not only one who obeys Christ but is actively involved in the expansion of Christ's kingdom in the lives of people.

When the church advances into unreached parts of the world, the challenge for the missionary is not finding a pastor for the newly established church but training people within the church to serve as shepherds. The same will be true of rural ministry. Instead of struggling to recruit pastors for rural churches, the church will need to focus on equipping and training individuals already present within the church to lead it.

Every community is unique, with its own distinct cultures, challenges, and religious perspectives. Even within a local community, people have different interests, needs, values, and desires. Connecting with the farmers in the community will be vastly different from connecting with the newcomers who have a completely different worldview. What works in reaching one group of people may be ineffective when reaching a distinct group, even though they live just a few miles apart. To meet this demanding diversity, the church will need to mobilize the whole congregation by equipping them for ministry. However, this will require a change in the church's DNA, which views the ministry as the work of professionals and the congregation as passive recipients of their efforts.

Historically, the church has served as an educational institution. It has been a place for people to come and receive a spiritual education passively. In the future, the church must evolve into a mobile service enterprise that sends its workers into the community to serve those in need. This begins with the pastor transitioning from a discipler (i.e., teaching people how to live godly lives) to an equipper (i.e., one who equips others for ministry). The congregation needs to transition from being a passive audience to active participants in the gospel's mission. This represents a significant shift in focus. It will not be an easy transition. It is easy to change a person's conduct, but it takes time, patience, and intentionality to change people's perception.

An Innovative Church Reevaluates the Mission of the Church

Innovation begins with the question, "Why do we do what we do?" When a church fails to evaluate its underlying assumptions, values, and traditions critically, it merely perpetuates the past. While a church may change its programs and structures, it will remain inward-focused because it still operates with the assumption that if it has the right program, then people will attend the church. The changes made are superficial in that they swap one program for another.

When a program does not achieve the desired results, they shift to another program that worked in another church. However, the problem goes deeper, for it goes to the underlying values and culture that prioritize the ministry to the membership rather than a mission to the world. Because the church has adopted a culture of consumerism, it judges the health of the congregation by "how it ministers to me and meets the needs of my family." This was not entirely ineffective, for in a Christian culture, people were looking for churches that would "meet their needs." However, in a post-Christian world, they turn to their therapist to bring answers for their life, to the government to provide for their needs, and to the local bar and club for their community.

It is not that people are anti-church; it is just that the church is off their radar. A church that focuses on ministering to its internal needs will soon be disconnected from its community. Even as the community increases in population, the church will experience a gradual death. When the focus is on the needs of the church constituents, they happily and gradually die. They blame their demise on the fact that people "just don't want to go to church anymore."

In reality, the problem is not just with the world; the problem is in a church that has lost its missional focus. To develop an innovative ministry, we need to ask three critical questions. The first is strategic, in which we develop new programs, ministries, and services. We ask the question, "*What* do we do?" The second is structural. Structural innovation involves how we do church, including the role of the pastor and the organizational structures of the church. In structural innovation, we are asking the question, "*How* do we do it?" The third level, which is the most comprehensive level, is systemic innovation. Systemic innovation involves examining our underlying beliefs and assumptions so that we reevaluate our strategy. It asks the question, "*Why* are we doing it?" As the rural church struggles today, we often focus on the first two questions. What we fail to recognize is that the changes in our culture require a fundamentally different approach to ministry. We need to start with the question, "Why do we do what we do?" Is it to serve ourselves, or is it to advance the gospel? An innovative church does not just seek new ways to minister to its members; it also looks for new ways to connect with people and advance the gospel in the community.

Conclusion

How do we develop an innovative ministry? How do we move forward into these uncharted waters? The answer lies in the next chapters. Instead of looking for programs that have worked elsewhere, we need to start examining our local community and adapting the ministry to the context of our local area. It begins by developing strategies to engage the community with the gospel that involve ministering to the needs of people within the community, not just the congregation (chapter 13). In chapter 14, we will examine how and why we must change from internal ministry to external missions.

13

Engaging the Community

As our society increasingly becomes secularized, the church becomes increasingly ignored as society continues to move it to the margins. Historically, the church has been recognized as a significant contributor to the community's well-being. As a community slowly dies, the organizational pillars of the church slowly disappear; the community school, the local factory, the local stores, and the local church are usually the last pillars to shutter their doors.

As culture becomes increasingly post-Christian, the church is seen by some as an outsider in the community where it once held significant influence. Community members do not view the church as a negative member of the community but rather as a nonessential one. As a result, the church is increasingly becoming isolated from the broader culture.

Even more tragic is that the church becomes increasingly isolated from the community it once served. As previously noted, fear can foster a fortress mentality, in which individuals withdraw from interacting with the community. Not only is the church becoming less engaged, but in some cases, it is retreating from the community as rural churches close at an alarming rate. It is estimated that four thousand churches shut their doors every year. Many of these churches are located in rural areas, struggling to maintain their presence due to declining attendance, aging buildings, and a lack of leadership.

As rural communities become less "Christian," the presence of churches in these areas diminishes. Instead of striving to establish and sustain churches in every community, isolation of the church occurs when regional congregations are promoted as the solution. Success is measured by the size of the building, the number of staff, and the abundance of programs. The more the church isolates itself from people and communities, the more it detaches from society and loses its influence. The gospel is intrinsically incarnational; it is grounded in the presence of people engaging their neighbors and friends with the gospel.

The Great Commission is not merely a mandate to share the gospel; it is a call to take the gospel to every corner of the world through the witness and lives of people. The task of the church is not to isolate itself and serve as a refuge for people seeking to escape the world. The church is called to deliver the gospel to the world. Ultimately, the church is missional, not organizational.

The goal of the church is not simply to be a place of worship for people to attend but to be a dynamic force used by God to advance the gospel in its community. This will necessitate a shift from being internally oriented to focusing on community ministry. David Horn rightfully warns,

> Perhaps for too long our churches have tended to be oases that have made pronouncements from afar but not actually been engaged in the life of the communities around them. This involvement includes actual interest and participation in the social, political, and educational missions of our cities and towns.[1]

Instead of focusing solely on the church's needs, the church must be more engaged with the community and its issues and struggles.

In the past, rural churches were called "community churches" because they were seen as a critical part of the community. Now the churches are becoming outliers, partly because the community no longer sees the church as essential to public welfare, but also (and tragically so), the church has withdrawn from being involved in the community.

The Rural Church Needs to Be Present as a Visible Outpost of God's Kingdom

To understand the importance of presence, we must grasp the nature of the church and its mission. Molton rightly points out that the church does not have a mission "but the very reverse: that the mission of Christ

1. Horn and McConnell, *Return to the Parish*, xxvi.

creates its own church. Mission does not come from the church; it is from mission and in light of mission that the church is to be understood."[2] The mission is to advance the kingdom of God so that it penetrates every community, in every life of every person. This stresses

> that the church's very existence has been sent into the world. . . . The fundamental point is that missions are not peripheral or additional to the church. The fact that it has been sent is of its essential nature, so much so that the sending is implicitly and explicitly formative in all aspects of its life—its worship, its koinonia, its engagements, its witness, its birthing of new communities, its sociopolitical engagements, its compassion and mercy.[3]

The church is tasked with being the physical manifestation of Christ to the world. The church is not defined by its structures, buildings, programs, or dynamic leadership. The vitality and legitimacy of a church are not determined by its building, the number of attendees, or the number of staff members. The church is a gathering of individuals to mutually support one another in spiritual growth and the advance of Christ's kingdom in the world. The church is to be the "visible, geographically-located outposts for Christ's kingdom and that coming assembly."[4]

A Missional Church is Centrifugal

Too often, the church falls into the trap of Israel. Instead of advancing the kingdom by spreading the gospel to the world, Israel insulated itself. Its mission to be a blessing to the world was reduced to only those who moved to Israel as a proselyte. Instead of being a centrifugal force expanding the gospel into the world, it became centripetal, requiring people to come to the gospel. For the church, the gospel mission is equally focused on the outward movement. It is to spread the good news to the world, engaging all people with it. It requires the church to move beyond one location and penetrate every community to advance the kingdom of Christ within that community. Christ affirms this in his high-priestly prayer. His design for the church is not to become an enclave for people to come and be protected from the world; rather, it is to be a redemptive force that engages the world (John 17:15, 18). He is sending the church into

2. Allison, *Sojourners and Strangers*, 147.
3. Allison, *Sojourners and Strangers*, 147.
4. Leeman, "Church Gathered," para. 2.

the world as he was sent into the world. Christ did not come to gather people to Jerusalem for a grand celebrative worship service. Christ came to dwell among us so that we might see his glory (John 1:14). In the Old Testament, God's presence was revealed through the tabernacle and the temple. It dwelt in a location that required people to come. In Christ, God now revealed his presence among human beings, walking where the Jews walked and living where the Jews lived. He did not remain in the temple; he walked among the people on the shores of Galilee and in the fields and small villages. He did not seek the people to come to him; he went to where the people lived and worked.

A Missional Church Is Dispersed

As Paul went throughout his missionary journey, he did more than preach the gospel; he also sought to establish

> communities of men and women who had come to faith in Jesus the Messiah and Savior, and who came together to study the Scriptures, to be instructed in the whole counsel of God, to learn and remember what Jesus Christ had done, to discover the will of God for their lives, and to celebrate God's salvation in Jesus Christ in prayers and hymns and spiritual songs.[5]

He established these churches not only in urban areas but also in rural areas. As Thomas Robinson points out, the advancement of the church was largely rural rather than urban. The fact that such a large segment of the early church was rural suggests that Paul not only planted churches in the cities he visited but also in the rural communities as he traveled through the countryside.[6]

To become missional, the church needs to disperse by taking the gospel into the world. Instead of focusing on consolidating into regional churches, the church should concentrate on establishing new churches and revitalizing existing ones that are dispersed within local communities.

5. Schnabel, *Paul the Missionary*, 32.

6. See Robinson, *Who Were the First Christians?*

A Missional Church Is Present

The local church is the channel through which the mission of reaching people with the gospel is achieved. Mike Regele rightly argues,

> The primary unit of mission as we move into the twenty-first century must be, indeed will be, the local congregation. No longer will the primary flow move from the local church up the denominational ladder and out to mission elsewhere. Just the opposite must occur, at least initially. Increasingly, denominational leaders are being forced to ask, "What must we do to serve the local congregation?" instead of asking, "What can we do to help the local congregation serve the denomination?" Mission is on our doorstep.[7]

However, this involves the presence of a local congregation. The church cannot reach communities in absentia. For the mission to be accomplished, the local church must be present in the community, allowing it to connect with the community and communicate the gospel in a manner relevant to the people it serves.

A Missional Church Is Visible

Today, the presence of God is revealed through the church as the church moves out into the world. The church is the visible representation of Christ sent to the world. For the gospel to advance, the church must go to the lost to communicate the truth (Rom 10:14–15). This will require a transition from a church-focused mentality, in which the life of the church is lived within the walls of a building, to a harvest-field mentality, in which the life of the church is lived in the midst of everyday life. Like Philip, the church cannot wait for the chariot to come to them; they are to go to the chariot, even if that means taking the gospel to a lone person riding a chariot in the wilderness (Acts 8:25–40). The necessary presence of the church within every rural community is a gospel necessity.

The Rural Church Needs to Be Present Relationally

To be present not only means the church is present physically, but it must also be present relationally. Having a church building in the local

7. Regele, *Death of the Church*, 219.

community is one thing; it is another to have the church fully connected to the people in the community. Christians need to develop relationships with people so they can examine the actions and attitudes of Christians as they live out the gospel in the daily struggles of life and see a different perspective. When they see the reality of the gospel lived out in daily life, they see a hope that they do not have and that they desire (1 Pet 3:15).

We Live in a Relationally Deprived World

Our world has become depersonalized and relationally anemic. Over the past forty years, society has shifted away from forming meaningful relationships within the community and has moved towards greater individualism and relational isolation, resulting in a lack of connection with the people living around us.[8] Dunkelman describes how the idea of "neighborliness" has changed:

> During the mid-2000s, two psychiatrists in the faculty of Harvard Medical School, Jacqueline Olds and Richard Schwartz, noted that the definition of "neighborliness" had evolved dramatically over the course of several decades. In the early post-war period, being neighborly meant reaching out to the people who lived next door—taking homed cake to the family moving into the house across the street, offering to watch the kids in a pinch, saying hello at an annual block party, or inviting acquaintances to join a Wednesday night bowling league. Over the years, however, the terms came to denote almost exactly the opposite. Today, "being neighborly" means leaving those around you in peace.[9]

We live in a culture relationally disconnected. As a result, people long for meaningful connections.

This is also true in the church. Roxburgh points out that in the past, "There was, then, an organic rhythmic connection between church and neighborhood."[10] As time passed, the church lost touch with its community and no longer had a connection with those surrounding the church. The church has become relationally distant from the rest of the community. The church is in the community but not a part of the community.

8. Roxburgh, *Joining God*, 65.

9. Roxburgh, *Joining God*, 66.

10. Roxburgh, *Joining God*, 66.

Moving forward, if the church is to make a missional impact, it will need to be relationally connected with the community. This involves learning to listen to the community, their struggles and challenges, so that the church can minister to them effectively. People are hungry for relational connections with others.

Relationships Are the Doorway to Evangelism

When Christ walked upon this earth, he connected with sinners. He spent time with them, engaging them with the hope of the gospel (Matt 9:10–17; Mark 2:15–22). The megachurch model—where we build it, and they will come—will become increasingly irrelevant in a world that sees the church as an outsider. This will require the church to be present in the community and build relationships that connect with people outside the church, rather than just within it. The strength of a rural church lies in its relationships.

People are not likely to attend a rural church solely because of its programs, excellent music, or dynamic preaching. In the past, the door to the church was through the programs. In the future, it will be through relationships. They are going to come because of a relationship they have with people who attend the church. The most effective tool for evangelism centers upon developing connections with people who do not attend church, so that we might influence them with the gospel.

Building relationships with people is crucial for establishing a foundation for presenting the gospel. Peter reminds us,

> In your hearts honor Christ the Lord as holy, always being prepared to make a defense to anyone who asks you for a reason for the hope that is in you; yet do it with gentleness and respect, having a good conscience, so that, when you are slandered, those who revile your good behavior in Christ may be put to shame. (1 Pet 3:15–16)

Paul likewise commends that we are to "walk in wisdom toward outsiders, making the best use of the time. Let your speech always be gracious, seasoned with salt, so that you may know how you ought to answer each person" (Col 4:5–6). Connecting with people is the basis for giving credibility to our message. Jason McConnell rightly points out,

> Paul knew that wise actions towards outsiders (nonbelievers) were essential for advancing the mission of the church. He

> understood that personal credibility directly impacts how a person receives the gospel message. . . . He wanted them to make the most of every opportunity to be good witnesses by earning credibility and cultivating relationships. It is impossible to gain true credibility apart from a personal relationship.[11]

This credibility is essential in a post-Christian culture when people have a negative view of the church and Christians.

Relationships Require Love and Acceptance

For the church to connect with people, it must also be welcoming to newcomers, both within the community and within the church. The strength of the rural church is the relationships people have with one another. However, this can also become a significant weakness. New people act and think differently, and they can disrupt the relational bonds within the church. As a result, they can be seen as outsiders and a threat to the unity of the church.

For the church to be relationally in the present, it needs to become relationally open. This means it not only welcomes new people into the circle of relationships but also accepts and appreciates the differences among them. As Basham points out,

> We can't preach a message that we believe all need and then be resistant when all kinds of people embrace it. Joining this family doesn't mean political alignment or cultural adherence; it's so much bigger than that. Our collective testimony is loudest when our individual testimonies are varied.[12]

A church that is present relationally in the community welcomes people regardless of their political or cultural ideology or lifestyle. Transformation into the image of Christ and adherence to biblical morality are not prerequisites for salvation but rather the result of salvation. While we do not compromise Scripture, we accept all people, despite their sin, so that the gospel might transform them to reflect the image of Christ. Being present in a post-Christian world involves building connections and relationships with people whose views we may not share or be comfortable with. When Jesus met the woman at the well, he reached across the cultural, ethnic, and religious divide and accepted her, despite her sinful

11. Horn and McConnell, *Return to the Parish*, 165–66.

12. Basham, *Rural Missions*, 78.

lifestyle, to bring her into the unified kingdom of Christ and transform her into the character of Christ.

The Rural Church Must Be Present Missionally

In a politically divided world, one increasingly hostile towards Christianity, it is easy to develop a fortress mentality. The world is unsafe, and therefore, it is a place to avoid. We start to see the world, with its anti-Christian values, as the enemy, and so we go to church to find security and protection from the world. However, as Paul points out, the enemy is not people who are opposed to the church. The enemy is the spiritual forces capturing the minds and hearts of people.

We live in a spiritual world in which Satan and his minions are actively distorting the truth and capturing the minds of people. In response, some seek to fortify the faith of people in the church to withstand the coming onslaught of secularism. This can lead to an "us against them" mentality. Trevin Wax rightly points out,

> But lest we forget, there's also the temptation to turn inward so that we focus only on our relationship with God and with each other, until an inward-focused apathy sets in, and we no longer know the power or promise of our identity as Great Commission believers. The inward turn can be just as problematic for our relationship with God, because unless we see ourselves on mission, we lose a holy desperation for the Spirit's power. Mission drives us back to our knees in repentance and prayer. Mission does not distract us from worship but drives us to it.[13]

He goes on to state,

> To abandon the missional understanding of the church—that God has a church as both expression and instrument of his mission of receiving glory by giving himself for the enjoyment of his people forever—is to diminish the connection between our identity and responsibilities as Christ's followers.[14]

While we need to rightly stand firm against the rising tide of secularism, we should not allow its presence to cause us to withdraw from the world in fear of its influence.

13. Wax, "Beauty and Power," para. 18.

14. Wax, "Beauty and Power," para. 22.

A Missional Church is Gospel-Driven

Those who embrace secularism are not the enemy; they are the prisoners captured by the enemy. The task of the church is to engage people with the gospel, freeing them from the spiritual bondage that ensnares them. To do so, we must move missionally beyond the church walls to engage people with the gospel. We must not be ashamed of the gospel or afraid of the giants. We can easily isolate ourselves from the community. Instead, being grounded in the truth of Scripture, we need to remain focused on our mission to proclaim the gospel and advance the church of Christ, recognizing that "the gates of hell will not prevail against it" (Matt 16:18).

A Missional Church Emphasizes Personal Evangelism

Being missional is not a program but a relational commitment. It is about getting each person to do their part in the evangelistic process. It is recognizing that evangelism is built upon building connections with people so that they see the reality of Christ in us to share that reality with them. When evangelism becomes a program, it depersonalizes our responsibility. It is no longer seen as the task of each individual interacting with neighbors and coworkers.

This is not to say programs are unnecessary; however, they should be carefully evaluated. They are helpful, but they are never a replacement for the importance of personal connections with others. When evangelism is reduced to a program, it is easy to view evangelism as a task for others—mainly the pastor—to develop and implement. However, evangelism does not begin with the pastor, the church, or a program. It starts by each Christian being missionally driven to share the hope of the gospel with their circle of friends and neighbors within the community. "If the local congregation is the primary unit of missions in the twenty-first century, then the individual members of the local congregation are the primary agents of the mission."[15]

A Present Church Is Present Organizationally

Being missional within the community does not happen by accident. It is intentional, and being intentional takes planning and commitment.

15. Regele, *Death of the Church*, 220.

When the ministries of the church are examined, in most cases, the focus is internal. Ministries are geared to serve those who attend the church. However, to become missional, programs must be examined, and ministries must be developed that serve the community and minister to those outside the church.

A Church That Is Organizationally Present Is Gospel-Driven, not Institutionally Driven

Becoming part of the community requires a change in our orientation. Often, the focus is on what is best to build the church. The focus becomes keeping the institution alive: the church building, the paid pastor, and the funding of programs. As a result, the community surrounding the church is abandoned because it cannot support the institution.

The goal of the church is not institutional survival but missional advancement. Instead of focusing on the internal organization and structure of the church, the focus should be on becoming a genuinely community-engaged church that serves the community. Regele rightfully argues,

> We must be willing to take our place as members of a community, being present to serve that community, not to build a big institution. If the mission is next door and across the street, then we need to give ourselves away to the people who live next door and across the street. Our institutional survival must be second—or better yet, irrelevant—to our thinking.[16]

The focus must shift from maintaining the church building's open status to sustaining the mission, and if necessary, being willing to abandon the institution for the sake of the mission. If sacrificing the building and institution to advance the kingdom is required, that is a sacrifice worth making. If the church learned one thing during the COVID-19 shutdown, it is that the church can thrive even without the building and its programs. It thrives when it connects with people.

A Church That Is Organizationally Present Serves the Community

David Horn and Jason McConnell take us back to the early founding of the nation, when there were parish churches and pastors, and the church

16. Regele, *Death of the Church*, 222.

was seen as an integral part of the community, central to the well-being of the whole community. They lament that

> no longer does the church exist center stage in the consciousness of the public square. Some of this may be because of what has been abdicated from within our churches, but more probably, the church has become marginalized from without by the increasing secular cultural life and institutions of our society.[17]

Thus, they challenge the church to a new parish thinking that

> comes with the realization that churches may need to expand their focus beyond the needs of the faithful within the church. . . . It may require rethinking its mission and priorities in very concrete ways. It may even require reallocation of resources away from the church, and in service to the community it now seeks to serve.[18]

This begins by ministering to the needs of people outside the church walls. Becoming present in the community organizationally involves developing ministries that engage the community by caring for people. A missional church understands that it is part of the social capital. As part of the social capital, the church can play a crucial role in supporting individuals who are confronted with a personal crisis or when the community is facing a tragic event. In doing so, the church moves beyond its walls and engages the community.

Through its involvement, the church develops positive connections with people. When Christ interacted with people, he ministered to their physical and emotional needs as a springboard to minister to their spiritual needs. As the church ministers to people's needs, the priority is always the gospel. The failure of the social gospel movement lies in its disconnection from the spiritual need for salvation and transformation. It became the end rather than the means to the end. Ministering to the physical and emotional needs of people must always have a redemptive purpose. That purpose is to develop relationships with people so that they would say, "I don't go to church anywhere, but if I did, I would go to that church where I talked to that pastor when my marriage was falling apart."

17. Horn and McConnell, *Return to the Parish*, xxiv.

18. Horn and McConnell, *Return to the Parish*, xxvi–xxvii.

Conclusion

In a volatile world of shifting morality, the rural church can retreat into the confines and safety of its walls or even withdraw from the community altogether by closing its doors to become part of a regional congregation. The more the church becomes isolated by culture, the greater effort must be made to connect people outside the church. The church can no longer assume that if we build it, they will come. People no longer view the church as an option. Therefore, every member of the congregation needs to see themselves for who they are: ambassadors of Christ called to represent and reveal him to the people they encounter as they live their daily lives.

We need to "de-program" evangelism and again revert to what we are called to do: personal evangelism. We are called to take the church into the world, building the kingdom of Christ by establishing a community of believers in every location and community worldwide. We are to strive to make the church available to every person by being the church in every community. This will require new approaches to ministry. The message and mission remain unchanged. How we share that message and fulfill that mission in a new world will require new methods and approaches. To this end, we must now turn.

14

Embracing a Missional Identity

Throughout this book, we have argued that rural communities and culture are facing a radical change that will confront the church with new challenges. However, the changes are not just cultural, moral, and external. They are not just changes in the world that surrounds the church. The changes are in the church itself. As we look to the future, at first glance, the future seems dark and foreboding, for along with the secularization of our culture, rural churches are struggling to exist. As a result, we focus on survival. But the church is not called to survive; it is called to transform people into disciples of Christ. We are called to advance the kingdom of Christ by being ambassadors for Christ, and we are given the ministry of reconciliation (2 Cor 5:18–20). In other words, we are acting on behalf of Christ to bring the reconciliation work of Christ's death and resurrection to those who are in spiritual need. Concerning this passage, Mark Seifrid writes,

> For the apostle, however, to bear the message of Jesus is to bear the dying and life of Jesus in his body. The Gospel is to be found nowhere but in an earthen vessel (4:7). It is therefore altogether likely that, in speaking of God "placing the word in him," Paul communicates to the Corinthians that he bears the message not only in his mouth but also in his body and life.[1]

This is not only true of Paul, but it is equally true for us today. We are given the responsibility in our lives to communicate in words and actions

1. Seifrid, *Second Letter to the Corinthians*, 259.

the ministry of Christ's reconciliatory work in our words, conduct, and life. It is through the life and message of his followers that Christ communicates the gospel to the world. We are to always be reading, "to make a defense to everyone who asks you to give an account for the hope that is in you" (1 Pet 3:15). This implies more than communication of the words; it implies living in such a way that the gospel is manifested in our actions and life. We are not the ones who "save people." This is the work of Christ applied through the inward conviction of the Holy Spirit. Rather, we are responsible for testifying to this work. From the beginning in Acts, the church has been sent by God to communicate the gospel (Rom 10:13–15). The benchmark of health and vibrancy is not the traditions, programs, or methods of ministry; it is our obedience and faith in Christ manifested in our daily life so that we are a visible testimony of Christ's redemptive work. However, we must recognize that the mission encompasses our total life, for salvation is a process, not an event.

Recognizing the Process of Evangelism

Growing up on the farm, we recognize that the harvest is not an event but a process that includes time, preparation, and work from the time the seed is planted to the harvest. Raising a crop is not just a matter of planting the seed. The seed must receive water to grow. Weeds must be sprayed so that the seed is not choked out, and the plants are fertilized. Last, time is needed for the seed to sprout, grow, and mature before the harvest is ready. It is only when the crop is mature that the harvest arrives. Paul points to this same process on a spiritual level when he writes, "I planted, Apollos watered, but God gave the growth" (1 Cor 3:6). We are the tools God uses to plant and prepare the soil, but he is the one who brings it to fruition. Fulfilling our mission begins with the understanding that the mission is a process, not an event. We often equate evangelism only with the harvest. We see it as an evangelistic event, such as Billy Graham calling people forward to accept Christ. We share the "Four Spiritual Laws" and ask them if they want to say the sinner's prayer for salvation. However, this fails to recognize the process involved in communicating the gospel. Becoming missional involves the whole process of planting the seed and engaging people so that they become more open to the gospel.

Assessing Receptivity to the Gospel

Being a witnessing community involves inviting people to accept Christ as their personal Lord and Savior. While this is the goal, we must recognize the process involved. To be missional, we need to understand the spiritual receptivity of people so that we can connect the gospel in a meaningful way that prepares them for the invitation. In a post-Christian world, where people no longer have a knowledge of the biblical message of Christ's salvation, we start by giving them an understanding of the nature and demands of a holy God, the nature of sin and its consequences, and the validity and necessity of Christ's redemptive work. This begins by assessing their receptivity and understanding of the gospel and finding the connecting point of their world with the gospel message. When interacting with the philosophers on Mars Hill, Paul did not begin with the death and resurrection of Christ; he started by connecting the gospel to their world of polytheism and the uniqueness of the God of the Bible (Acts 17:22–34). Evangelism is not a set program that follows a specific formula. It is the process of communicating the gospel in a way that is meaningful and relevant to the people that we are seeking to reach. This starts with relationships rather than programs.

Evangelism starts with relationships. The old cliche is true that people do not care how much you know until they know how much you care. In rural communities, people are suspicious of strangers. They are reluctant to embrace an outsider. Before they will listen to us, they must first accept and trust us. Trust can only be built through personal connection. Throughout his ministry, Jesus spent time building relationships with sinners. The one accusation that the religious leaders could rightfully bring against Jesus was that he was a friend to sinners (Matt 11:19; Luke 7:34). Jesus did not just preach a message on the hills of Galilee; he also visited people in their homes, socialized with them (Luke 19:1–10), and shared a meal with them. Evangelism is not just a sermon preached in the pulpit; it is a message communicated through our dealings with them. We gain a hearing in the community by becoming engaged in the community. Effective evangelism requires us to be integrated into the community's social capital, gaining their trust so that they will listen to our message.

Second, preparing the soil requires a visible demonstration of the gospel in our lives that provides a context for the gospel's authenticity to be fully revealed to others. Before people hear the gospel, we need to show them the reality of the gospel in our own lives. Peter implies this when he encourages "always being prepared to make a defense to anyone who asks you for a reason for the hope that is in you" (1 Pet 3:15). They see in us the difference the gospel makes in our lives as we face the same struggles and issues they encounter. They see we have confidence and hope amid the trials that are lacking in their life. In our lives, we give context to the message of the gospel by demonstrating the transformational nature of the gospel. This draws them to the gospel as they face the hopelessness of their own lives.

Developing an Evangelism Strategy for a Rural Church

Have you ever heard a statement such as, "Only X percent of Christians ever share their faith?" Usually, it's a relatively small number, such as 5 or 2 percent. Or maybe you have heard this one: "If half of the Christians will just win one person to Christ each year, we can win the whole world in ten years." I'm not saying these statements are inaccurate, but I want to move beyond using guilt to motivate people to witness. The truth is, most Christians already feel guilty about not witnessing more.

True evangelism stems from the overflow of our spiritual life. As for me, I was once sentenced to death, but I've been given life in Jesus. I got to tell somebody!

Methods vs. Strategy

What we're discussing here is the distinction between evangelism *methods* and evangelism *strategy*. Starting with the method is like a doctor prescribing a treatment without conducting a thorough examination. We would like to perform the examination first.

Most evangelism methods come from a suburban setting and are based on the law of large numbers. For example, if I were to go down the street of a big city, witnessing to everyone I met, I could keep going until I finally found somebody willing to listen to me. It doesn't matter if they get mad at me.

But in a rural setting, I must understand the law of interwoven relationships. Let's say I go to a town of one thousand people. I go to the mayor first and say, "Let me tell you about Jesus." If I make him mad, I just made the principal of the school angry, because that's his wife. I also made the chief of police mad, his brother. The mayor's sister-in-law, who runs the one store in town, is now angry at me. Once I make one person mad, I've killed my witness in the whole community.

We need to think carefully about strategy, for it is more than just employing an evangelism method. An evangelism strategy involves two aspects. First, is how to get everyone in the church involved in the evangelism process. This means helping the timid develop relationships that can become opportunities for honest conversations about the gospel. Second, an evangelism strategy includes how to move people along the spectrum from antagonistic to the gospel to responders to the gospel.

A Spiritual Process

People who are lost are somewhere along a spiritual spectrum. On one end are people who are antagonistic toward Jesus. The next place on the spectrum is uninterested. The next place on the spectrum is a person interested in the gospel. Then the moment of conversion! Most evangelism methods focus just on the conversion end of the spectrum. But in rural settings, you must build for conversion. Of course, every conversion is a miracle from God, and sometimes God uses us to gently guide someone along.

One time, my dad's preacher asked, "Who do you know in the community that would be the most unlikely to go to church?" Dad said, "George won't ever go to church." Dad had invited him to church a couple of times, and George's response was emphatic, "I'll never go to church, don't ask me again." Then the preacher said, "Start praying for him." Dad responded, "That's a waste of time and energy. He's antagonistic." But he started praying for George.

The next time Dad saw George, he asked again, "Would you like to go to church?" And George said, "What would I have to wear?" Dad said, "Just come as you are." George showed up the following Sunday. And on the second Sunday, George gave his life to Christ. Three weeks later, he was baptized. By the time George passed away ten years later, he was teaching a class in the church. It's a miracle that anyone comes to Christ!

Now, George jumped from uninterested to interested to conversion in just a matter of three weeks. But as we know, that's the exception, not the rule. Most of us are working with people who are years in the process. And you can't go to them and apply some new evangelism method you've just learned. In rural areas, building relationships is a key part of moving them along that spectrum.

Three Types of Evangelists

There are three types of people in each church. There's the gifted evangelist. There's the timid evangelist. And there's the non-evangelist. The gifted evangelist is easy to spot. They come to every evangelism training event held at the church. They're constantly looking for that surefire method. They'll go to conference after conference. They come back and say, "Hey, preacher, we ought to do this new method of evangelism," and get mad when you are slow to respond.

Timid evangelists will share the gospel with their cousins or close friends when the situation is just right. They will reluctantly attend evangelism training classes but seldom put into practice what they learn.

Non-evangelists have not shared the gospel with another person. Additionally, they will not attend any evangelism training. I have a friend who is a classic example of a non-evangelist. My friend became a Christian at the age of forty-five. He's a quiet man and just a "good old country boy." He'll tell you, "I'm not good with words." My friend will never come to a witness training event. He has to have a relationship with someone and feel safe enough before he'll talk, much less witness to someone.

The non-evangelist or timid evangelist hardly ever turns into a gifted evangelist. It's like trying to change their DNA when you're trying to move them from one end of the spectrum to the other. It's just not going to happen. So, we must think differently to involve them in an evangelism strategy.

I asked my friend one day, "How do you witness?" He said, "Wa termelons!" I said that makes no sense. He went on to elaborate, "When my watermelons get ripe, I fill up my pickup truck with watermelons. I then go through the community and hand them out to everyone. I then invite them to church." His philosophy is to get them to church where an evangelist can talk with them. For my friend, handing out watermelons in the community has become part of his church's evangelism strategy.

Small Steps of Courage

The timid evangelists are probably going to need more than a project like growing watermelons. They need a safe place where they can exercise thirty seconds of insane courage. Here is a suggestion. Ask them to tithe one night a month and invite someone over for dinner who doesn't attend church. For the timid evangelist, this is a stretching exercise. They may need some training before they can do this. They need to understand that the unchurched will come for ice cream or a cookout when they won't come for Sunday school.

The thirty seconds of courage come when it is time to eat. The timid evangelist can say something like, "I go to __________ Church, and I want to invite you to come to our church on Sunday. If you come, I'll meet you at the door and walk in with you. Now I'm going to pray for our food." They pray, and that's all.

Here's a second suggestion for the timid evangelist. Take the five houses on each side of them. Go to each door and say, "Hello, my name is ___________ and I am from ____________ Church. Our Church has started a prayer ministry, and I want to pray for you and your family. Is there anything in your life I can pray for right now?" On rare occasions, people will turn you away. Most of the time, they'll share something. The key to this ministry is to pray with them right there. But pray a short prayer, such as, "Lord, this person's mother is dying. We pray for them in this terrible situation that you give them peace. Let them know that you love them in a very real way. Amen."

Start with a few houses and pray for them. Then go back in a month and say, "I've been praying for your mother. How'd that go? Oh, she passed away? I'm so sorry. Let me pray for you and your family." The neighbor might be thinking about how serious death is. Now they know a church has been praying for them and loves them. The goal is to get them to think, "I don't go to church anywhere. But if I were to go to a church, I would go to the church that is praying for me."

Creating a Culture of Evangelism

As soon as someone becomes a Christian, I teach them to share their faith, even before I teach them to pray. I want them to go back to their friends and say, "I once was blind, but now I see." Remember the Bible story of the lame guy? He said, "I don't know how it happened, but it was this man named Jesus" (John 9). After they're comfortable sharing their testimony, teach them to include a Bible verse, such as John 3:16. Other methods can be introduced later, but provide people with something real and simple.

We should also constantly celebrate evangelism from the pulpit. One day, I asked my non-evangelist friend to talk about his watermelons. I didn't say, "Tell us about your evangelism method," because he would never share from that invitation. Instead, I said, "Friend, take just a minute and tell us about your watermelons." He said, "I grow watermelons, y'all." I asked, "What do you do with those watermelons?" "I give them to people and invite those people to church." Then I said to the congregation, "You can do this, too."

Prepare each person to minister at their level and challenge them without using guilt. This is how Jesus did it. Jesus offered the invitation, "Come and see." His strategy was look, listen, and learn. He didn't teach his disciples a method. He taught a strategy that matched each specific person, even though the message was still the same.

In a rural setting, focus less on methods. Focus on relationships and encourage people to take one step forward at a time. When people work within their specific giftedness for evangelism, they can be very effective for Christ.

15

Reaching an Ethnically Diverse Rural Community

I (Jeff) grew up in a rural county in southern, middle Tennessee in the 1960s and 70s. When I was a child, the demographics of my county were simple. Twenty-nine thousand people were white, 2,200 were black, and 76 people were "other." Where I lived, land was revered. People did not sell their farms, and new people did not move in. The county was fairly isolated, and farms were passed down from one generation to the next.

When I was a child, Franklin County had no "Mexican" restaurants. I cannot recall any Mexicans living in my county. (I was in college the first time I went to a Mexican restaurant. My wife and I were dating when we had fajitas for the first time.) Racial issues in my county were black and white.

In recent years, significant changes have occurred. Franklin County now has twelve Hispanic restaurants (not counting Taco Bell). To put this in perspective, Franklin County has more Hispanic restaurants than Dollar General stores (ten). Several of these "Mexican" restaurants offer authentic Latino foods from countries other than just Mexico, such as pupusas and arepas.

Franklin County has experienced a significant influx of Hispanic immigrants, driven by the area's expansive nursery industry and a growing demand for lawn care services. Nursery work is difficult, involving hours of digging and lifting heavy plants. Additionally, it is low-paying and menial work. The great majority of Hispanics in my home county have come to work these kinds of jobs.

In 1970, the Tennessee Valley Authority built a dam on the Elk River in our county and formed Tims Ford Lake. This picturesque lake transformed the entire landscape of my home county, offering affordable and beautiful locations for building houses. This paved the way for large and expensive subdivisions to be built, offering lakefront property at affordable prices. These home sites appealed to two groups of people. First, it appealed to people in surrounding urban areas, such as Nashville and Huntsville, Alabama, who were looking for an affordable place to have a vacation home. Franklin County is about an hour from Huntsville and an hour and a half from Nashville, making it the ideal distance for a getaway lake house.

Second, Franklin County has become a desirable destination for retirees from the upper Midwest, including those from cities such as Chicago, Detroit, and Cleveland. Not only does Franklin County offer affordable lakeside lots, but the state of Tennessee also has no state income tax, making it a particularly desirable place to live. Additionally, Franklin County has become a desirable destination for people from the upper Midwest, as the return trip to visit families still in the region now takes only one day, compared to two days or more from Florida. The final appeal is that Franklin County has four seasons, with winter being relatively mild.

Thus, a number of people who initially planned to retire in Florida moved to Tennessee to enjoy the amenities that Franklin County had to offer. The old-timers refer to these people as "half-backs."[1] They initially moved to Florida and then relocated halfway back to enjoy the amenities that Franklin County, Tennessee, has to offer.

While Franklin County remains overwhelmingly white, its demographics have undergone significant changes. With twelve Hispanic restaurants, two Chinese restaurants, and three nail salons, the nonwhite population has grown dramatically. Added to these numbers are the multiple convenience stores throughout the county run by families primarily from South Asia.

1. I use the term "old-timers" to refer to the families that have been in Franklin County for generations. This is not the same as "old money." For example, my family has been in Franklin County since the early 1800s, and we own some land. That does not mean we have money. Growing up, we were called "dirt poor." We owned some dirt, but we were financially poor.

The influx of predominantly white people moving in from other states and foreign-born immigrants has had a profound impact on the county. These new residents of Franklin County have influenced local politics, the tax base, and almost every aspect of the county where I grew up. Since I graduated from high school in 1979, the population of my county has grown by over 40 percent.

I recently met with some pastors from my county, and I told them I have good news and bad news. The good news is that people are moving to Franklin County, and the potential for a church to grow is significant. The bad news is, these new people are not like us. To reach them, one of two things will have to happen. Your church will need to adapt its ministry approach, or you may need to establish new churches designed specifically to reach these new demographic groups.

Nationwide

The influx of immigrants and people from urban areas to rural counties is not just specific to my home county. Rural America is experiencing growth in many regions throughout North America. Much of that growth is from an influx of Hispanics moving into rural America. In many areas of the Great Plains,

> Hispanics are arriving in numbers large enough to offset or even exceed the decline in the white population in many places. In the process, these new residents are reopening shuttered storefronts with Mexican groceries, filling the schools with children whose first language is Spanish and, for now at least, extending the lives of communities that seemed to be staggering toward the grave.[2]

Once confined to the difficult jobs found in meat-packing plants, chicken processing factories, farms, feedlots, and other menial jobs, Hispanics are pushing into smaller towns and buying cheap property. Between 2000 and 2010, the rural Hispanic population in the Great Plains grew by 54 percent.[3] While every county in the western half of Kansas except one saw a significant decline in the white population, the vast majority experienced double-digit growth in the Hispanic population.[4]

2. Caballero, "Latinos Reviving Small Towns," para. 6.
3. Caballero, "Latinos Reviving Small Towns," para. 11.
4. Caballero, "Latinos Reviving Small Towns," para. 13.

While the number of Hispanics moving into remote, rural, and small-town areas may not compare with the number of Hispanics moving into urban areas, even numerically modest increases can represent a significant increase in population growth and in the percentage of Hispanics to the overall population.[5]

While Hispanics make up the vast majority of immigrants moving to rural areas, they are not the only ones. Asians are also moving to rural areas in smaller numbers than Hispanics, but in significant numbers. Asians typically do not migrate to rural areas to work in agricultural-related industries. Instead, they tend to come to rural areas to run small businesses such as Chinese restaurants, convenience stores, nail salons, and local hotels.

Another recent trend in the US is the increasing number of young people, aged twenty-four to forty-four, who are relocating to rural areas. From 2020 to 2023, approximately 63 percent of counties classified as rural or small metro experienced an increase in the population of this age group, and the top ten counties with the most significant growth in this age group were all rural.[6] This trend is nationwide, including the South, with states like South Carolina, North Carolina, and Tennessee leading the way. Areas around Flint, Michigan, are also seeing an increase, as well as along the eastern front of the Rockies from Montana to New Mexico.

While the decline of population is still a problem for some parts of rural America, most rural areas of the country are experiencing growth due to immigrants moving in and young people able to work from home, seeking cheaper places to live. Rural areas, once isolated from the world, are now having the world literally come to them.

Why Is Being Multiethnic Important?

Almost every evangelical Christian is aware of the Great Commission's command that Christians go and make disciples of all nations. It is another thing entirely to invite them into our church to worship with us and to be a part of the leadership of our church. Most Christians enthusiastically support going "over there" to share the gospel with people who have never heard. But when we start talking about having "them" become part of "us," the conversation stalls.

5. Jensen, "New Immigrants Settlements," 7.
6. Sheidlower and Kaplan, "Forget LA and BK," para. 1.

A famous missions text is Rev 7:9, where people from every nation, tribe, people, and language are worshiping together around the throne. The emphasis is often on the gathering of people from different nations. But what is equally important from this text is that people from different nations are worshiping side by side. They are not segregated by language, race, or country. People from every tribe and nation will be worshiping *together*!

Multiethnic churches are living examples of how Christians will be worshiping in heaven. Their example of multiethnic worship is why they are important today. Every church should strive to become multiethnic.[7]

Keys to Developing a Multiethnic Rural Church

If the world is coming to rural America, what is the rural church's response to this influx of new people? For some, the safest thing to do is ignore them, hoping that they will one day move away.

A more effective strategy is to develop new churches to reach specific people groups. For workers immigrating to the US and holding jobs where English is not required, starting language churches may be the most effective way to share the gospel with them in their own language and culture.

Embrace the Difference Between Groups

Another alternative is to seek ways to incorporate new people from the community into the life and ministry of the local rural church. However, to do so will require the "C" word: *change*. Honestly, being a multiethnic church does not happen without being intensely intentional. Left to ourselves, we tend to gravitate toward worshiping with people who are similar to us in terms of religious beliefs, history, and educational and economic backgrounds. To stretch ourselves to include others from different nationalities and worldviews requires an intentional love that brings them into the fellowship.

Christians tend to equate uniformity with unity. Often, the goal in a church is for everyone to think alike, vote alike, and act alike. Any

7. Many books have been written on multiethnic churches including the biblical basis. With limited space, I wanted to provide one quick foundation for having multiethnic churches.

variation from the unwritten norm is met with looks of disapproval, if not subtle hostility. One of the significant challenges in a rural church is to accommodate differences in ideas while maintaining unity.

Uniformity has often impeded witnessing. Christians can isolate themselves to the point that they do not have any significant relationship with someone who is not a Christian. A church can also isolate itself not only from the lost but also from other Christians, to the point that fellowship with them is frowned upon when they do not meet our requirements for uniformity.

To overcome the stranglehold of uniformity, the local rural church must be willing to embrace people from diverse backgrounds. First steps to breaking through the wall of uniformity might be as small as allowing someone to sing in Spanish or pray in Chinese. While allowing someone to participate in worship using their native language is not the end goal, it might be a visible beginning on a journey to embrace different cultures.

I once pastored a church of around two hundred people from all around the world. It was common to have ten languages spoken on any given Sunday. One of our most popular events was a Thanksgiving potluck where people brought things from "home." We had jambalaya alongside bulgogi, a Virginia ham, and Italian fettuccine. The idea was to celebrate each person's culture and heritage. Again, another small step toward embracing others.

My dad provided another example of embracing people from a different culture. A few years ago, one of the old farms in my county went up for sale. That was news enough. However, the new owners were Hispanic, which made news throughout the county. One day, my dad stopped by to introduce himself. The new farm owners were having a big dinner in the backyard and asked my dad to join. He said he had no idea what he was eating. But at the end of the meal, he invited everyone to church. They were surprised by his invitation and appreciated his stopping by and joining in with their dinner. My dad was doing his best to embrace people from another culture.

The key to embracing other cultures is to ensure that the dominant culture is not perceived as the "correct" or "ideal" culture. For a church with a long-held culture, it is difficult to give up some of its culture and traditions to embrace aspects from other cultures into the life of the church. It is easy to incorporate someone praying or singing in another language, but that is not fully embracing people from another culture. It is much more challenging to incorporate a newcomer with a distinctive accent, whether from Mexico or New York, into the church's leadership structure. The danger is that they may want to change things. And the truth is, things may need to change. Remember, the goal is not to maintain the status quo but also not to compromise the gospel. Traditions must not become gods in an evangelical church to the point that they keep the church from reaching the changing culture around it.

Involve Everyone

It is much easier to embrace people from different cultures into the worship service than it is to involve them in ministry. It is possible for a church to act like toddlers and participate in parallel play when it comes to people from different cultures. The normal flow of things can be disrupted in a church when people from different cultures come together and seek to be equal participants in the church's ministry. Traditions provide powerful barriers to involving everyone in a church.

To involve everyone means the church must be willing to ruthlessly evaluate everything it does to see if its actions are merely maintaining traditions or are designed to help the church reach the entire community for Christ. Traditions that exclude others due to their ethnic heritage or due to their being new to the community must be changed in order to allow the church not only to embrace others from different backgrounds but to actively involve them as well in the ministry of the church.

A fine balance exists between tokenism and genuine involvement of everyone. No one likes being treated like a token. The goal for a church is to make sure that whatever position a person takes in the church, it is because brothers and sisters in the church believe this person is the God-called person for the job, and the person feels called by God to do that job. The rural church must wholeheartedly believe, "There is neither Jew nor Greek, there is neither slave nor free, there is no male and female, for you are all one in Christ Jesus" (Gal 3:28).

Ultimately, involving others from different backgrounds means that the existing leadership must learn how to relinquish some control. To do so, existing leadership must recognize that the church is not their church but God's church. No one is the guardian of God's church. It is God's church, and he will protect it and provide for it. The church will remain open as long as he wants it to stay open, and it will close on the day he wants it to close.

Often, the desire to protect the church stems from a fundamental inability to trust God with his own church. It may be that God is using "outsiders" to make some much-needed changes in his church. Not allowing people with varying backgrounds into leadership positions in the church may be a way of going against God.

To begin to trust others with the future of the church does not mean handing everything over and walking away. What it does mean is the historical matriarch or patriarch must transition from the role of protector of the church to become one of multiple voices, where each voice is a valued part of the church's decision-making process.

Involving everyone will require an intentional act of inclusion. It is easy for a rural church to repeatedly ask the same people to perform the same tasks. More than one pastor has shared with me that their church has terminal elders or deacons. These deacons or elders, once appointed, serve until they die. There is no rotation of leadership. This creates a problem where potential leaders are excluded from leadership and influence in the life of the church.

Don't Tolerate Racism

Most Christians today understand that racism is wrong. No person is allowed to think any other person is "less" in some way. We are reminded once again of Gal 3:28, where no distinctions by race, nationality, or ethnic group are to be tolerated.

Addressing racism in the church comes with many political rabbit holes. While trying to avoid these distractions, political, social, educational, and economical, racism still exists in a more subtle format today. The way I usually hear it is when someone talks to me about "those people" in a way to differentiate between two groups of people.

The key to understanding racism is to understand what it means to be prejudiced. The term comes from two words: "pre," which means "before," and "judge." So, the term means to prejudge a person or a group of people. The truth is, all people prejudge to some extent. It is a shortcut for trying to understand someone or a group of people.

To eradicate racism, a rural church must be diligent in taking the time to listen and learn about the various cultures within its community. Listening means to listen honestly without judgment. The goal is to hear and understand their stories of how God has led them to this place in their lives. Additionally, it entails listening for opportunities to help outsiders become insiders within the church.

For missionaries on the field and for pastors moving from one culture to another culture to serve, one of the most challenging things to do is move from "they" to "we." "The people I serve, *they* do this strange thing" to, "In my church, *we* do this strange thing." It moves the missionary, the pastor, from being an outside observer to identifying as part of the group. Moving from "they" to "we" also helps to eliminate racism. For I cannot be prejudiced against my own people.

Not tolerating racism does not mean participating in protests or writing emails to senators. It means not allowing church members to talk about "those people" or to use stereotypes of any kind.

Practical Ideas of How to Become Multiethnic

Many Christians are open to becoming a multiethnic church but do not know how to begin. What follows below are some ideas to get a church started. The goal is for these ideas to help a church begin thinking about multiethnic ministry, resulting in a church developing its own unique plan for engaging the people surrounding it. These ideas are not meant to replace a church earnestly seeking before the Lord his desire for an individual church.

While it may sound trite, any church seeking to reach everyone in its community for Christ must first begin with earnest prayer. The first thing to pray for is open eyes. Ask God to reveal to you the people living within the community who are not fully integrated into it. Matthew 9:36 starts with, "When he saw the crowds." A church can become so self-focused that it fails to see the crowds. Praying for open eyes is the first step toward developing a multiethnic church.

Once a church begins to see the crowds, Matt 9:36 says that Jesus had compassion for the crowds. The second stage of prayer is when seeing leads to compassion, and compassion leads a church to seek God's plan. Seeing the crowds invariably leads to the question: What can we do?

A common first step for many churches is to develop English as a Second Language (ESL) classes. These classes provide an easy way to offer assistance to those with limited English skills while teaching scriptural truth. Biblically based ESL models abound. Through the process of teaching ESL classes, relationships are formed, and opportunities to learn about a new culture allow both the teacher and the student to learn from each other.

Another simple first step is to offer the use of the church's kitchen and fellowship hall to a group of people. People living in a different culture like to get together with people from their home culture to eat food from home. (I am well acquainted with this concept, living overseas in another culture. Nothing was better than having people over and making biscuits and gravy.) Many immigrants live in small homes and often lack the means to feed a larger group. By offering the use of a kitchen and fellowship hall, a church takes a significant first step to becoming multiethnic.

Closely related to this idea is to invite someone from a different culture to your house for a traditional "American" meal. After all, it is a great privilege to introduce someone from a different culture to biscuits and gravy. Food is a great way to break down barriers between cultures. Not only have I made biscuits and gravy for people who had never eaten such a Southern delicacy, but I have also invited Latinos to come to my house and make pupusas for my family and me, now one of my family's favorite foods.

To put it in perspective, when visiting my parents recently, I met a couple from China. They had lived in the town next to where I grew up for eighteen years but had never once been in an "American" home. No one had ever invited them to dinner, and no one ever invited them to church. They indicated they would love to visit if invited.

One of the greatest things Christians can do is listen to others. We are trained to share the message of Jesus with others. But first, we need to listen and earn the right to be heard. Witnessing almost always takes place within a relationship. For those who have immigrated to a new community, nothing is better than when someone from the community takes time to listen to their story. People want to be seen and heard.

How to Involve People in Church

I once had someone tell me it is difficult to get in the front door of a small rural church, and it is difficult to sneak out the back door. Rural churches often have relationships that go back generations. The difficulty arises when someone new and different shows up at the church and wants to participate in the church's life. For old-timers, these individuals have not been there long enough, and relationships have not been established sufficiently to allow them to be involved in the decision-making process. The newcomer does not know enough stories, doesn't understand the "inside jokes," and "doesn't understand how things are done around here."

The onus is not on the newcomer to force themselves into the life of a rural church. The responsibility for incorporating new people belongs to the long-time members of the church. They must be willing to allow new people with new ideas to be an integral part of the church's life and ministry.

A couple of ways to involve new people are to invite them to participate in worship, such as leading in prayer, singing a special song, or sharing their testimony. These allow people to hear from the new person and learn their story. This begins the relationship-building process necessary in most rural churches.

However, to fully incorporate new people into the life and ministry of the church requires that new people have a voice in the church's ministry. To have such a voice will require them to participate in committees or teams that determine the church's ministry. Placing newcomers in leadership positions will almost guarantee that they will be stretched by old-timers, as these newcomers invariably bring new ideas.

The key to new people developing into leaders requires the old-timers not to micromanage the new leaders. New people must be able to have a voice that is heard and appreciated. Many well-meaning old-timers tend to micromanage leadership teams with the goal of protecting the church. Trusting God and trusting newcomers is difficult for some. It is difficult to remember that someone at some point in the distant past trusted the future old-timers with the leadership of the church.

Conclusion

Revelation 7:9 is a promise that people from every nation, tribe, people, and language will be worshiping around the throne in heaven. Worship in heaven is the model for all churches today. Thus, all churches, including rural churches, should strive to be multiethnic in worship and in their ministries. Worship in a rural church today is more than just a service; it is preparation for worship in heaven. Personally, I want to be as prepared as possible to fully worship when I get to heaven. So, I need to gather with people from different nations, tribes, and languages from around the world.

The Bible models for us multiethnic worship, and the Great Commission requires us to make disciples of all nations. No excuse is acceptable for not reaching out to the world when they live in our own community. We cannot send missionaries to the far ends of the earth while ignoring those in our midst. We have a clear biblical mandate to go and a clear biblical mandate to make sure all hear a clear and contextually relevant presentation of the gospel.

With the biblical mandate in mind, we simply cannot ignore the swelling numbers of immigrants moving into rural areas, whether they are from another country or from another state. If the gospel is for everyone, Christians are mandated to reach all nations. The church must make serving the crowds of people coming into rural areas from other places a priority. Excuses such as "we don't know how to reach these people" will no longer suffice.

The rural church must be proactive in learning new ways to minister and be willing to change to reach the lost effectively. The goal of the church is not to maintain traditions, programs, or any other comfortable practice that subtly excludes others. The goal of the church is to make disciples of all nations. Churches are required to adapt their methods to meet the changing needs of their community and the evolving culture.

Today, many rural churches face a crossroads due to the lack of financial and human resources needed to sustain the church, despite God's promise that the harvest is abundant. It is a shame when the abundant harvest is ignored simply because "they are not like us."

To move forward, rural churches must consider how to become multiethnic. It is our God-given task!

Conclusion

Embracing the Challenge of Change

When we look back at the history of the rural church, we see a history of change and adaptation to the spiritual needs of the rural community. From the beginning, when the Pilgrims first landed upon Plymouth Rock, the vastness of the country and the spiritual needs of small rural communities that began to dot the landscape required the church to develop fresh and new approaches to reach people with the gospel. As the nation moved westward, a spiritual void began to grow. Into this void stepped the itinerant preacher, who traveled from community to community on horseback, with the simple task of preaching the gospel and establishing a congregation within each community. Men, like my (Glenn's) great-great-grandfather George W. Daman, would travel the rural road to help small communities establish a congregation to preach the gospel. Formerly, he was a man of music who played in the dance halls and bars. However, after his conversion, as he would express it, he "stopped doing the work of the devil" and instead spent his life in the service of God. For George, his office was his horse, and his congregations were the people of the Sandhills of Nebraska. There were no programs, no prescribed methods or strategic plans. For them, the task was simple: preach the gospel to people who were on the fringes of civilization. As an itinerate preacher, he would help start churches in Curlew, Tilden, Meadow Grove, Battle Creek, Pierce, and Paddock, Nebraska. At the end of his life, it was said of him that he "was a wonderfully loved man. A big man with a heart just as big." For the itinerant preachers, the call was simple: take the gospel to the remote places, preach the gospel, and start churches.

Along with itinerant preachers reaching rural communities, there were "sky pilots" who had a passion for the rugged loggers working in the end-of-the-road logging camps. There were men such as Frank Reed, Frank Higgins, John Sornberger, and Dick Farrell who abandoned the institutional church and became itinerant "sky pilots," who traveled about the logging camps of the Western Adirondacks, north woods of Minnesota, and the logging camps of western Montana, eastern Washington, and northern Idaho. They did not come with a program; they came with a heart for rugged loggers, which required that they be as tough as the men they sought to reach. Concerning Dick Farrell and John Sornberger, Harry Rimmer would write, "Dick Farrell had been a prize fighter, and every one of this group was capable of giving a good account of himself in a brawl. But they avoided trouble when they could. Their purpose was to preach Christ, not to win fights—although none of them ever ran from trouble of any sort."[1] They were driven by a simple task: to reach the loggers with the gospel. Dick Farrell would eventually travel to northern Idaho, where he would take the gospel to the logging camps that dotted the region. Along with having a passion for the logging camps, he also preached and held evangelistic services in small farming communities. It was while preaching in one such community that a young man came forward to accept Christ. Farrell would then help establish a church in the town, which this young man would attend. The young man who came forward to accept Christ that night was named Wayne Daman (my father), and the church he helped start is the church I attended in my youth. The church still remains active over seventy-five years later, and my brothers and their families still attend. I am in ministry because of the passion these individuals had for the neglected small communities that dot the rural landscape.

As we look to the future of rural ministry, we must recognize that rural America is not an idealized countryside of rolling green hills but a spiritually barren land where the gospel is desperately needed. We need to realize that rural communities are the new mission field, requiring a new missional vision. If rural America is going to be reached with the gospel, it will require a change in our focus. In the past, we have condemned (and even closed) rural churches because they did not maintain the attendance necessary to cover the costs of the building and the pastor. Because of the lack of "growth," denominational leaders saw the death of the church as necessary and sought to replace it with dynamic regional "Walmart" churches. While these churches were successful in gathering

1. Rimmer, *Last of the Giants*, 33. See also, Reed, *Lumberjack Sky Pilot*.

large crowds of believers, they often overlooked the unchurched in rural communities. The church adopted the world's philosophy that numbers, financial success, and numerical growth are measures of health. The church became a franchise to build, and the rural "franchise" was not sustainable. As a result, even though rural communities retained their moral conservatism, it became a spiritual desert. We would rather build dynamic churches than invest in forgotten people.

As the church moves forward, it is not only confronted with a changing culture but also the need to adapt and change as it seeks to maintain relevance in a world that has become increasingly indifferent to the church. Just as the itinerate preachers in the previous generations adapted and developed new approaches to reach forgotten communities, so the church today needs to adapt and create new strategies and methods to reach rural America. Rural America is becoming a mission field. To reach people with the gospel, we will need to adjust our approach to rural ministry and shift our perspective on the church. However, change is never easy, for it brings a sense of loss and a feeling of uncertainty. We like to maintain the status quo because it is comfortable and safe.

We need to follow the example of the early church in Acts. In Acts 6, the early church was likewise in danger of shifting from a mission-driven and message-focused church to an institutional church driven by its programs. People were demanding more efficient programs to minister to their needs. The Hellenistic Jews were complaining because native Hebrews were getting preferential treatment in the distribution of food and other necessities for life. While the apostles recognized the legitimacy of the complaint and the importance of caring for the widows, they also recognized that this could become a distraction. It could derail the ultimate mission of the church. They recognized the importance of caring for people but also maintained the priority of advancing the gospel.

In the ministry of the church, it is easy to revert to maintaining the church, running programs, ministering to the congregation's needs, and preserving the church's structure. While these are important, we can lose sight of our calling, which is to advance the kingdom in rural communities. We are called to take the gospel to the "ends of the earth" (Acts 1:8). The word "ends" refers not just to the most distance places but also to the most insignificant and least important areas. Within God's economy, every individual is essential. We are not just called to reach the masses; we are also called to reach every individual. There is no unimportant ministry, unimportant place, or unimportant person. The task of the church is to proclaim the transforming gospel to the "outposts" of society. An institutionalized church, one driven by programs, systems, structures, and numbers, focuses on where we can "get the biggest bang for our buck." A missional church is driven by the need to reach all people with the gospel of Christ. The advancement of the church in rural communities is not just a cultural, sociological necessity; it is a theological necessity that is woven into the very fabric of our soteriology and ecclesiology.

We are not challenged with adapting a new program, but with adopting a new outlook on ministry. We do not just need new methods in a post-Christian culture; we need a new vision, one that is driven by the desire to see all people come to Christ.

A Return to the Past

In many ways, what we are advocating is not a radical new approach to ministry but a return to the past in which the church is focused upon engagement rather than programs, on advancing the kingdom of Christ rather than maintaining its structures. When the church began in the book of Acts, its focus was simple: to engage people within the community with the hope and transformation offered by the gospel. Ministry was not done in the confines of the walls of a building; it was done in the thoroughfare of life. The apostles went to the synagogues, to the marketplace, to the homes of people. The church went to the people rather than expecting the people to come to the church. As our culture increasingly embraces postmodernism, there will be greater opportunities for the church to share the distinctives of the gospel. This is done not through programs or methods but by interacting with people and building relationships with them so that they can see the reality of our faith and the hope that we have (1 Pet 3:15).

The Importance of One

A mission-driven church recognizes that it is not the number of people in the pew but the importance that God places upon every individual. If only one person is living in an isolated area, is it worth changing our structures and ministries to reach this person? Is the risk of disruption, conflict, and uncertainty worth it? To answer these questions, we must ask another question: What value does God place on each individual? In the parable of the lost sheep (Matt 18:12–14), we see the answer. To find the one lost sheep, the shepherd not only leaves the ninety-nine, but he also places them at risk for attack. In God's economy, the value of the one is equal to the value of the ninety-nine. Theologians debate the extent of the atonement, whether the atonement was universal or just for the elect. However, in the debate, we lose sight of the individual nature of the atonement. The death of Christ is not applied corporately to a group of people; it is applied individually to each one who responds to the gospel. When Christ died on the cross, he not only died for the world but also for every person. He knows each one of us by name and has a personal relationship with us. As Demarest rightly points out, "Christ's suffering and death at Calvary was a very personal and individualized event. While impaled on the cross, his suffering eye was on the world, but it was also lovingly directed toward you, the reader, and toward me, as his sheep."[2] In ministry, it is easy to fall prey to the value of the crowds. As long as we are reaching the crowds, even at the cost of the individual, we justify it. However, God places value on each person. There is a cost to change; instead of focusing on the cost, we must consider the impact on every person we affect. If we need to adapt and change our ministry to reach one individual, the risk and reward are worth it.

As we move forward in ministry, we must embrace change to minister to those who are lost. Within the church, it is comfortable to maintain the status quo, but in the process, we become disconnected from the people we are seeking to reach. If Christ loved us enough to set aside his divine rights and become a servant to die on the cross, how much more should we be willing to change our ministry to reach people in our community with the gospel of Christ?

Never Devalue the Value of Two

A mission-driven ministry never devalues the church, no matter its size. Sam Rainer rightly points out, "If we believe any person is worth saving, we must also believe any church is worth saving."[3] We see the value of each person when the angels rejoice whenever one person is redeemed. Christ points to the value of even the smallest church when he promises that he will be present when only two people gather as the church.

2. Demarest, *Cross and Salvation*, 194–95.

3. Rainer, *Church Revitalization Checklist*, 1.

When two individuals meet together to mutually encourage one another, they become the local manifestation of the universal church. A church is not determined by the size of the building, the variety of programs, or the number of individuals on staff. The church encompasses believers mutually encouraging one another in the faith and advancing Christ's kingdom in their sphere of influence. A church of just two people is so important to Christ that he is personally present when they gather (Matt 18:20).[4] The value and vitality of the church is defined by the presence of Christ and the mission it has to reach its community. If the value of one person is essential in developing our soteriology and missiology, then the value of two is essential in forming our ecclesiology. The task of the Great Commission is not to take the gospel to people and then have them travel to a centralized church. The Great Commission is to advance the church and the kingdom of God by establishing churches in every place where people have embraced the gospel. The church can still be the church without structure, but the church cannot be the church without presence.

Throughout this book, we have argued that in a postmodern world, we will need to change our mode of ministry. We will need to adapt our approach to ministry to reach people with the gospel. If all we do is reach one individual, if all we do is plant one church with two individuals in attendance, then it is worth the risk, the challenge, and the cost. What is the value of each individual? What is the value of the smallest church? In the sight of God, their value is infinite.

Assaulting the Gates of Hell

Our natural tendency in the face of the onslaught of postmodernism is to shrink back into the protected shell of the church to insulate ourselves and our children from the perils and assaults of secularism. We become fearful of the future and fearful of the next generation. We desire to keep ourselves and our children safe. However, engaging in the Great Commission is not safe; in fact, Christ promises us the very opposite. To engage the world is to face persecution, even death. The church is never

4. While the focus of the passage is upon church discipline, the promise itself is a general statement regarding the presence of Christ when believers gather together as the church. In this case, the two individuals are gathered to act in an official capacity of the church by enacting church discipline. A minimum of two individuals is all that is needed to act as representatives of the universal church within the local setting to execute church discipline. See Grudem, *Systematic Theology*, 996n11.

persecuted because of what it does within the walls of the church; it is persecuted because it challenges the world with the gospel. Yet this is our calling. The Great Commission is a call to enter the world of insecurity, knowing that our security does not come from our isolation but from the sovereign God who calls us to proclaim the gospel. When we are proclaiming the message that Jesus "is the Christ, the Son of the living God," we have the assurance that even the gates of Hades will not prevent the advancement of the gospel and the church (Matt 16:16–18). Security is not found in embracing safety but in embracing risk. In risking everything, we discover the security of God (Matt 16:24–27). The church that seeks to isolate itself in order to protect itself from the world is a church that has signed its own obituary. The church that risks everything to advance the Great Commission is a church that attains both vitality and security. In a radically changing world, the most important question is not how do we protect ourselves from the world, but how do we engage the world with the gospel in a fresh and relevant way?!

Bibliography

Adamy, Janet, and Paul Overberg. "Rural America Is the New 'Inner City.'" *Wall Street Journal*, May 26, 2017. https://www.wsj.com/articles/rural-america-is-the-new-inner-city-1495817008?msockid=25700429d08d69e819cc1146d114686f.

Allison, Gregg R. *Sojourners and Strangers: The Doctrine of the Church*. Wheaton: Crossway, 2012.

Anderson, Leith. *A Church for the 21st Century: Bringing Change to Your Church to Meet the Challenges of a Changing Society*. Minneapolis: Bethany House, 1992.

Appalachian Mountain Ministry. "Looking for Missions? Make Appalachia Your Mission Field." https://web.archive.org/web/20190820032620/https://appalachianmountainministry.org/the-importance-of-the-church-getting-involved/.

Arlund, Pam. "Acts 1:8 Sequentialism." Anglican Frontier Missions. https://anglicanfrontiers.com/articles-on-mission-frontiers/.

Arndt, William F., and F. Wilbur Gingrich. *A Greek-English Lexicon of the New Testament*. 2nd ed. Chicago: University of Chicago, 1979.

Austin, Jon. "How the Church Growth Movement Has De-Churched Christians." Reformed Journal, May 1, 2023. https://reformedjournal.com/how-the-church-growth-movement-has-de-churched-christians/.

AZ Quotes. "John Wesley Quotes." https://www.azquotes.com/quote/1320088.

Bader-Saye, Scott. *Following Jesus in a Culture of Fear*. Grand Rapids: Brazos, 2020.

Bailey, Liberty Hyde, et al. "Report of the Country Life Commission." Washington Government Printing Office, Feb. 9, 1909. https://www.fca.gov/template-fca/about/1909_Report_of_The_Country_Life_Commission.pdf.

Bailyn, Bernard. *Voyagers to the West*. New York: Knopf, 1986.

Balance, M. "The Site of Derbe: A New Inscription." *Anatolian Studies* 7 (1957) 147–52.

Barna, George. "American Worldview Inventory 2022." Cultural Research Center at Arizona Christian University, May 24, 2022. https://web.archive.org/web/20260207042307/https://www.arizonachristian.edu/wp-content/uploads/2022/05/AWVI2022_Release_06_Digital.pdf.

———. *The Power of Vision: Discover and Apply God's Plan for Your Life and Ministry*. Ventura: Regal, 1992.

Barna Group. "What Makes Innovation So Challenging for Church Leaders?" Nov. 7, 2024. https://www.barna.com/trends/church-innovation-tips/.

Barnett, Mike, ed. *Discovering the Mission of God: Best Missional Practices for the 21st Century*. Grand Rapids: IVP Academic, 2012.

Barth, Al. "A Vision for Our Cities." Redeemer City to City, Jan. 1, 2009. https://redeemercitytocity.com/articles-stories/a-vision-for-our-cities.

Basham, Will. *Rural Missions: Insights From A Rural Church Planter*. N.p.: Rural Church Voices, 2021.

Belknap, Helen O. *The Church on the Changing Frontier*. New York: George H. Doran, 1923.

Bible Hub. "Village." https://biblehub.com/topical/v/village.htm.

Bolsinger, Tod. *Canoeing the Mountains: Christian Leadership in Uncharted Territory*. Downers Grove, IL: InterVarsity, 2015.

Borden, Paul. *Hit the Bullseye: How Denominations Can Aim Congregations at the Mission Field*. Nashville: Abingdon, 2003.

Brown, David L., and Louis E. Swanson. *Challenges for Rural America in the Twenty-First Century*. University Park: Pennsylvania State University Press, 2003.

Caballero, Axel. "Latinos Reviving Small Towns on the Plains." Cuentame Arts, Nov. 15, 2011. https://mycuentame-bravenew.nationbuilder.com/latinos_reviving_small_towns_on_the_plains.

Capital One Shopping Research. "Mall Closure Statistics." Dec. 3, 2025. https://capitaloneshopping.com/research/mall-closure-statistics/.

Castle, Emery N., ed. *The Changing American Countryside: Rural People and Places*. Lawrence: University Press of Kansas, 1995.

Census.gov. "Table 4. Population: 1790 to 1990." https://www2.census.gov/programs-surveys/decennial/1990/tables/cph-2/table-4.pdf.

Clayton, Ingrid. "What Is the Fawning Trauma Response?" Psychology Today, Mar. 24, 2023. https://www.psychologytoday.com/us/blog/emotional-sobriety/202303/what-is-the-fawning-trauma-response.

Clement. "Letter to the Corinthians (Clement)." In *Ante-Nicene Fathers*, vol. 9, edited by Allan Menzies, translated by John Keith. Buffalo, NY: Christian Literature, 1896. Revised and edited for New Advent by Kevin Knight. https://www.newadvent.org/fathers/1010.htm.

Compeer Financial. "Where Are Young People Moving: The Small Town Relocation Trend." Aug. 25, 2026. https://www.compeer.com/articles/2022/march-2022/three-reasons-gens-x,-z-and-millennials-are-moving-to-small-towns.

Connaughton, Aidan. "Americans See Stronger Societal Conflict Than People in Other Advanced Economies." Pew Research Center, Oct. 13, 2021 https://www.pewresearch.org/short-reads/2021/10/13/americans-see-stronger-societal-conflicts-than-people-in-other-advanced-economies/.

Cormode, Scott. *The Innovative Church: How Leaders and Their Congregations Can Adapt in an Ever-Changing World*. Grand Rapids: Baker Academic, 2020.

Critchfield, Richard. *Trees, Why Do You Wait? America's Changing Rural Culture*. Washington, DC: Island, 1991.

Daman, Glenn. *The Forgotten Church: Why Rural Ministry Matters for Every Church in America*. Chicago: Moody, 2018.

———. *Leading the Small Church: How to Develop a Transformational Ministry*. Grand Rapids: Kregel, 2006.

———. *Shepherding the Small Church: A Leadership Guide for the Majority of Today's Churches*. Grand Rapids: Kregel, 2008.

Daman, Glenn, and Jeffrey Clark. *The God of Small Places*. Eugene, OR: Wipf & Stock, 2026.

Data Commons. "Washtucna." https://datacommons.org/place/geoId/5376440.

Deaton, Todd "The Rise of the Digital Church." Baptist Courier, May 5, 2022. https://baptistcourier.com/2022/05/the-rise-of-the-digital-church/.

Demarest, Bruce. *The Cross and Salvation: The Doctrine of Salvation*. Wheaton: Crossway, 1997.

Duignan, Brian. "Postmodernism." Encyclopedia Britannica, Dec. 19, 2025. https://www.britannica.com/topic/postmodernism-philosophy.

Earls, Aaron. "Small Churches Continue Growing—but in Number, not Size." Lifeway Research, Oct. 20, 2021. https://research.lifeway.com/2021/10/20/small-churches-continue-growing-but-in-number-not-size/.

Easum, Bill. "Too Many Pastors Are Wasting Their Lives." Effective Church Group. https://effectivechurch.com/too-many-pastors-are-wasting-their-lives/.

Easy Sociology. "The British Class System: An Outline and Explanation." Feb. 2, 2024. https://easysociology.com/sociology-of-inequalities/the-british-class-system-an-outline-and-explanation/#google_vignette.

Eikenberry, Kevin. *Flexible Leadership: Navigate Uncertainty and Lead with Confidence*. Dallas: Matt Holt, 2025.

Erickson, Millard J. *Christian Theology*. Grand Rapids: Baker, 1985.

———. *The Postmodern World: Discerning the Times and the Spirit of Our Age*. Wheaton, IL: Crossway, 2002.

Etheredge, Craig. "The Forgotten—Model Jesus as the Model for Ministry." https://discipleship.org/blog/the-forgotten-model-jesus-as-the-model-for-ministry/.

Farm Progress. "Number of Farms in U.S. declines in 2020." Mar. 3, 2021. https://www.farmprogress.com/farm-operations/number-of-farms-in-u-s-declines-in-2020.

Finke, Roger, and Rodney Stark. *The Churching of America, 1776–2005: Winners and Losers in Our Religious Economy*. New Brunswick, NJ: Rutgers University Press, 2014.

Fitchen, Janet M. *Endangered Spaces, Enduring Places: Change, Identity, and Survival in Rural America*. San Francisco: Westview, 1991.

Ford, Kevin G. *Transforming Church: Bringing Out the Good to Get to Great*. Carol Stream, IL: Tyndale House, 2007.

Ford, Kevin G., and Jim Singleton. *Attentive Church Leadership: Listening and Leading in a World We've Never Known*. Downers Grove, IL: InterVarsity, 2024.

Forsetti's Justice. "Rural Christian White America Has a Dark and Terrifying Underbelly." Raw Story, Feb. 6, 2018. https://www.rawstory.com/2018/02/insider-explains-rural-christian-white-america-dark-terrifying-underbelly/.

Fulkerson, Gregory M., and Alexander R. Thomas. *Urbanormativity: Reality, Representation, and Everyday Life*. New York: Lexington, 2019.

Furedi, Frank. *How Fear Works: Culture of Fear in the Twenty-First Century*. London: Bloomsburg, 2019.

———. "The Only Thing We Have to Fear Is the 'Culture of Fear' Itself." Spiked, Jan. 2007. https://www.spiked-online.com/2007/04/04/the-only-thing-we-have-to-fear-is-the-culture-of-fear-itself/.

Goins-Phillips, Tre. "DC Talk's Kevin Max Is Now 'Exvangelical,' Says He's Been 'Progressing' for 'Decades.'" Christian Broadcast Network, May 18, 2021. https://cbn.com/news/news/dc-talks-kevin-max-now-exvangelical-says-hes-been-progressing-decades.

Goldman, Steven L. *Science Wars: The Battle over Knowledge and Reality*. New York: Oxford University Press, 2021.

Grudem, Wayne. *Politics According to the Bible: A Comprehensive Resource for Understanding Modern Political Issues in Light of Scripture*. Grand Rapids: Zondervan, 2010.

The Guardian. "The Guardian View of American Christianity: Change and Decay." Jan. 15, 2017. https://www.theguardian.com/commentisfree/2017/jan/15/the-guardian-view-on-american-christianity-change-and-decay.

Guinness, Os. *Dining with the Devil: The Megachurch Movement Flirts With Modernity*. Grand Rapids: Baker, 1993.

Harney, Kevin G., and Bob Bouwer. *The U-Turn Church: New Direction for Health and Growth*. Grand Rapids: Baker, 2011.

Hawks, Howard, dir. *Sergeant York*. Burbank, CA: Warner Brothers, 1941.

Heifetz, Ronald A., et al. *The Practice of Adaptive Leadership: Tools and Tactics for Changing Your Organization and the World*. Cambridge: Harvard Business, 2009.

Historical Association. "Social Structure." https://www.history.org.uk/student/categories/495/module/4536/overview-of-elizabeth-i/4543/social-structure.

Horn, David, and Jason R. McConnell. *Return to the Parish: The Pastor in the Public Square*. Eugene, OR: Cascade, 2022.

Hunter, James Davidson. *Culture Wars: The Struggle to Define America*. New York: Basic, 1991.

Huston, James. "Early National America, 1789–1830: Laying the Foundation for Nineteenth-Century Agricultural Growth." In *A Companion to American Agricultural History*, edited by R. Douglas Hurt, 37–46. Hoboken, NJ: John Wiley & Sons, 2022. https://onlinelibrary.wiley.com/doi/abs/10.1002/9781119632214.ch3.

Irving, Washington. *Rip Van Winkle and Other Stories*. New York: Puffin, 2011.

Jefferson, Thomas. *Notes on the State of Virginia*. Boston: Lilly and Wait, 1832. https://tile.loc.gov/storage-services/service/gdc/lhbcb/04902/04902.pdf.

———. "Thomas Jefferson to John Jay, 23 August 1785." Founders Online. https://founders.archives.gov/documents/Jefferson/01-8-02-333#.

Jensen, Leif. "New Immigrant Settlements in Rural America: Problems, Prospects, and Policies." Carsey Institutes, University of New Hampshire. Reports on Rural America 1.3, 2006. https://scholars.unh.edu/cgi/viewcontent.cgi?referer=&httpsredir=1&article=1016&context=carsey.

Jethani, Skye. *How Churches Became Cruise Ships: A Survival Guide for the Seasick Christian*. Self-published, 2015. Kindle ed.

Jewison, Norman, dir. *Fiddler on the Roof*. Hollywood: United Artists, 1971.

Johnson, Jamie. "From Mall Madness to Sadness: Why Shopping Centers May Soon Be Obsolete." Business.com, Oct. 23, 2024. https://www.business.com/articles/why-shopping-centers-will-soon-be-obsolete/.

Jones, Jeffrey M. "U.S. Church Membership Falls Below Majority for First Time." Gallup, Mar. 29, 2021. https://news.gallup.com/poll/341963/church-membership-falls-below-majority-first-time.aspx.

Keller, Timothy. *Why God Made Cities*. New York: Redeemer City to City, 2013.

Kittel, Gerhard, and Gerhard Friedrich, eds. *Theological Dictionary of the New Testament*. Translated by Geoffrey W. Bromiley. 10 vols. Grand Rapids: Eerdmans, 1964–1976.

Knowlton, Christopher. *Cattle Kingdom: The Hidden History of the Cowboy West*. New York: Houghton Muffin Hardcourt, 2017.

Leeman, Jonathan. "The Church Gathered." Gospel Coalition. https://www.thegospelcoalition.org/essay/the-church-gathered/.

Leibovich, Mark. "Palin Visits a 'Pro-America' Kind of Town." *New York Times*, Oct. 17, 2008. https://archive.nytimes.com/thecaucus.blogs.nytimes.com/2008/10/17/palin-visits-a-pro-america-kind-of-town/.

Lewis, C. S. *The Lion, the Witch, and the Wardrobe*. London: Geoffry Bless, 1950.

Lutzer, Erwin W. *No Reason to Hide: Standing for Christ in a Collapsing Culture*. Eugene, OR: Harvest House, 2022.

Macdonald, John. *Calling a Halt to Mindless Change: A Plea for Commonsense Management*. New York: Amacom, 1998.

Maraniss, David. *When Pride Still Mattered: A Life of Vince Lombardi*. New York: Simon & Schuster, 1999.

Martin, Rachel. "A Throwaway Line Led 'Washington Post' Reporter to Call Rural Midwest His New Home." NPR, Sept. 11, 2019. https://www.npr.org/2019/09/11/759513032/a-throwaway-line-led-washington-post-reporter-to-call-rural-midwest-his-new-home.

McLaren, Brian. *A New Kind of Christianity: Ten Questions That Are Transforming the Faith*. New York: Harper Collins, 2010.

Melotte, Sarah. "Rural People Don't Practice Religion More Than Their Urban Counterparts, Survey Shows." Oct. 23, 2023. https://dailyyonder.com/rural-people-dont-practice-religion-more-than-their-urban-counterparts-survey-shows/2023/10/23/.

Miller, Paul. *The Religion of American Greatness: What's Wrong with Christian Nationalism*. Downers Grove, IL: IVP Academic, 2022.

Merriam-Webster. "Christendom." https://www.merriam-webster.com/dictionary/christendom.

———. "Pluralism." https://www.merriam-webster.com/dictionary/pluralism.

———. "Secularism." https://www.merriam-webster.com/dictionary/secularism.

Nations Encyclopedia. "United States—Agriculture." https://www.nationsencyclopedia.com/Americas/United-States-AGRICULTURE.html#google_vignette.

Oberlensky, Nick. *Complex Adaptive Leadership: Embracing Paradox and Uncertainty*. New York: Routledge, 2014.

Orozco, Ellis. "Theological Education and the Decline of the American Church." Stark College and Seminary. https://stark.edu/theological-education-and-the-decline-of-the-american-church/.

Overstreet, Jeffrey. "Why God Loves Cities: Timothy Keller Challenges Church Leaders at the Cape Town Lausanne Congress." Seattle Pacific University Response. https://spu.edu/depts/uc/response/new/2011-spring/features/god-loves-cities.asp.

Parrott, Roger. *Opportunity Leadership: Stop Planning and Start Getting Results*. Chicago: Moody, 2022.

Paxson, Fredric. *History of the American Frontier, 1763–1893*. Troutdale, OR: Independently re-published, 2022.

Pew Research Center. "Modeling the Future Religion in America." Sept. 13, 2022. https://www.pewresearch.org/religion/2022/09/13/modeling-the-future-of-religion-in-america/.

———. "Online Religious Services Appeal to Many Americans, but Going in Person Remains More Popular." June 2, 2023. https://www.pewresearch.org/religion/2023/06/02/online-religious-services-appeal-to-many-americans-but-going-in-person-remains-more-popular/.

———. "Religious Landscape Study." 2025. https://www.pewforum.org/religious-landscape-study/state/kentucky/.

Pigg, Kenneth, ed. *The Future of Rural America: Anticipating Policies for Constructive Change*. New York: Routledge, 2019.

Plummer, Robert L., and John Mark Terry. *Paul's Missionary Methods: In His Time and Ours*. Downers Grove, IL: IVP Academic, 2012.

Pratt, Zane. "How Theology Drives Missions." Midwestern Theological Seminary, Oct. 15, 2021. https://www.mbts.edu/2021/10/how-theology-drives-missions/.

The Progressive Rancher. "Growing the Number of People Fed by U.S. Farmers." Jan. 24, 2025. https://progressiverancher.com/growing-the-number-of-people-fed-by-u-s-farmers/.

Radmacher, Earl. *Celebrating the Word*. Portland: Multnomah, 1987.

Rainer, Sam. *The Church Revitalization Checklist: A Hopeful and Practical Guide for Leading Your Congregation to a Brighter Tomorrow*. Carol Stream, IL: Tyndale, 2021.

Rainer, Thom S. "Five Reasons Why 2025 Will Be Pivotal Year For Many Churches." Baptist Courrier, Jan. 27, 2025. https://baptistcourier.com/2025/01/five-reasons-why-2025-will-be-pivotal-year-for-many-churches/.

Ramsay, W. M. *Cities of St. Paul: Their Influence on His Life and Thought, the Cities of Eastern Asia Minor*. London: Hodder and Stoughton, 1908.

Reed, Frank. *Lumberjack Sky Pilot*. Utica, NY: North Country, 1965.

Regele, Mike. *Death of the Church*. Grand Rapids: Zondervan, 1996.

Rendle, Gil. *Quietly Courageous: Leading the Church in a Changing World*. Lanham, MD: Rowman & Littlefield, 2018.

Renn, Aaron. *Life in the Negative World: Confronting Challenges in an Anti-Christian Culture*. Grand Rapids: Zondervan, 2024.

Rimmer, Harry. *The Last of the Giants*. Abbotsford, WI: Aneko, 2015.

Ritner, Jon. *Positively Irritating: Embracing a Post-Christian World to Form a More Faithful and Innovative Church*. Cody, WY: 100 Movements, 2020.

Robinson, Phil Alden, dir. *Field of Dreams*. Universal City, CA: Universal Pictures, 1989.

Robinson, Thomas A. *Who Were the First Christians?: Dismantling the Urban Thesis*. New York: Oxford University Press, 2017.

Roper, Willem. "Rural Life Desire Rises in 2020." Statista, Jan. 6, 2021. https://www.statista.com/chart/23855/rural-urban-living/.

Roy, Megan. "Major Tenets of Postmodernism." Postmodernism. https://mroypostmodernism.weebly.com/tenets.html.

Roxburgh, Alan J. *Joining God, Remaking Church, Changing the World: The New Shape of the Church in Our Time*. New York: Morehouse, 2015.

Russell, Michael B. "The Great Commission: Recognizing the Church as a Decentralized Virtual 'Spider Plant' Proclamation of the Gospel." Leadership Advance Online 24. Regent University, 2013. https://www.regent.edu/acad/global/publications/lao/issue_24/4lao-russell.pdf.

Santayana, George. *The Life of Reason or the Phases of Human Progress*. New York: Charles Scribner's Sons, 1905.

Schnabel, Eckhard J. *Paul the Missionary: Realities, Strategies, and Methods*. Downers Grove, IL: IVP Academic, 2008.

Seifrid, Mark A. *The Second Letter to the Corinthians.* Piller New Testament Commentary. Grand Rapids: Eerdmans, 2014.

Selyukh, Alina. "Amazon Dethrones Walmart as the World's Biggest Company by Sales." NPR, Feb. 19, 2026. https://www.npr.org/2026/02/19/nx-s1-5719173/amazon-walmart-biggest-company-by-sales.

Sheidlower, Noah, and Juliana Kaplan. "Forget LA and BK: The Rural Places Where Young Americans Are Moving." Business Insider, Nov. 13, 2024. https://www.businessinsider.com/gen-z-millennials-rural-small-towns-cities-colorado-texas-montana-2024-11.

Smith, Ben. "Obama on Small-Town Pa.: Clinging to Religion, Guns, Xenophobia." Politico, Apr. 11, 2008. https://www.politico.com/blogs/ben-smith/2008/04/obama-on-small-town-pa-clinging-to-religion-guns-xenophobia-007737.

Stetzer, Ed. "America's Hidden Mission Field: Why We Need Rural Churches." Christianity Today, Oct. 27, 2018. https://www.christianitytoday.com/edstetzer/2018/october/americas-hidden-mission-field-why-we-need-rural-churches.html.

Strong, James. *The Exhaustive Concordance of the Bible: Showing Every Word of the Text of the Common English Version of the Canonical Books, and Every Occurrence of Each Word in Regular Order.* Electronic ed. Ontario: Woodside Bible Fellowship, 1996.

———. *Strong's Greek Dictionary of the New American Exhaustive Concordance.* Updated ed. La Habra, CA: Lockman, 1998.

Svendsen, Lars. *A Philosophy of Fear.* London: Reaktion, 2008.

Sweet, Leonard. *SoulTsunami: Sink or Swim in New Millennium Culture.* Grand Rapids: Zondervan, 1999.

Tabbernee, William, ed. *Early Christianity in Contexts: An Exploration Across Cultures and Continents.* Grand Rapids: Baker Academic, 2014.

Ushchan, Michael V. "43 Years of 'Li'l Abner' Makes for Serious Reading." United Press International, May 27, 1988. https://www.upi.com/Archives/1988/05/27/43-years-of-Lil-Abner-makes-for-serious-reading/7671580708800/.

Vaters, Karl. *De-Sizing the Church: How Church Growth Became a Science, Then an Obsession, and What's Next.* Chicago: Moody, 2024.

Vine, W. E. "Village." Blue Letter Bible. From *Vine's Expository Dictionary of New Testament Words.* https://www.blueletterbible.org/search/Dictionary/viewTopic.cfm?topic=VT0003239.

Vreeland, Derek. "Why Biblical Inerrancy Doesn't Work." Missio Alliance, Apr. 12, 2019. https://www.missioalliance.org/why-biblical-inerrancy-doesnt-work/.

Wagner, E. Glenn. *Escape from Church, Inc.* Grand Rapids: Zondervan, 1999.

Walrath, Douglas Alan. *Leading Churches Through Change.* Nashville: Abingdon, 1979.

Wax, Trevin. "The Beauty and Power of a Missional Church." Gospel Coalition, Aug. 28, 2019. https://www.thegospelcoalition.org/blogs/trevin-wax/beauty-power-missional-church/.

Wells, Barney, et al. *Leading Through Change: Shepherding the Town and Country Church in a New Era.* St. Charles, IL: ChurchSmart Resources, 2005.

Wells, David. *No Place for Truth: Or Whatever Happened to Evangelical Theology?* Grand Rapids: Eerdmans, 1994.

White, Thomas, and John M. Yeats. *Franchising McChurch: Feeding Our Obsession with Easy Christianity.* Colorado Springs: David C. Cook, 2009.

Wikipedia. “Homestead Acts.” https://en.wikipedia.org/wiki/Homestead_Acts.

Wilkinson, Kenneth P. *The Community in Rural America.* Boulder: University of Colorado, 2023.

Witmer, Stephen. *A Big Gospel in Small Places: Why Ministry in Forgotten Communities Matters.* Downers Grove, IL: InterVarsity, 2019.

Wolfe, Stephen. *The Case for Christian Nationalism.* Moscow, ID: Canon, 2022.

Wuthnow, Robert. *In the Blood: Understanding America's Farm Families.* Princeton, NJ: Princeton University Press, 2015.

———. *Small-Town America: Finding Community, Shaping the Future.* Princeton, NJ: Princeton University Press, 2015.

www.ingramcontent.com/pod-product-compliance
Lightning Source LLC
LaVergne TN
LVHW050625100826
845148LV00011B/1741

* 9 7 9 8 3 8 5 2 7 6 4 0 0 *